CHOOS[...]
COSTA RICA
FOR RETIREMENT

Help Us Keep This Guide Up to Date

Every effort has been made by the author and editors to make this guide as accurate and useful as possible. However, many things can change after a guide is published—establishments close, phone numbers change, facilities come under new management, housing costs fluctuate, and so on.

We would love to hear from you concerning your experiences with this guide and how you feel it could be made better and be kept up to date. While we may not be able to respond to all comments and suggestions, we'll take them to heart and we'll also make certain to share them with the author. Please send your comments and suggestions to the following address:

The Globe Pequot Press
Reader Response/Editorial Department
P.O. Box 833
Old Saybrook, CT 06475

Or you may e-mail us at:

editorial@globe-pequot.com

Thanks for your input, and happy travels!

Choose Retirement Series

Choose Costa Rica for Retirement

Fourth Edition

Retirement

Discoveries

for Every

Budget

The Globe Pequot Press

Old Saybrook, CT

John Howells

Cover and text design: Laura Augustine
Cover photos: (upper left and lower right) Kevin Schafer©Tony Stone; (upper right) Brian Sytnyk©Masterfile

Library of Congress Cataloging-in-Publication Data

Howells, John 1928-
    Choose Costa Rica : a guide to retirement or investment / by John Howells.
    — 4th ed.
        p. cm. — (Choose retirement series)
    Includes bibliographical references and index.
    ISBN 0-7627-0310-5
    1. Retirement, Places of—Costa Rica. 2. Investments, American—Costa
    Rica. 3. Costa Rica—Guidebooks. I. Title. II. Series.
    HQ1063.2.C8H67   1999   98-27082
    917.28604'5—dc21   CIP

Manufactured in the United States of America
Fourth Edition/Second Printing

CONTENTS

COSTA RICA

INTRODUCTION

This book is the fourth edition of *Choose Costa Rica* and the result of almost twenty-five years of travel in and writing about Central America. The two years since the last edition of this book have seen many changes in Costa Rica, and this new, thoroughly revised edition reflects this.

Before I began doing nonfiction books, I was a freelance writer; my specialty was writing travel articles on Latin America. Why Latin America? Partly because of the pleasantly warm climates (I hate cold weather) but mostly because of the gorgeous scenery, exotic foods, and friendly people who live there. Places like Mexico, Guatemala, and Costa Rica naturally beckoned with tropical warmth and picturesque surroundings. I always hated it when my research was completed and I had to return home! Thankfully, my wife and I have solved that problem. We purchased a condominium in Rohrmoser, a suburb of San José, Costa Rica, and recently constructed a home near the beach on the Pacific side of the country. We spend five months a year in Costa Rica.

Choose Costa Rica is intended for not only retirees but also those nearing retirement age who are casting about for ideas for the future. This book is also designed as a guide for those individuals who manage to have part or all of the year free for doing exactly what they feel like doing. It's for the professor on sabbatical, the schoolteacher on a summer vacation, the construction worker with chronic winter unemployment, the executive who can take a leave of absence. This book is also for the self-employed individuals who can trust their businesses to others while they enjoy life *now* instead of waiting for the "someday" that may never come. *Choose Costa Rica* is especially oriented toward those who seek a "new start," who might wish to invest time and resources into launching a new business career as well as enjoying a fascinating lifestyle in an exotic foreign country.

Although this is partly a travel book, the emphasis is on "how to do it" rather than "where to stay." A hotel, bed-and-breakfast, or restaurant may be mentioned from time to time but only as an adjunct to the narrative and should not be taken as a personal recommendation.

About prices quoted throughout this book: They are accurate as of the time of writing, based on the current dollar exchange rates in Costa

Rica. In the summer of 1998 the Costa Rican currency, the colón, was worth about 250 colones to the dollar.

After you read through this book, maybe you'll understand why Costa Rica has such a good reputation among North Americans and Europeans. You might even find a niche there for you and your family. A word of caution: Costa Rica isn't for everyone. There are those who can't resist comparing conditions in Costa Rica with those in the United States or Canada. Remember, Costa Rica is still a developing Third World country. There's a world of difference. For those of us who love Costa Rica, we thank our lucky stars for the difference!

Note: Unless otherwise stated, all phone and fax numbers in this book are in Costa Rica and require that you dial the proper access and country code to reach.

SWITZERLAND OF THE AMERICAS

As the jetliner droned over the Nicaraguan border crossing into Costa Rica, I eagerly looked forward to touching down at the Santa María Airport for another visit to Costa Rica. As I tried to identify the landmarks below, eager to catch a glimpse of the bowl-like mountain valley that contains the sprawling city of San José, I heard the lady in the aisle seat sniff disgustedly as she tossed aside a guidebook on Costa Rica.

"Why can't these books simply describe Costa Rica?" she complained peevishly. "Every place is described in superlatives or else it is 'just too beautiful for words.' You'd think the authors were poets instead of travel writers! Give me a break!" The empty seat between us held four discarded books, all travel guides to Costa Rica.

A frown creased my forehead as I realized that my mission on this trip was to complete the research for yet *another* book on Costa Rica to add to the stack. Perhaps her complaint was a message I needed to take to heart; clearly, I wouldn't want to evoke similar reactions from my readers. But after a few moments of thought, a truth dawned upon me: It's *impossible* to describe Costa Rica without using superlatives, because the country *is* a superlative!

People who have traveled all over the world affirm that Costa Rica's beaches are unsurpassed anywhere. Its varied climates offer choices of weather as perfect as you could hope to find anyplace on earth (unless you are a skier, of course). Steep-sloped mountains—topped by cloud forests, ferns, and exotic wildlife—tower over fertile farmland dotted with hundreds of neatly maintained homesteads. Flowers bloom everywhere; often trees bear so many colorful, scented blossoms that green leaves are hidden. As if this weren't enough, the small towns are every bit as neat and clean as the countryside and are blessed with friendly Costa Rican hospitality. This is truly a country of superlatives.

One of the more common descriptions of Costa Rica is "the Switzerland of the Americas." At first glance, Costa Rica differs so much from Switzerland that one might wonder how it earned this title. True, both countries are of similar size (although Switzerland is actually a bit smaller—one of the world's few countries with that distinction). But Costa Rica is lushly tropical, continuously swathed in luxurious green vegetation, a place where coffee, sugarcane, and mangoes thrive and where snow never falls. Costa Rica would seem to be the opposite of Switzerland, with its snowcapped peaks and rocky terrain.

Yet the more one travels in Costa Rica, the more apparent are the parallels with Switzerland. Both are peaceful, progressive countries where democracy and stability are hallmarks. Although Costa Rica's tropical beaches are incongruent with the Swiss terrain, the higher mountains rival the rugged beauty of the Alps. The lake area around the Arenal Volcano could easily pass for parts of Switzerland—during the Swiss summertime, at any rate.

Even closer similarities between the two countries appear in their philosophy of life and economic structures. Both are places of small farms and small businesses, with an air of prosperity and a feeling of equality among citizens. Both countries have renounced aggressive militarism, diverting resources—those that would otherwise be consumed by wars—toward education, medical care, and services for the good of all. In short, both places are affluent, happy, and tranquil. Both are locations where North Americans can feel at home, safe, and welcome.

There are differences, of course. Costa Rica is closer to the United States and Canada, making it somewhat more accessible than Europe. Costa Rica also enjoys a dramatically lower cost of living than Switzerland. And best of all, Costa Rica has a climate that can be enjoyed year-round by those of us who hate wearing snow boots and earmuffs. The higher elevations enjoy springlike temperatures all year; brightly colored flowers seem to glow in the crystal-clear atmosphere. The countryside is so fertile that fence posts sprout and become trees despite all the farmers' best efforts. Crossing over the mountains, you drop down to tropical lowlands where North Americans own plantations of coffee, macadamia nuts, black pepper, and other exotic crops for export. Beaches flank either side of the country, dotted with small communities where North Americans and Europeans live in communion with surf and jungle.

A Unique History

Costa Rica stands out in this hemisphere in many ways, but its biggest contrast is with its Central American neighbors. When you drive across the border into Costa Rica or when you step off an airplane arriving from another Central American country, you know immediately that you are in a special place. Relative affluence stands out in contrast to the grinding poverty of most other Central American locations. People living in neighboring republics point to Costa Rica as an example of the kind of world they would hope to imitate. "If Costa Rica can be prosperous, democratic, and free," the envious neighbors ask, "why can't we?"

Clearly, there are light-years of difference between Costa Rica and the other Central American countries. How did it get that way? Why does Costa Rica have so much less poverty and so large a middle class in comparison with neighboring countries? The answers to these questions can be found in a series of historical events, some accidental, some planned.

In 1502, when Columbus happened upon Costa Rica during his last voyage to this hemisphere, he anchored at present-day Limón and dispatched an expedition ashore. Chances are, Columbus himself waited on the ship for a report from his landing party. His explorers returned with news of an inhospitable jungle and impossible swamps, plus ferocious natives who owned but a few paltry ornaments of thinly pounded gold. In short, the Limón Coast offered little to excite the imagination of these avaricious explorers. They quickly moved on without attempting colonization.

According to legend, Columbus gave his new discovery the name *Costa Rica* or "rich coast." Some historians think the name may have come from another explorer—Fernández de Córdoba, as he charted the Pacific side of the isthmus some thirty years later. Impressed by the magnificent forests, fertile lands, and abundant wildlife of the Nicoya Peninsula, he coined the term *Costa Rica* as he established a settlement in 1539. The Caribbean Coast that Columbus discovered was left virtually untouched and ignored by Europeans for several centuries. In part due to the isolation of this Pacific Coast settlement, and in contrast with the fast colonization of other parts of the Americas, Costa Rica grew very slowly.

It was the custom for the Spanish Crown to grant huge tracts of land to the conquistadores as a reward for their services. Indians were considered a part of the land, and although not exactly slaves, they essentially belonged to the enormous haciendas—they were forced to work as peons for the aristocratic conquerors. In places like Peru, Mexico, and Guatemala, the Indians meekly accepted their new rulers and continued working the same lands as before, paying tribute to new overlords. However, the Indians of Costa Rica (like their cousins in North America) proved to be determined, fierce fighters who resisted the idea of accepting the intruders as their superiors. Experts in defending their heavily forested lands, the natives simply withdrew farther into the jungle when defeated. They clearly weren't interested in tilling fields for the pink-faced intruders. Archaeological evidence suggests that at least some tribes were headhunters, possibly culturally related to the Jívaros of Colombia, whose warriors dangled their enemies' shrunken heads around their necks as ornaments. In short, these people were unlikely candidates for being docile field laborers.

This left the newcomers in a position they hadn't counted on. Instead of being lords over huge estates and overseeing gangs of laboring peons, the Spanish conquistadores were forced to work the land for themselves! This required hard manual labor and a marginal existence on small, family-run farms. From the beginning all were equal in their struggle for existence. Even the royal viceroy had to raise chickens and tend his own garden to avoid starvation. Small wonder that many early settlers moved on to easier pickings; others ignored the country completely.

Costa Rica's development got off to an inauspicious start, and the country remained a backwater of Spanish colonization, all but forgotten over the ensuing centuries. It grew in its own way, ignoring the ineffective Spanish governors sent by the royal court of Madrid. Costa Ricans lived quiet lives, isolated and unaffected by events in other colonies. In fact, when Spain granted independence to the Spanish colonies in 1821, Costa Rica was the last to know (and probably cared the least). For all practical purposes, it had always been on its own. Independence was no novelty.

Fortunately, Costa Rica's first president turned out to be a progressive thinker, a visionary who wanted to see the country develop socially and economically. He was convinced that growing coffee for export could be a major economic breakthrough, a key to modernization. Coffee profits could build roads, schools, and cities.

But the country was scantily populated. More people were needed to grow coffee in order to fulfill the president's dream. Consequently, free land was offered to anyone willing to plant coffee trees. Since coffee production in Costa Rica is ideally suited to small farms, European families began immigrating to take advantage of Costa Rica's opportunities. They came from Italy and France as well as from Spain. Instead of huge plantations owned by a few wealthy families, as in other Central American republics, hundreds of small farms sprang up, selling coffee beans to merchants who processed and exported the product. This resulted in a tradition of independence and equality, with a preponderance of middle-class farmers and a few moderately wealthy, coffee-exporting families. The spread between rich, middle class, and poor was much narrower than anywhere else in the hemisphere and remains so to this day.

Troubled times in Europe during the last half of the nineteenth century sent new waves of economic and political refugees to the Americas, seeking a chance to "start over." The standing offer of free land to grow coffee was irresistible. The ranks of small farmers grew even larger. These refugees, often imbued with contemporary Europe's liberal intellectual and political philosophy, contributed substantially to the notions of freedom, democracy, and individual rights that were already in place.

This is not to say that Costa Rica didn't develop a wealthy oligarchy of elite families whose position rested upon their control of coffee exports. But because of their tradition of being "self-made" families and their respect for hard work, their mentality was different from that of the arrogant Spanish conquistadores who worshiped royalty and privilege.

Free and compulsory education was an early development, starting in 1869 and setting a tradition of literacy that ranks Costa Rica higher than most other countries of the world—including the United States. A university was founded in 1844, staffed in part by intellectuals who fled Europe's political and economic maelstrom. These and other modern European traditions developed in Costa Rica in stark contrast with the medieval, feudal heritage of Mexico and other Central American countries.

A Peaceful Democracy

Costa Rica is a country where North Americans feel very much at home. It is a country of law-abiding citizens, a place where you don't feel shivers of apprehension at the approach of a policeman or a heavily armed soldier. (You have to have traveled in a brutal police state to appreciate this last statement.) Costa Rica is a country where juvenile gangs and graffiti are the exception, not the rule. It's a place where your conscience isn't continually assaulted by obvious poverty, children begging in the streets, or social injustice. It's a place where North Americans feel comfortable living in just about any neighborhood, not forced to huddle together in enclaves of other expatriates for mutual support. That's not to say Costa Rica is crime-free (is there such a place?), but compared with most other places in this world, the country has a safe feeling.

One reason we North Americans are attracted to Costa Rica is that Costa Ricans are so much like us. They think like us, act like us, and hold much the same values. They are open, friendly, and egalitarian. Most North Americans feel at home in Costa Rica. (The only other Latin country where I feel this way is Argentina.)

Because of these ingrained attitudes, Costa Rica has avoided the problems that have mired its sister Central American republics in a quicksand of turmoil and tragedy. Costa Rica's devotion to democracy and peaceful cooperation with its neighbors has enabled the country to retain its enviable position as a showcase of prosperity, respect for law, and personal freedoms.

A century-and-a-half tradition of free and honest elections forms the basis for today's political life. Instead of frequent coups d'état, so common in neighboring countries, Costa Ricans change their government by balloting. Although members of the same affluent families usually win election, they are civilians and intellectuals and for the most part are working for the good of the country as a whole, not just for one particular class. In 1889 a revolution threatened when the defeated incumbents considered not recognizing the election results. But at the last minute, they decided to accept the will of the people, thus reinforcing a tradition of democratic process.

A truly significant event that totally separated Costa Rica from the ranks of other Latin American nations occurred in 1948. The ruling party decided not to recognize the results of an election and refused to give up power, ordering new elections because of the closeness of the vote and accusations of fraud. A crisis of democracy threatened. Pepe Figueres, a charismatic member of one of the wealthy families, stepped forward to lead an uprising against the illegal government and its attempt to use the army to hold on to power. The result of this successful revolution (the first and only in Costa Rican history) was a decision to abolish the army and replace it with the *Guardia Civil*, a civilian-controlled police force that augments the local police. In some smaller towns the Guardia Civil is the only police force.

This was a brilliant and bold step. Barracks were turned into schools. Ex-soldiers were given jobs building roads. Money that would normally be absorbed by military corruption and graft was devoted to highways, education, and medical care. Today a huge percentage of the national budget goes to education and culture. Public money pays for four universities, three symphony orchestras, and five autonomous state publishing houses. Of the gross national product, about 10 percent is spent on medical care; Costa Rica has an average of one physician for every 700 inhabitants.

Some North Americans shake their heads in dismay at the lack of a standing army. They ask, "Without a military, how can you defend your country from aggression?" The answer is simple. The function of a Central American military has never been to deter aggression; the military's duty is to protect the *rulers* of the country from its *citizens,* to keep the people in line, and to maintain privileges for the military and the country's financial elite. Democracy doesn't stand a chance when armed soldiers can bully candidates, threaten voters, conduct elections, and then count the ballots! Are we actually surprised when generals are elected president?

Election Day is Costa Rica's most important holiday, a riotous celebration with a joyous spirit that goes far beyond mere politics. Voting is mandatory (nonvoters pay a token fine), but few citizens would think of passing up the fun and excitement of an election. Weeks prior to Election Day, all parties campaign vigorously, with folks everywhere waving their party's flags, cheering enthusiastically when a car displaying a favored flag drives past, or booing good-naturedly when an opposition flag passes by. On the day of an election, all stores, bars, and businesses are closed. All public transportation is free. Buses, taxis, and even private cars are expected to stop when someone indicates he or she wants a ride to a polling booth. In practice, most autos will stop for anyone who waves and asks for a ride in whatever direction the auto is headed. After all, this is a fiesta!

It's interesting to note that many Costa Ricans, when they move from their hometowns to another part of the country, do not change their voting registration to their new address. Because transportation is free, this is an opportunity to return to their hometowns to vote, to visit friends and family, and to party at the same time. Reunions and celebrations are a vital part of Election Day.

Voters must dunk their thumbs into indelible ink to prove they've voted (and cannot vote again), and this purple digit is worn as a proud badge of civic duty. Automobile drivers honk their horns and wave their discolored thumbs in the air as they drive along the streets, to show everyone they have voted, while shouting, "Have *you* voted yet?" There are so many horns blowing on Election Day that it sounds like New Year's Eve at midnight, all day long.

The result is a country intensely dedicated to notions of democracy. All segments of the political spectrum, from extreme Right to far-out Left, are represented; all are totally legal. Yet middle-of-the-road parties always garner most of the votes. Despite vigorous campaigning, the radical Left and extreme Right parties garner but a small percentage of the vote. The crucial point is this: The electorate has a *free choice.* Voters can vote Right, Left, or Center—depending on which party presents the best ideas. Because citizens can change their government at will, Costa Rica is revolution-proof. (Popular revolutions occur *only* when people can't change their government except by violence.) Because voters have choices, middle-of-the-road parties compete to endorse the best programs in order to elect their candidate, and extremist parties are forced to soften their rhetoric in order to attract support.

The end result is a free, prosperous, and peaceful country.

Don't misunderstand—I'm not implying that Costa Rica has no poverty or that Costa Rican workers are highly paid. But compared with the situation in most other Latin American countries, workers here enjoy excellent working conditions, relatively high wages, and government guarantees of fair treatment from employers. Even those living below the poverty level live far better than in most other Third World countries, better, in my opinion, than the millions of people living below the poverty level in the United States. You'll see few if any "street people," panhandlers, or beggars on Costa Rican streets. Children never beg. As a friend observed, "Among the world's poor, Costa Rica's poor are the most affluent."

Welfare is an unknown concept in Costa Rica. Family and friends are always there to help in case of disaster. Jobs are plentiful and unemployment a fraction of that in most highly developed countries. Food is abundant; medical care and education are free. Much agriculture here depends on illegal aliens from Nicaragua to harvest crops and tend banana plantations; Costa Rican workers prefer not to do this kind of backbreaking work. (Does this sound familiar to Californians and Texans, who depend on illegal Mexican immigrants for their crops?)

Open-air markets have a tradition of giving food to the poor, with vendors handing out their surplus to those asking. If a family wants land to grow food, the government does its best to set them up with a farm. Can you now understand that, given all this, welfare isn't necessary?

Although wages are higher here than in neighboring countries, they appear to be extraordinarily low to us Norteamericanos. How can workers be expected to survive on as little as $50 a week, much less be considered well-off? The answer is that even though the cash salary is small, fringe benefits connected with the job make a big difference. In addition to their cash salary, workers are guaranteed items such as sick leave—at the rate of 50 percent of their salary—from the first day of illness up to a lifetime of disability. Workers receive a month's *aguinaldo*, or Christmas bonus, every year and a minimum of two weeks' paid vacation every year. Medical care is free. Women receive six weeks' maternity leave (at full salary), and all receive a Social Security pension upon retirement. It isn't necessary to put aside money for the children's college tuition, because education is free, a basic right provided by the government. Since medical care is free, a worker can spend his entire salary on living expenses without having to put a portion aside for medical emergencies or illnesses.

All these benefits are guaranteed by law, and everybody knows exactly what their rights are. Since there's usually a chronic shortage of help in many regions of Costa Rica, anyone who really wants to work can find a job. The result is that employers have to pay more than minimum wages in order to attract competent workers. This is in contrast to other Latin American countries, where the minimum wage and the maximum wage are usually the same.

When you measure these benefits and put a cash value on them, you'll find that Costa Rican workers are ahead of many North Americans. In the United States an inadequate medical insurance policy can cost a worker more money than many Costa Ricans' total monthly earnings! Since few low-paid U.S. workers can afford insurance, one short visit to a hospital can push them into hopeless poverty. Sick leave? In the United States and Canada, only large, affluent companies can afford such extravagance. Up north paid vacations are not mandatory; they're granted only at the discretion of an employer.

Easy Access

For the past several years, North American tourism overseas has been on the decline, particularly travel to Europe. Out-of-sight prices overseas discourage many North Americans from traveling or living abroad. At one time Europe was considered a bargain place for travel and retirement, but prices in many European countries have risen steadily and now exceed those in North America. When traveling in France, Germany, or Italy, my wife and I feel like poor folk.

In the midst of this softening of foreign travel and retirement, Costa Rican vacations become more and more popular. Tourism increased by 336 percent from 1988 to 1994. In 1995 and 1996 the growth slowed—actually declined several points—but then in 1997 and 1998 the upward movement resumed.

Another thing tourists appreciate about Costa Rica is the ease with which they can enter the country. A Canadian or U.S. tourist traveling with a valid passport has only to present it at the airport for a ninety-day visit, which can easily be extended.

Without a passport a tourist card is needed, and it can be obtained by presenting a birth certificate and identification with a current photo, such as a driver's license. Some tell me they've been granted a tourist card with a voter's registration card. Tourist cards are available at any Costa Rican consulate, from your travel agency, from your airline, or even at the airport when you disembark from the airplane. But I highly recommend carrying a passport. It's inexpensive and serves as the ultimate in identification, especially for renting and driving a car, cashing traveler's checks, and performing other financial transactions. You'll be surprised how many times you'll be asked for your passport or to write your passport number on an official form.

Your Costa Rican visa is for ninety days. It's usually an easy matter to obtain one visa extension for an additional three months; a travel agent can take care of this matter for you. If you don't care to bother with an extension, you can simply exit the country and take a seventy-two-hour break before returning. Many choose to visit Nicaragua, the San Andres Islands (which belong to Colombia), or Panama. Be aware that in 1995, the Ministry of Immigration threatened to tighten the rules on folks who do too many of these in-and-out trips to avoid applying for residency. At the time of writing, the rules are still being applied leniently. This will be discussed in more detail later in this book, along with the rules and procedures for getting permanent residence.

Speaking of permanent residence, according to a U.S. State Department source, about 40,000 monthly Social Security checks are sent to retirees living in Central America. This doesn't tell us much about North American retirees or investors, since many of these 40,000 are naturalized citizens or aliens who returned to their country of birth to retire. However, a large number of native-born Canadians and U.S. citizens choose to work, operate a business, or retire in Central America. As best as I can tell, about 20,000 North American citizens live in Costa Rica—some full-time, others making their homes here seasonally. My estimate is that 6,000 of them are retirees living here year-round. Exact figures are impossible to come by. The percentage of Canadian versus U.S. citizens is difficult to state with precision, but you can be confident that plenty of Canadians are represented. A few North Americans live in other Central American countries—Guatemala, Honduras, Belize, and even El Salvador and Nicaragua—but their ranks are scanty compared with those in Costa Rica.

Because of its small size and economically homogeneous native population, Costa Rica lures a much larger percentage of North Americans (and foreigners in general) who are "starting over" or living part-time in this exotic semiparadise. Furthermore, you'll find these newcomers scattered all around the country—almost every nook and cranny has a few of us living there—instead of concentrated in enclaves or colonies, as is the case in many other foreign countries.

Like Mexico, Costa Rica eagerly welcomes tourists, seasonal residents, and retirees—but Costa Rica places fewer restrictions on newcomers. The government makes it easy to own property or start a business. You can do either even while holding just a tourist visa. To become a *pensionado* in Costa Rica, you need only to prove $600 a month retirement income. For those who aren't retired but would like to live in the country or manage a business, the requirement is $1,000 a month income. Happily, these amounts can easily cover a couple's basic living expenses, something unthinkable in most other parts of the world. Just consider the living standard you'd maintain in the United States on $600 or even $1,000 a month! In Costa Rica on $1,000 a month, you can afford a maid and a gardener, at least part-time.

Two other conditions make Costa Rica special as a destination for part-time or full-time living. Most important is the almost perfect weather. The central plateau is wonderfully temperate, with thermometer readings virtually the same year-round—with highs in the seventies. Beaches are exquisitely tropical, yet like Hawaii, not overly hot or humid.

The second favorable condition is Costa Rica's exciting investment climate. Instead of placing barriers to prevent foreigners from going into business, as do most other countries in the world, Costa Rica encourages foreign investment. To lure investors, the government offers tax incentives and duty-free imports. Again, you don't have to be a citizen or even a legal resident to own property or conduct a business. You can do it on a tourist visa! Not many desirable countries permit you to do this.

Preplanning for Costa Rica

One publication I strongly recommend for anyone considering Costa Rica for anything more than a short vacation is San José's English-language newspaper, the *Tico Times*. If you read every issue, from front to back, including the advertisements, by the time you actually get to Costa Rica, you will know so much about the place that you will feel as if you are returning home. The classified ads keep you up to date on rental costs, housing prices, and what secondhand furniture and appliances sell for. Display ads tell you what you should pay for a hotel room or a bed-and-breakfast, the best places to dine, or where to go for a beach excursion. The news columns are well written, with complete and unbiased news of what's happening in Costa Rica as well as in neighboring countries—news not available in U.S. or Canadian newspapers. Featured are articles relating to foreign residents, governmental actions, or changes in law that may affect them, as well as news of social activities and club events. An extensive letters-to-the-editor section prints opinions of tourists and residents alike, telling of exceptionally nice places to go and which places are rip-offs, giving opinions about the country, kudos and complaints, political views, and just about anything else you can imagine. By all means, start your subscription several months before you leave.

A second essential publication for your initial trip is a good travel book. U.S. and Canadian bookstores are loaded with excellent travel guidebooks packed with information you need on bus and plane schedules, hotels, and places you'll want to visit—in accurate, nonflowery language. It's best to purchase your guidebooks before leaving home; they are sometimes overpriced in Costa Rican bookstores. You'll need this additional information because *Choose Costa Rica* is not intended to be a comprehensive travel book; it's a guide to retirement, long-term living, and investment in the country.

Choose Costa Rica also tries to avoid making recommendations on business services such as real estate agencies, simply because of the impossibility of being able to vouch for reliability or character. Personnel can change; brokerages are sold; and Costa Rican real estate agents aren't bound by the strict rules of ethics common in the United States and Canada. Your job is to investigate, conduct inquiries, and make your own, on-the-spot selections. When business services are mentioned, it isn't as an endorsement of their reliability but simply as a starting place for checking out the field. At the time I interviewed these business representatives, I was impressed by their knowledge—but that says nothing of their competence or honesty. These are judgments you must make for yourself.

Finally, I emphatically urge that you make no decisions about permanent moves or business investments without spending several months "on location," getting to know the country, meeting the people, and learning what it's all about. Before making any financial moves, find a good lawyer, one recommended by someone in the North American community. Above all, don't hand your money to someone simply because he or she also comes from Omaha or Ottawa and has an honest face. Honest faces and firm handshakes are the mark of successful swindlers! Costa Rica has suffered its fair share of sweet-talking Gringos with designs on your pocketbooks. There's something about a foreign country that tends to bring out latent larceny in some people. Later on in this book, we'll discuss ways to protect yourself from theft.

Why "Ticos"?

Throughout this book you'll see the term *Tico* used when speaking of Costa Ricans. This is the appropriate nickname for a Costa Rican citizen, just as *Gringo* is used for North Americans in general, and *Yankee* for a citizen of the United States. The term *Gringo* is an accepted nickname, for both Canadian and U.S. citizens—no one takes umbrage by it, because Ticos mean it in an almost affectionate way. And Costa Ricans call themselves *Ticos* when distinguishing themselves from foreigners, instead of the more cumbersome *Costariquense*.

The name *Tico* comes from an archaic practice of using the sound *-tico* on the end of a word as a diminutive instead of the normal *-tito*. For example, whereas a Mexican would say *momentito* for "just a tiny moment," some Costa Ricans (not all) might say *momentico*. Thus, a kitten would be a *gatico* in Costa Rica but a *gatito* in Mexico. Not all Costa Ricans use this ending, but enough do to keep the tradition alive.

One uniquely Costa Rican term, solidly ingrained into the language, is *pura vida*. I suppose this would translate as "it's a great life," but in effect it means "OK," "cool," "all right," or sometimes as emphatic "aw-right!" A clerk in a store, rather than asking, "Would you like anything else?" might instead ask, "*Pura vida?*" A gas station attendant might ask, "Is your oil *pura vida*, or should I check it for you?"

What's Costa Rica Like?

Costa Rica is a small country, even though it doesn't appear so from the standpoint of the traveler who is driving a rental car from one end of the country to the other, over winding roads, uphill and down. Every turn in the road brings a new vista, something else to contemplate. Actually, the country contains a little less than 20,000 square miles, much of it almost unpopulated.

Travel articles and guidebooks traditionally describe Costa Rica as being "the size of West Virginia," but that's not really accurate. Some travel writer must have said that years ago, and others automatically repeat this misinformation. The truth is, Costa Rica is smaller than West Virginia by 20 percent. To be more accurate, let's say that Costa Rica is about the size of New Hampshire and Maryland, with poor little Rhode Island tossed in for good measure. Would it help to say that Costa Rica is about half the size of Kentucky? If that makes the place sound small and insignificant, we can balance out the equation by pointing out that Costa Rica is larger than Albania, Denmark, Belgium, Holland, Israel, or Switzerland (plus a handful of countries you and I have never heard of).

Yet few other countries of any size offer such a diversity of scenery and climate or such a wide variety of flora and fauna. Probably no other country in the world devotes as large a percentage of its territory to national parks and wildlife refuges. About 27 percent of Costa Rica's land is thus protected. These preserves range from cloud forests to tropical beaches, from volcanic craters to jungle swamps and inland waterways. The national park system is a major attraction for tourism.

Costa Rica's bewildering assortment of wildlife includes 850 species of birds—more than three times as many as in the United States and Canada combined. Representative mammals are monkeys, coatis, jaguars, and ocelots, as well as sloths, tapirs, and agoutis. One evening down on the Pacific Coast, a large anteater ambled in front of my car, its long snout almost touching the ground in front and an equally heavy tail drooping behind, looking very prehistoric. Turtles, colorful frogs, and toads of all descriptions are found, as are crocodiles and iguanas. Snakes? Of course. They range from huge boa constrictors to tiny coral snakes. Experts say there are more varieties of butterflies in Costa Rica than in all the African continent; more than 2,000 species have been collected so far and more are being discovered. The number of orchids and bromeliads confuses the mind. This is truly a naturalist's paradise.

Many tropical countries offer beaches and vacation accommodations, but nowhere else in the world can a tourist find such a combination of beaches, mountains, friendliness, and tropical wonder that's accessible year-round.

The Costa Rican government recognizes these unique assets and actively involves its citizens in both the preservation and the exploitation of nature at the same time. How do you protect as well as exploit the environment? Just one example: By hiring local people to guard and preserve endangered turtle nesting beaches, jobs are created. Beach villages then become tourist attractions, complete with motels, restaurants, and shops, thus creating even more jobs. Visitors from all over the world can now visit cloud forests, turtle nesting beaches, and nature preserves—in comfort. In the process, they leave much-needed foreign currency with Costa Rican businesses and banks.

Many North Americans and Europeans are scrambling to join this bandwagon and, with government encouragement, are investing heavily in tourist businesses, particularly in motels, restaurants, and endeavors of a like nature. Some enterprises become instant successes, with full bookings and plenty of business. One Canadian, who started a motel on the Caribbean side of the country a few years ago, showed me the registration book for his twelve-unit facility, saying proudly, "This place has an occupancy rate of 98 percent during the tourist season and over 60 percent during the off-season." I asked for a room but was told, "Not until next week. I'm booked solid." This process of expansion did, however, slow significantly in 1995. The tourist industry didn't collapse or anything like that, but instead of an expected 10 to 20 percent increase in tourism, people were shocked when there was only a 2 percent boost. In 1997 and 1998 tourist business began to rise again, although not as dramatically as before. (Details about starting and operating businesses in Costa Rica are presented in Chapter 10.)

A Country of Contradictions

Before readers are left with the impression that things are perfect in paradise, that Costa Rica is the best of all worlds, let's examine some contradictions.

The first contradiction: Even though the Costa Rican government is totally committed to preserving the environment and tries to control illegal deforestation, it also permits foreign companies to bulldoze forests in order to make more banana plantations. The government puts large tracts of land into biological and wildlife reserves, forest reserves, national parks, and Indian reservations, yet at the same time, farmers and agribusiness cut down forests on private tracts at a faster rate than anywhere else in the world. The economy destroys in the name of progress, while the government tries to preserve in the name of conservation. But at least the government does try, and its efforts are improving.

Another contradiction: The growth of ecotourism in Costa Rica brings hundreds of thousands of visitors to enjoy the ecological wonderlands, but large numbers of visitors tramping through delicately balanced wilderness systems threaten to destroy the very ecological treasures that lure them to Costa Rica in the first place. For this reason, the government raised admission fees to national parks in an effort to cut traffic to some extent. Some say the increase was merely to bring in more revenue—that may well be true—but it did indeed lower the number of visitors and traffic in national parks. The fee increase had a beneficial side effect in directing more business toward private ecological parks and developments. However, the tourist industry raised strenuous objections to the higher fees, claiming they hurt business. So the government offered a deal: "You cut the hotel rates 15 percent, and we'll reduce national park entrance fees by 60 percent." The result is that entrance fees to national parks, which had ranged from $5.00 to $15.00, are being reduced to a fixed price of $6.00 for all visitors, and more than a hundred hotels have agreed to lower their room rates by 15 percent.

Yet another contradiction in Costa Rica is the high incidence in petty crime among such a peaceful population—particularly in larger cities. In fact, the major criticism this book has received in the past was that it did not place proper emphasis on the crime rates. I have to admit that I've had a propensity to overlook this issue, probably because I feel that the problem is lightweight compared with the situation in other Latin countries and is almost insignificant when matched with the crime rate in most U.S. communities of similar sizes. Any increase in crime rates can be considered a natural phenomenon that parallels the rise of crime back home, although on a more minor scale. We'll discuss crime in more detail in Chapter 7.

Some will disagree, but to me a bigger annoyance than petty crime is Costa Rica's substandard roads and heavy automobile traffic in the cities. From time to time, public anger initiates a concerted campaign to eliminate the monster chasms and bottomless pits that are euphemistically referred to as "potholes." Once stirred into action, government workers do a remarkably fast job of smoothing things over. Unfortunately, when they turn their attention elsewhere, the potholes begin making a determined comeback. Someday they'll make a movie: *The Pothole That Ate San José.* To be perfectly fair, I must admit that in the spring of 1998, the roads were in relatively good shape. Of course, the big presidential election was scheduled for February 1.

Combine treacherous pavement with too many automobiles on the Meseta Central's street system and you have a situation that encourages taxi rides into congested parts of San José. Fortunately, cab rides are cheap, and more than 7,000 taxis roam the streets, so you don't have a long wait between rides. The problems of potholes and heavy traffic in the city will always be another of those fly-in-the-ointment nuisances you'll have to accept if you want to live in paradise. Nothing's perfect. The farther you get from downtown San José, the less the annoyance. When you are really deep into rural areas, the biggest obstacle to driving might be a herd of cattle being driven down the gravel road, or a sow and litter of piglets ambling across the way.

Another situation that could become a problem as foreign population increases is foreign ownership of most of the coastal lands. Although the Costa Rican people are friendly, gentle, and welcoming, they cannot help but feel some level of resentment as they see foreigners bid up the price of property until it is out of their price range. (The big-money players are heavily represented by German, Swiss, and Italian buyers.) At present this level of resentment is low, and it's balanced by an appreciation for how foreign investment creates jobs and bolsters the economy. Where my wife and I own property, the local people tell us they'd rather see foreigners own the land, because Ticos tend to clear-cut the forest to make room for cattle. Cattle ranches create few jobs, but businesses and residences bring full employment and prosperity to all.

Visitors and foreign residents can do little to resolve these contradictions, but they need to be aware that problems do exist and may crop up in the future. The best they can do is try to minimize their impact upon the natural resources of the country. None of these problems have gotten completely out of hand, and solutions are constantly being sought by the

Costa Rican government. But as is the way in any democracy, the going is slow and cumbersome. Just be aware that not everything is perfect in paradise—but for my money, it's still paradise!

Menu of Climates

For such a small country, Costa Rica has an astonishing variety of climates. From the misty mountaintops of Talamanca and Monteverde to the dry northern Guanacaste province, from the permanent spring weather of the Arenal area to the jungle lushness of the Caribbean Coast, Costa Rica has every kind of climate one might desire. The exception is frozen snow and bitter cold; but you don't want that anyway. Yes, there are seasons, but the differences between them are minimal, mostly measured in differences in rainfall rather than in temperature variation. Unlike many other world vacation spots, Costa Rica isn't a one-season destination; almost any time of the year can be a perfect time to visit. For those who live here full-time, the seasonal changes add spice to retirement. September and October are probably the least popular months, though, for these are the rainiest ones.

In Costa Rica people transpose the meanings of winter and summer. They call the months of December, January, and February "summer," or the "dry season." These are the months that children take their "summer vacation" from school. To a Costa Rican, "winter" means June, July, and August! Conversations can become very confusing when Costa Ricans and North Americans discuss the seasons, with summer and winter having opposite meanings for each. To avoid misunderstandings, I generally say, "June, July, and August" instead of "winter," or better yet I'll say "dry season" or "rainy season"—then everybody knows what I mean.

The dry season, which actually begins around the end of November and lasts until the end of April, isn't parched and arid, as the name might imply. Occasional showers keep plants and lawns pleasantly green and flowers blooming in the higher parts of the mountains, where most folks live. On the Caribbean Coast and the area around Lake Arenal, the "dry season" is just a figure of speech; rain knows no seasons here. Some Pacific coastal areas are truly dry during December, January, and February, very much like California summers, when rain rarely falls.

The "winter" months of June, July, and August—also referred to as the "green season"—are actually cooler than the "summer" months. This is because of frequent rains and almost daily afternoon cloud cover.

A common misconception is that "rainy season" means continuous downpours. Typically, even in the most rainy parts of the country, the day begins with glorious sunshine, with blossoms glowing in the sparkling clean air and birds singing happily. Then clouds roll in after lunch, and rain starts falling between 2:00 and 4:00 P.M. (In some places you can almost set your clock by it.) A heavy downpour sends people indoors for a couple of hours. Then sunshine returns, and the world is once again refreshed. Other sections of the country enjoy sunshine all day, with the rain falling mostly at night. This is the "best" rain, for falling asleep to the drumming sound of raindrops on the roof is a delight. Seldom does it rain *every* day; several days in a row can be perfectly dry.

Because most North Americans customarily think of the tropics as a place to visit in their winter season—to escape the snow and ice of their homelands—they are often surprised to find that the rainy months of June, July, and August are the favorite time of year for many who live in Costa Rica. "You can't really appreciate this country until you've experienced our winter months," says Graham Henshaw, an expatriate from England. "Everything is green now in January, but when the rains start in May, the grass changes to an even brighter emerald color. Flowers that only bloom in July and August are absolutely stunning. Winter is my favorite time of year."

To further complicate matters, what is true of the mountain valley environment around San José isn't necessarily true on the Caribbean side, which can be flooded with sunshine while the capital is awash in *aguaceros* (rainstorms) and vice versa. The truth is, no matter what time of year you choose to visit, you're guaranteed a serving of nice sunny weather—and probably some rain as well.

Weather in the tropics is largely determined by altitude. At ocean level the climate is a year-round summer; at moderate elevations year-round spring is a better description. The higher you go, the cooler it gets. A sweater or jacket can be worn almost every evening of the year in higher elevations. Your travel wardrobe should include shirts, sweaters, and jackets you can peel off or pile on, depending on whether you're dining at a beach restaurant, visiting a volcano, or traveling somewhere in between. Be sure to bring raingear and sturdy shoes if you plan any jungle exploring, plus sunscreen for visits to mountains or beaches; the tropical sun is persistent at all altitudes.

On the northwestern Pacific side, the dry season is exactly that, with very little rain falling from early December until the beginning of May.

The grass turns brown, and many trees lose their leaves, just as they do in North America in the winter. But the reason for leaf loss is to conserve water, not because of frost and freezing weather. Most trees are evergreen, but even some of these lose a portion of their leaves. It isn't as bleak as it sounds, for many of these trees replace leaves with brilliantly colored blossoms, as this is the time of year to attract bees, butterflies, and other pollinating insects.

Even on the dry Guanacaste Coast, you'll find microcosms of green environments tucked away in the interior valleys, where sporadic rains are coaxed from the westerly Pacific winds. Farther south along the Pacific Coast, the dry-season rainfall is even more frequent, keeping things pleasantly green during the driest months. (At the end of this chapter, you'll find a weather chart that provides statistics on the microclimates of Costa Rica.)

Insects and the Tropics

An odd thing about the weather checkerboard of Costa Rica is that, contrary to what one might think, the more humid areas are not necessarily the most insect-plagued. Of course, bring your insect repellent, but I'm convinced that you need it less in most places in Costa Rica than you do in the American Midwest or places in Canada. Along the forested Pacific Coast and the Nicoya Peninsula—where the insect varieties are amazingly abundant—mosquitoes and flies pester you far less than in the dry, almost desertlike parts of Guanacaste. On the humid Caribbean Coast, where rain can fall almost any time of the year and where bugs can get so large you'd think they've been taking hormones, household cockroaches and flies are not nearly as plentiful as I've seen in Houston or New Orleans. (I've seen many kinds of beetles but surprisingly few ordinary cockroaches in my Costa Rican travels.)

In parts of Costa Rica, even in the most tropical locations, insects are so benign that many natives don't bother with screens on their windows. Of course, the rainy season in some areas will make a liar of me, so best carry repellent. This is particularly advisable when staying in one of the areas where dengue fever has been reported (mostly around the outskirts of Puntarenas and near Liberia). There's a vigorous campaign under way at present to eliminate the mosquito that spreads the flulike ailment.

Why flies and mosquitoes are relatively scarce might seem puzzling. But I believe the answer is that the physical environment in Costa Rica is largely intact. The natural enemies of pests like flies and mosquitoes haven't been eliminated by pesticides, chemicals, and other methods, as they have back home. By day, birds of all descriptions flit back and forth, snacking on insects, keeping them in balance with nature. Many birds consider houseflies to be special treats. By night, squadrons of bats keep up the good work, finishing off mosquitoes before they get a chance to do much damage. According to one naturalist, a small bat can catch about 600 mosquito-size insects per hour, and a large colony of bats will consume thousands of pounds of insects every night! (There are more than thirty species of bats in Costa Rica, thank you very much.)

Meanwhile, lizards, geckos, and chameleons patrol the walls and corners of houses, cleaning up cockroaches and water bugs before they have a chance to infest the kitchen or make a condominium out of your bathroom. The fearsome-looking praying mantis sometimes prowls about the edges of rooms, snapping up bugs that the lizards miss. Ugly as the mantis is, we love 'em!

My wife and I have additional help in keeping our Costa Rica home bug-free. From time to time our house is invaded by army ants. They march in broad formation up a concrete column to the veranda and spill over the floors in a busy wave of housecleaning. They remove moths and other night-flying insects that committed suicide against the porch lights the previous night, and they scour the baseboards, corners, and ceilings in search of bugs, beetles, and insect eggs. Scorpions flee in terror; they have no defense against army ants—if they tarry, they are dismantled and served as snacks. Even snakes fear the ants. We simply stay out of their way or prop our feet out of range while we read a novel, until their twenty-minute cleaning expedition is finished. We say goodbye and thank them as they continue on their way to their next housecleaning duties.

Not that insects can't make one suffer. Some very small creatures made my last trip to the Pacific beaches memorable for several weeks. These were the dreaded "no-see-ums," a generic name given to any tiny bug that bites without your knowing you are being attacked but makes you suffer afterward. In this case, they were probably some kind of miniature sand flea because they got me on the ankles and lower legs. However, it was my own fault; I should know better than to stroll along the beach at dusk without repellent on my bare legs.

Now I'm going to reveal a personal discovery concerning these bites: It's a salve called Panalog. This is an all-purpose antibiotic and fungicide that veterinarians routinely prescribe when treating cats and dogs for infections, rashes, and general skin problems. If you have a dog or cat, you'll probably have some at home. I've found that a dab of Panalog on a mosquito or no-see-um bite not only stops my itching but heals the puncture almost immediately. According to my brother, who is a veterinarian, the only known side effects of Panalog are an occasional urge to chase Pontiacs and a tendency to scratch behind your ear with your hind foot.

It's claimed that Costa Rica has more species of insects than anywhere else in the world, and I believe it. Once in Cahuita—on the Caribbean Coast—I was about to enter my cabin when I encountered an enormous beetle. It was about the size of a large teacup, shaped like a giant ladybug, and the color of an olive drab army helmet. Feeling brave, I gingerly picked it up by its back, correctly figuring that its wicked-looking legs couldn't reach around the shell. I carried it to a nearby restaurant and proudly displayed my beetle to the people sitting at the bar, figuring that I'd raise a few eyebrows. The bartender looked at my discovery with a bored expression as he remarked, "Yes, those little ones are females." It turned out that I was holding a rhinoceros beetle, possibly the largest bug of the entire insect world. They tell me the male, which fortunately I never happened to confront, grows to a length of 10 inches, sports enormous horns, and is colored in brilliant metallic hues. Harmless, though.

Earthquakes

All along the mountain chains that stretch from the tip of South America to Alaska, you will feel earthquakes. As a Californian, I've become accustomed to them and seldom experience more than a slight feeling of excitement when windows start rattling and my desk sways a bit. We Californians expect to have several minor quakes a year, and every twenty-five years or so, a big one.

So it should come as no surprise that Costa Rica has its share of shakes and tremors—actually, more than its share. The really big ones here are spaced by decades instead of generations. Yet Costa Ricans are just as calm about earthquakes as Californians are. After all, compared with the 700 or so tornadoes that slam the midwestern and eastern parts of North America, claiming eighty to a hundred victims each season, an occasional shaker seems relatively mild.

The last big tremor—a whopping 7.4 on the Richter Scale—hit the

Caribbean Coast near the city of Limón in April 1991. Older structures suffered the most damage, particularly those not constructed to modern-day standards. However, by the beginning of the next tourist season, much of the damage had been repaired, hotels were operating, roads were open to traffic, and tourism was going full blast.

A few months after the quake, I visited Cahuita, not too far from the epicenter. Expecting to see a lot of damage and hear horror stories, I was delighted to learn that there were no fatalities in the village and that, except for one major building (which had been made of nonreinforced cement) and a few other smaller structures, the town came through relatively unscathed. Cahuita construction is of wood, which may shake, rattle, and twist but doesn't usually tumble down.

Costa Rica's 7.4 shaker claimed about forty lives, one of the worst ever. But compare this earthquake with the one in Iran the year before; it was 7.5 on the Richter Scale and claimed more than 50,000 victims. A horrible 6.9 quake in Armenia in 1989 killed 25,000 people; one in Costa Rica the following year was just as strong yet nobody was killed. Why the difference?

One answer to this question, besides lower population density, is sensible construction methods. Costa Rican homes and businesses are designed with earthquakes in mind. Costa Rica has prohibited the use of adobe in constructing homes for more than eighty years. This is the only nation in the hemisphere with a ban on adobe, a material that has a tendency to collapse and bury earthquake victims. Wood, reinforced concrete block, or stressed cement is infinitely safer. Instead of picturesque tile roofs, which can crush inhabitants under tons of heavy beams and broken tile, most Costa Rican roofs are of ordinary-looking corrugated aluminum, plastic, or iron. These lightweight roofs may slide about during a quake, but they won't collapse and kill people by burying them.

An interesting feature of the 1991 quake was an uplifting of the coastline. The force raised the land as much as 5 feet near the town of Puerto Limón and 1.5 feet at Puerto Viejo. Coral reefs are now dry land, at the edge of surf where fishermen once hauled in crab, shrimp, and red snapper. This lifting of the land from the sea is a wonderful example of how the Central American land bridge was formed some two or three million years ago when quake activity began pushing the land ever higher. Geologists find coral fossils on mountaintops now 9,000 feet above sea level.

Temperatures and Rainfall for Selected Costa Rican Locations

Alajuela

AVG.	JAN.	FEB.	MAR.	APR.	MAY	JUN.	JUL.	AUG.	SEPT.	OCT.	NOV.	DEC.	ANNUAL
					(In degrees Fahrenheit and inches)								
HIGHS	81	83	85	85	82	81	81	81	80	80	80	81	81
LOWS	62	62	63	63	64	64	64	63	63	63	63	63	63
RAIN	0.3	0.5	0.6	3	11	11	7	10	1	14	20	1	92

Golfito

HIGHS	91	92	92	91	90	89	89	90	89	89	89	90	90
LOWS	71	72	73	73	73	72	71	71	71	71	71	71	72
RAIN	6	6	8	11	19	18	18	22	28	28	23	12	199

Cahuita

HIGHS	86	86	87	87	87	87	86	86	87	87	86	86	86
LOWS	68	68	69	71	71	71	71	71	71	71	69	69	69
RAIN	13	8	8	11	11	12	17	13	6	8	16	18	141

Nicoya

HIGHS	91	93	95	96	91	89	89	89	87	87	87	89	87
LOWS	69	71	71	73	73	71	71	71	71	71	69	69	71
RAIN	0.2	0.4	1	3	11	13	10	12	16	16	5	1	89

Manuel Antonio

HIGHS	87	87	89	89	89	87	87	87	86	86	86	86	87
LOWS	69	69	71	71	71	71	69	69	71	71	71	69	71
RAIN	3	1	2	7	16	17	18	19	21	26	16	7	153

San José

HIGHS	73	75	77	78	78	78	77	77	78	77	75	77	77
LOWS	59	59	60	60	62	62	67	62	60	60	60	59	62
RAIN	0.4	0.2	0.5	2	9	12	9	10	13	13	6	2	77

MESETA CENTRAL

Nuevo Arenal
Lake Arenal
Tilarán
Santa Ana
San Ramón
Poás
La Garita
Atenas
Alajuela
San José
Orotina
Heredia
San Pedro
Escazú
San Isidro del
General

THE MESETA CENTRAL & BEYOND

Those North Americans who make Costa Rica their home—part-time or full-time—fall into two categories. They either insist on living in the temperate zone or shun that for the more romantic, although warmer, tropical zone. Each group can't understand why the other group want to live where they do. Costa Ricans themselves are also divided about which is best, tropical or temperate. As proof of this division, half of the entire Tico population chooses to live in the higher reaches of the country, more or less in the middle, in an area known as the Meseta Central. Roughly half of the expatriates from the United States and Canada also prefer living here.

The Meseta Central is surrounded by the mountain range that starts near Costa Rica's border with Nicaragua and marches south until it crosses the border of Panama. This range is known as the "Cordillera," a picturesque complex of high ridges, valleys, peaks, and tablelands—perpetually covered with green vegetation and teeming with wildlife. The mountains vary from rounded promontories to the rugged peaks of the Talamanca Range, dominated by 12,600-foot Cerro Chirripó. Valleys and rolling tablelands are interspersed between steep mountains and volcanic formations, providing fertile agricultural space. The largest complex of valleys is the Meseta Central.

San José, the largest city in Costa Rica, nestles in a wide depression about halfway down the Cordillera, at an altitude of 3,750 feet above sea level. The city of 275,000 inhabitants is surrounded by dozens of satellite towns and villages and by small cities such as Heredia, Alajuela, Escazú, and Cartago perched at various elevations on the uneven plateau. About 15 miles wide by 40 miles long, this break in the mountains is called the "Valle Central" (Central Valley) or the "Meseta Central" (Central Plateau), depending on who is speaking. From just about any point in this area, you are treated to views of the high mountains that form a half-bowl around the Meseta Central. This is not only where most Ticos live but also the most heavily populated area in Central America.

Towns and villages surrounding the capital have grown to the point that it is sometimes difficult to tell exactly where one ends and another begins. Although greenery and small farms are abundant, much of the Meseta Central blurs into a loose suburban complex.

Why so many prefer the Meseta Central is a question answered in two words: superb climate. This is the land of perpetual spring. Daily high temperatures are almost always in the seventies—creating newspaper headlines on occasions when the thermometer climbs into the high eighties. Low temperatures are always in the sixties. Understand, these aren't average temperatures, which can give a distorted picture, but average high and low readings. Because Costa Rica is so close to the equator, temperatures vary little between summer and winter.

Even this weather doesn't please everyone; some prefer temperatures in the eighties and even nineties, while others feel more comfortable in the sixties and low seventies. Fortunately, in Costa Rica it's possible to "fine-tune" your weather simply by moving a few kilometers in one direction or another. Since temperatures and weather patterns are determined by altitude in the tropics, just a few meters higher or lower elevation make a difference. A fifteen-minute drive from anywhere on the Meseta Central brings you to a slightly different climate, with more or less rainfall and warmer or cooler temperatures.

It seems as if each town or community here brags of having the "best climate in the world." Each is perfect for at least some folks. Alajuela is proud of being a few degrees warmer than San José, while Escazú is happy about being a few degrees cooler. Poas boasts about being even cooler than Escazú, and La Garita brags about its rating by *National Geographic* of having one of the three best climates in the world. The wonderful thing is that all these choices, however slight, are freely available to you. (The weather chart at the end of Chapter 2 illustrates this diversity of weather.)

San José

San José, the capital and business center of Costa Rica, is a comfortable place to live despite its large population. Although downtown streets throng with shoppers and automobiles, neighborhoods a few blocks away can be tranquil residential areas. San José doesn't suffer from the widespread slum zones that plague many U.S. cities. You'll find modest neighborhoods, to be sure, and a few run-down areas but not the starkly depressing ghettos so apparent in some large U.S. cities. Truthfully, I've found few residential neighborhoods in San José where I would feel uncomfortable or ashamed to live. There is a slight smog problem in the downtown streets—mostly caused by belching diesel trucks, buses, and taxis. Continuous cross-breezes keep the atmosphere superclean, except in the immediate vicinity of a bus or truck. Some residents disagree with my denial of San José smog. But having lived in Los Angeles and visited places like Athens and Rome, I just don't trust air I cannot see.

As you might expect, the farther from the business center, the better the housing. However, this isn't because of a decaying city core, as is the case with some U.S. cities; it's because the center is taken up with businesses, hotels, restaurants, and uncountable shops and stores. For some reason, people from all over the valley feel a compulsion to do their shopping in downtown San José. This is partly from habit and the fact that shopping is something of a social event. By the thousands crowds of shoppers amble along the streets and avenues, checking out window displays, making purchases, and gossiping with friends. Most could shop in their own neighborhoods, but it's more fun this way, and here is where you will find those scarce items you need. So many pedestrians pack the main downtown avenue (Avenida Central) that the city has been forced to turn part of it into a mall. During peak periods pedestrians turn the rest of the downtown section into a virtual mall by filling the streets, forcing drivers to detour around Avenida Central.

Although just about any neighborhood in San José is comfortable, North Americans are predisposed to congregate in some of the more costly areas. This is understandable, since they tend to be more affluent than Costa Ricans and can better afford upscale neighborhoods. The western edge of San José attracts a large number of foreign residents, particularly around the Sábana Park area (Sábana Sur and Sábana Norte), the upscale neighborhood of Rohrmoser, and some areas of Pavas. Better supermarkets, nicer restaurants, and amenities such as tennis clubs and attractive parks make this a very livable part of the city. The *Tico Times* classified section frequently lists homes and condos for sale or rent in Pavas and Rohrmoser. Typically, rents for condos start around $400, and homes can go as high as $1,500 a month for a supernice place. Still farther out, toward the airport, is Cariari, a luxury area with a golf course and country club.

Directly across the valley, the towns of Escazú and Bello Horizonte match Rohrmoser for elegance and expensive housing. Just to the east of downtown San José, Barrio Escalante is an affordable neighborhood of stately older homes. This used to be the "in" place for wealthy Ticos years ago and is now in the process of adapting to middle-class families. Still farther out on the eastern edge of the city, Los Yoses and San Pedro supply moderate to expensive housing, with some of San José's most exclusive neighborhoods. San Pedro provides a university atmosphere, with many rentals available at student budget levels.

By shopping around you can usually find housing that will fit your pocketbook and lifestyle. Remember that ads in the *Tico Times* are directed toward North Americans who can afford to pay more. For less expensive places, check the classified ads in *La Nación;* that's where Ticos find their rentals. San José has several apartment complexes renting furnished places by the day or week that make excellent "base camps" while one is looking for permanent quarters or trying out Costa Rica as a place to live.

Finding Your Way

Searching for an address in and around San José and its suburbs can be an exercise in frustration; few buildings have street numbers, and no one pays attention to them when they do. Even worse, many streets have no names, or at least no street names posted on the corners. Suppose you are looking for the García residence, whose address is listed as "From Caballo Blanco 250 mts. West, 300 South." To understand where this house is located, you need to know the location of a store called Caballo Blanco, then go 2½ blocks (250 meters) to the west and then 3 blocks south (300 meters). At that point, you need to ask someone which house belongs to the García family.

This confusion isn't restricted to residences; businesses use the same system. On maps, advertisements, and business cards, the word *calle* is often abbreviated as *c*, *avenida* as *a*, and *central* as *ctl*. The distance from a point is given in meters (abbreviated with an *m*), although sometimes people give it in *varas* instead of meters, both meaning a long pace or step about a yard long. (A *vara* is a bit shorter than a yard, about 33 inches, an ancient measurement in use before the introduction of the metric system.)

Examples of address insanity: The address of the Hotel Presidente would be "c ctl, av 7–9," which translates "on Calle Central between Avenidas 7 and 9." The address of the bus terminal for Alajuela is "a 2, c 12–14," meaning "facing Avenida 2, between Calles 12 and 14."

Directions and addresses can be vague to the point of impossibility. This is particularly true away from the orderly grid of north-south, east-west streets. An address might be described thus: "From the gasoline station, go

100 meters north and 75 *varas* to the east." Which gasoline station? My favorite address is on a real estate agent's business card. It says "50 *varas* south from where the Mas Por Menos supermarket used to be."

It doesn't do any good to complain; Ticos understand the system perfectly and actually become confused when you use logical addresses. Often when I take a cab downtown, asking to go to "Avenida Segundo and Calle Primera," the driver responds with a puzzled frown. When I add "Teatro Nacional," his face lights up with understanding and away we go.

Away from the City: Alajuela

Although many foreigners live in the city of San José, the majority prefer one of the smaller communities surrounding the city. These towns range from expensive to moderately priced places to live. For some mysterious reason, at least six of these towns have the same name—San Isidro—which adds to the confusion of finding your way around! San Antonio is another favorite place-name that is scattered about like leaves in the wind.

One of the less expensive yet pleasant places for foreigners to live is Alajuela. Situated on the western edge of San José, this small city is convenient to the airport and a twenty-minute bus ride from downtown San José. Clean, modern buses run every few minutes during the day, stopping at the airport on the way to and from San José. (If you have a small amount of luggage, this is an inexpensive way to get downtown from the airport.)

Your first approach to Alajuela can give a misleading impression. The highway comes in on a higher level than the town, providing an unfortunate panorama of tin roofs in every direction—some new, some rusted, some painted red to resemble tile, but mostly of corrugated iron or aluminum. Now, in the United States, a tin roof usually implies cheap construction, structures such as storage sheds or temporary buildings. But as explained in Chapter 2, this is earthquake country; those picturesque tile roofs can be deadly when they collapse. You may see occasional tile roofs, but you can be reassured that underneath all that pretty tile is a steel-reinforced cement roof. Since the temperature never gets hot or cold, the insulation value of a heavy tile roof is beside the point.

Alajuela's focal point is a large park in the center of town (called the Parque Central, of course), a pleasant place shaded by tall trees, with chessboards built into some of the cement benches that surround the park. If you would like to meet North American retirees to ask for information about

Alajuela, this is the place to come; sometimes there seems as much English spoken here as Spanish. This is the place to find out about housing rentals, who is leaving for the States, who has a car for sale, and who can recommend a gardener or a maid. A reputable money changer sits on a bench across from the bank in case you want to deal with him rather than stand in line. In the evenings a mixture of classical and pop music can be heard by the park's bandstand, where professional musicians entertain a couple of times a week. A new addition to the expatriate scene in Alajuela is a bar/restaurant called Señor Gazpacho, run by Tom Best and Ken Green from San Diego, who always wanted to have a Mexican restaurant. It turns out that 90 percent of their customers are Ticos who also like Mexican food. If you spend enough time sitting at one of the outdoor tables, you'll eventually meet every Gringo in Alajuela.

Alajuela has several rather attractive neighborhoods, none very expensive, yet all classy in appearance. One area we inspected is called Trinidad, about a fifteen-minute walk from the park. In 1996 I revisited an American and his Costa Rican wife at their attractive Trinidad home, consisting of three bedrooms, two baths, a maid's room, and a garage. Three years earlier he had estimated the value of his home at $35,000. When asked what the home's present-day value might be, the owner, a retired orchardist from Florida, said, "Remember, I told you that property here is bound to go up. Today I figure $47,000 would be a fair price." In similar U.S. neighborhoods it would cost triple that, at least. Another nice-looking neighborhood is near the local sports stadium, with prices even lower. All these homes have attractive landscaping, some with wrought-iron fences.

Housing costs in Alajuela seem to be exceptional bargains, considering the quality of the area. Other places available during my last visit: a two-bedroom, two-bath home for $29,000 and a four-bedroom place for $58,000. An interesting aspect of Alajuela's housing market is that $250 to $500 a month can rent a satisfactory home, one that would sell for between $30,000 and $50,000. (These prices were quoted for the previous edition of *Choose Costa Rica* and, according to Alajuela residents, are still accurate.)

Heredia

When I first started visiting Costa Rica, Heredia was located way out in the country—a small town containing a scattering of nice homes with acreage on the outskirts. Today the town has expanded toward the sprawl of San José, Alajuela, and other nearby communities. Some of the outskirts are still somewhat rural and countrified, but smaller homes have intruded between the large estates, partially filling in the openness of yesterday. Today Heredia is a sister city of Alajuela, as far as retirees are concerned. It's a place of modestly priced homes as well as some truly spiffy domiciles.

The center of Heredia, like its neighboring city of Alajuela, features a large, friendly *Parque Central* (central park) complete with weekly band concerts. This park is shaded by stands of enormous mango trees and has the usual park benches for informal meetings and gossiping. Like the Parque Central in Alajuela, Heredia's Parque Central has a large church at one end—a cathedral, actually—that has watched over the quietness of the square for more than 200 years.

Heredia's famous market is large, featuring quality meats and exceptionally fresh vegetables, fruits, and greens of all descriptions. Much of the market's exotic produce is grown by local residents in their backyards. Saturday is market day, and selections are bountiful as well as fresh-picked. People from all over the valley come here for their weekend shopping. The market is near the Parque Central and dates back 100 years. Like most other cities on the Meseta Central, Heredia homes don't have street numbers. But instead of saying "150 meters north," it's customary to say "150 meters *arriba*," for the town slopes uphill toward the north. "Two hundred meters *abajo*" would, of course, mean 200 meters to the south.

Heredia doesn't attract quite as many foreign retirees and residents as Alajuela does, at least not in the central part of town. The foreign community seems to be scattered in and around the city or in the nearby communities. Continuing *arriba* is the town of Barva, location of the large coffee producer Café, where many tourists visit for a tour of a coffee plantation. Up the slope toward the extinct Barva Volcano, many lovely homes are tucked away among the tropical vegetation that crowds the side of the narrow highways.

From Heredia's northern edge, hills and mountains rise steadily toward the Poás Volcano. All along these foothills are winding roads that travel past beautifully maintained homes, alternating with evergreen forests, small farms, and verdant pastures. This is one of my favorite parts of the Meseta Central (I almost bought a coffee farm here a few years ago). As the roads climb higher into the mountains, temperatures become progressively cooler, thus allowing prospective home buyers and renters precise adjustment in their environment.

Some foreign residents live on small coffee farms here, with excellent views of the valley and with orchards of citrus, avocados, and tropical fruit supplementing truck gardens for home use and income. At present coffee-producing property has gained in value because of the high prices the crop is bringing on the world market.

Incidentally, those foreigners who own rural parcels and who spend half the year in Costa Rica and the rest of their time in their home country are sometimes anxious to rent their property in their absence to ensure that someone will keep an eye on their place and protect it from vandalism. Some attractive rental deals can be worked out in these instances.

Other Towns and Villages

To the south of Heredia and Alajuela, several smaller towns and open countryside sprinkled with small farms and beautiful homes draw Ticos and foreigners wanting to escape the city's crush.

The road from Heredia to Turrucares is particularly striking, with lovely, high-quality homes interspersed with small, neatly kept farms and residences. Our taxi driver, who was renting his cab and services by the day, drove us there and proudly pointed out some of the prettier homes along the way. "I was born in this area," he said proudly. And then, with a hint of sadness in his voice, he added, "Of course, it is too expensive for me to live here now."

More to the west, Atenas and La Garita are pleasant places that are gaining in popularity, particularly with foreigners who prefer cooler weather. (Some folks are hard to please!) These towns sit along the alternate highway that winds down through Orotina, toward the Pacific beaches. Right now the traffic through this area is often snarled and frustrating (frightening on Sunday evenings, when everybody's returning from Jacó Beach), but when (and if) the superhighway past Ciudád Colón is completed, coast-bound traffic will bypass the Atenas–La Garita area and make it an exceptionally desirable place to live. It's nice here now, even with traffic, lightly settled, with luxury properties interspersed with modest-priced, livable homes. The commercial centers of both towns are particularly neat and attractive. Some friends considered buying a wonderful three-bedroom house on a large lot on the outskirts of Atenas recently for $46,000; had we not already owned more property than we needed, we'd have bought it ourselves.

The town of Grecia sits a few kilometers north of the Pan-American Highway, along a picturesque road that traverses coffee fields and deep valleys. The center of town features a lovely square in front of one of the country's most unique churches, apparently made of sheet iron, probably manufactured by the Eiffel company of France, during the period when they were prefabricating churches for export around the world. This is a peaceful-looking place, with wide streets and prosperous neighborhoods.

Drive another few kilometers and you come upon the famous town of Sarchí. The village and surrounding area is celebrated for its wood products and small furniture factories. More than a dozen stores and outlets display an enticing assortment of quality furniture and decorations made of tropical woods. As far as I know, few North Americans make their homes in Sarchí, although it looks like an enjoyable place to live. But many visit there regularly to furnish their homes. Our beach home and our condo near San José are both decorated in contemporary Sarchí.

For those who like to be nearer the big city but are so fussy that even Escazú temperatures are too warm, there is a cooler alternative where living is pleasant and heavy exhaust fumes from diesel buses seldom foul the air. This is the Poás area, partway up the side of the mountain and volcanic crater of the same name.

To get to Poás, a winding, scenic road takes you past fields of produce and coffee, past comfortable houses with spectacular views. Along the way are roadside stands vending the specialties of the mountainside farms. Strawberries, enormous and sugar-sweet, are year-round treats here, displayed on stands along with homemade cheeses, candies, and fresh veggies from backyard gardens. As you gain altitude, the air becomes cooler and slightly crisp. The panorama of the valley in the distance looks impressive indeed. The vegetation becomes even more lush; enormous plants with leaves 6 feet across hang over the roadside, and flowering trees filter the sunshine overhead.

Finally, the road tops a grade and enters the town of Poás. This is a quiet, middle-class town of workers, farmers, and, lately, North American *pensionados* and *rentistas*. Its unimposing, no-nonsense business center lacks spiffy boutiques and gourmet restaurants, yet maintains a folksy, neighborly atmosphere, with adequate commercial conveniences.

The Poás area isn't for everyone, only those who view temperatures over seventy degrees as beastly hot. If any place in the Meseta Central can be described as "the place of eternal spring," it would have to be the area around Poás. I've been told that temperatures almost never rise above seventy-five degrees; neither do they drop below sixty, day or night, summer or winter.

Escazú

For North Americans who prefer the higher elevations, Escazú is the premier retirement and residential location. Only 8 kilometers from San José and fifteen minutes or less driving time, depending upon traffic, the town of Escazú is far removed from the city hustle and bustle. Nestled at the base of a magnificent backdrop of ancient volcanic mountains, Escazú has always drawn the affluent and those seeking tranquillity away from the city. Somehow this area has managed to preserve remnants of the peace and beauty of its agricultural past yet provide a modern backdrop for suburban living. As one hotel advertises, "Close to the capital, but worlds away." Of all the suburbs where foreigners choose to live, Escazú is the most popular and is well stocked with English-speaking expatriates.

Three mountains hover over Escazú. The tallest is Cerro Rabo de Mico, at 7,770 feet, and the most spectacular is Pico Blanco, at 7,250 feet, with a dramatic, sheer rock face that has challenged the skill of many a mountain climber. Residential streets on the edge of town ascend the mountainside bravely, with each gain in altitude presenting an even better view.

The total population of the Escazú area is said to be 40,000, but it doesn't appear nearly that large. It looks more like a cluster of sprawling villages, with quaint old adobe buildings painted in a traditional two-color motif. Incidentally, the 3-foot, colored stripe you'll see painted along the bottom of a house is believed to ward off evil spirits and witches. It must work, because I've encountered few evil spirits or witches during any of my visits.

Escazú is actually divided into three separate towns: San Miguel de Escazú, San Rafael de Escazú, and San Antonio de Escazú, each having its own church and patron saint. The red-domed church in San Miguel de Escazú was constructed in 1799 and has survived numerous earthquakes since.

As San José grew and spread out, artists and those in search of serenity began moving to Escazú. No longer the peaceful retreat of yesterday, the area retains a reputation as an artists' colony as well as a retirement center. Escazú's higher elevations are ideally suited for those who think that San José's climate is too warm. It is also high enough that the occasional light smog that sometimes touches San José remains far below. For these reasons, a large number of North Americans choose Escazú and the surrounding towns as their place of residence. Here is where the U.S ambassador's residence is located. Two famous country clubs provide the area with golf, tennis, and a focal point for the society set. Escazú is the center of much of Costa Rica's social life.

An odd-sounding place for newcomers to go for orientation and assistance is Escazú's very active American Legion Post. This is the largest such entity outside the United States and is combined with a VFW post, making it even larger. More than just a veterans' organization, this group reaches out to all foreigners and Costa Ricans, offering "a socially active, bilingual fellowship of warm, interesting, international people." You needn't be an American Legion member or even a veteran to be welcome; this may be the only American Legion post in the world in that respect. A Lions Club, a Rotary Club, and several other service organizations also make their headquarters in this picturesque setting. All these organizations welcome nonmember visitors. The clubhouse is a popular stop for newcomers seeking a welcome and introduction to the community of Escazú and the neighboring town of Santa Ana. I always recommend clubs and charity associations as valuable windows of opportunity for making friends and building a network of social contacts.

Escazú (and its environs) has a sophistication that makes it stand out among San José's suburbs as a prestige address. Although it admittedly has some of the more expensive places to live, modestly priced homes and apartments are also available throughout the community. Those who choose to live here say they wouldn't think of settling anywhere else. "We have the best of all worlds," explained a couple who owns a small house on the slope of Pico Blanco. "We live in the country, with a gorgeous view of the city below, yet we are just five minutes away from stores, restaurants, or whatever we need." They pointed out that although they are close to San José, they rarely go there on other than essential business. Well-stocked supermarkets, shops, doctors, dentists, and a first-class health clinic serve the community's needs quite well.

Restaurants of all descriptions abound, including European, barbecue, Chinese, and even a Cajun restaurant for the Yuppie trade.

Although new homes are sprouting on the fringes of Escazú, the municipality requires that construction near the town's center conform to colonial or traditional style. Most buildings are 1-story, 2-story at most, fulfilling a sense of rural, Costa Rican countryside living.

"Property here is probably the most expensive of anywhere in the valley," explained one of Escazú's many real estate agents. "Everyone wants to live here. You can pay $95,000 and more for a nice three-bedroom home that you could buy for $45,000 elsewhere, but this is a quality area." He pointed out that there is no real "foreign colony" in Escazú, because Gringos tend to spread throughout the community, interspersed with Ticos and other foreigners. Although some prefer to live in "sealed-in" developments—compounds with high walls and twenty-four-hour guards—more folks live in ordinary homes or townhouses. A two- or three-bedroom condo in one of the exclusive compounds might start at around $80,000 and go up from there (way up), whereas a similar place in an ordinary building might start at $60,000. Those who choose to pay more for the security feel it is worth it, since they can comfortably leave their places unoccupied for months at a time while they return home for visits. Others rely on neighbors and friends to take care of things while they are gone.

Escazú is a great place to make your headquarters while exploring the Meseta Central. There are several nice hotels here, small and often relatively inexpensive. Several bed-and-breakfasts in Escazú are priced as low as $35 a night. Getting into San José and environs is easy, since bus service is frequent.

Rohrmoser

Rohrmoser is at the upper end of the housing market in the immediate San José area, and it is Escazú's main competition for upscale residences. For some folks there is no competition; Rohrmoser wins hands-down. Here homes and condos consistently command rents and sales prices higher than elsewhere in the metropolitan area. Unlike Escazú, Rohrmoser looks more like a modern city suburb, in that it has sidewalks and boulevards instead of mostly narrow roads and streets with dirt shoulders. (For some that's an advantage; for others it's not charming enough.)

Homes and apartment buildings here are much newer, with some condo development and home building still under way. Started by a German developer, Rohrmoser begins at the end of Sábana Park and runs along both sides of Rohrmoser Boulevard until it reaches the ultra-modern shopping center of Plaza Mayor. From that point west Rohrmoser is on the northern side of the boulevard, and Pavas is on the eastern side. The U.S. Embassy, incidentally, is in Pavas, on Pavas Highway.

Many North Americans live in Rohrmoser, but the largest percentage of your neighbors will be Tico professionals who like the convenience of being close to the business center of the city. A big advantage of locating here is that it is just a ten-minute drive to downtown San José (five minutes by taxi), yet has a quiet and safe feeling. Adding the security is the presence of private guards who are hired by homeowners on the block. With everyone contributing, the cost of twenty-four-hour security is affordable and comforting.

Santa Ana

Another part of the Meseta Central that attracts North Americans to become residents is Santa Ana, a sunny mountain valley just another 6 kilometers to the west of Escazú. The altitude here is lower than at either Escazú or San José, making it slightly warmer and drier. A number of small rivers cross the rolling valley, and rounded mountains provide a scenic backdrop.

Santa Ana's setting is also more rural than Escazú's, with crops such as sugarcane, rice, beans, and coffee growing all around this town of 20,000 residents. Roadside stands sell braids of garlic and onions, garden-fresh vegetables, and jars of rich local honey. (Despite Africanized bees' nasty reputations, they produce high-quality honey and more of it than ordinary bees.) All roads converge upon a central area, giving Santa Ana the feeling of a downtown center, rural yet sophisticated. High above the town, on the mountain Cerro Pacacua, is a 20,000-acre forest preserve and bird sanctuary, keeping nature ever present in the local ambience.

A few generations ago—before it became an easy thing to drive to the beach for vacations—San José's wealthy families maintained summer homes in Santa Ana. This was the place to spend weekends and school vacations, a place for the upper crust to host parties and entertain lavishly.

This old tradition left its traces on today's community, with nice homes scattered about the area. Some rather attractive developments, complete with swimming pools, gardens, and twenty-four-hour security, are found here. This is the place for polo matches and international equestrian competitions. Seasonal festivals bring an impressive parade of horseback riders, who ride their high-stepping steeds along the streets to the central plaza where the main celebration is under way. (Don't try to drive along the parade route on festival day; horses have the right-of-way.)

Santa Ana has a deserved reputation as a working artists' colony, with a number of writers and amateur artists present as well. The town is famous for ceramics, and production of excellent pieces is a major industry, with almost thirty workshops and 150 local people engaged in the art. Excellent restaurants, a first-class supermarket, and shopping of all descriptions are at hand, eliminating the need to go to the crowded world of downtown San José for odds and ends. Yet when such travel is necessary, it's but an easy 10-mile drive along one of the country's few stretches of superhighway. One of the largest and most elegant shopping malls in the country is found between Santa Ana and Escazú on this highway: the Multi-Plaza. It's worth a visit.

Of all the Meseta Central retirement locations, I suspect that communities from Santa Ana west to the town of Ciudád Colón may have the best potential for development and property appreciation. The reason for my belief is a planned extension of the divided highway from San José through Ciudád Colón that will someday hook up with the Pacific Coast Highway 34. This highway, by the way, is one of the few made of cement, instead of the usual mixture of asphalt, gravel, and brown sugar (or whatever they mix with asphalt to make a dissolvable road surface). It's lasted without damage—not even a tiny pothole—for about fifteen years. Surely, the government transportation bosses will someday realize the value of cement highway construction as opposed to disappearing asphalt surfaces.

Anyway, traffic moves right along on this highway, zipping back and forth to San José with surprising ease (surprising for Costa Rica). When the highway is extended to the Pacific, this will dramatically cut the driving time to the popular beach communities of Jacó and Quepos. With Pacific beaches just an hour's drive from Santa Ana, the convenience will make the area even more attractive as a place to live, and real estate could become a good investment. When I mention this possibility to my Tico friends, they shrug their shoulders and say, "Don't count on that highway in the near future. We'd be delighted if they'd just fill the potholes on the roads we have!"

San Isidro del General

At first glance, this town would seem to be a rather unusual place for North Americans to choose as a place for residence or retirement. There is nothing spectacular about San Isidro del General; it is an ordinary, small Costa Rican city. It's neat and orderly, with the ubiquitous mountain views common to most other parts of the country. Few vacationers visit San Isidro, and those who have passed through the town may get it mixed up with one of the half-dozen other San Isidros in the mountains. But those North Americans who have discovered San Isidro's secrets love living here. The climate is considerably warmer than that of San José, which suits some folks just fine, and the pace far slower.

Located on a wide ridge, not far from the high peak of Cerro Chirripó, the town enjoys a continuous breeze that keeps the air clear and aromatic with flower-blossom perfume. Daytime temperatures are pleasantly warm for my tastes (maybe hot for some folks), and evenings are tempered by cool air flowing down from Chirripó Peak. Although San Isidro is not as serene and idyllic as some other Costa Rican towns, once you are away from the main square—and the inevitable cars, motorcycles, and trucks circling the square in search of a parking space—the pace slackens to a very peaceful stride.

Like most older Costa Rican towns, San Isidro features a main square in its center, the usual well-kept park. Since the park is the social gathering place for local residents, it isn't surprising that the members of the North American community use it as their social focal point as well. The open-air restaurant of Hotel Chirripó faces the park, and at any given time you can count on at least some of the tables being occupied by English-speaking patrons.

Real estate and rentals are exceptionally inexpensive here. Since it is off the ordinary tourist routes, with no beaches, and lacking in discos and other flashy attractions, San Isidro is likely to remain inexpensive. On one visit I talked with an American who had just completed building a small, two-bedroom home and was eager to find a tenant. He was offering to rent it for almost nothing just to have someone in there to take care of it while he returned home.

Several North Americans have taken advantage of the climate and low-cost real estate, living on small farms on the outskirts of town or along the highway toward the beach at Dominical. The views along this road are absolutely spectacular, with neat, prosperous-looking farms and picturesque homes in the mountain valleys below looking like toys along a model train set. At the time of my last visit, one American from Texas, who was married to a Tica lady, operated a motel, restaurant, and bar on the highway, midway between San Isidro and the ocean.

Lake Arenal District

The northern portion of the Cordillera mountain chain, until recently ignored by North Americans, has one of the best potentials for growth of any place in Costa Rica. Certainly that's my opinion and one shared by many other North Americans who are buying property around Lake Arenal as quickly (and quietly) as they can. Those who know about Lake Arenal would love to keep it a secret, but truth will out! The character of this region is so different from that of other parts of Costa Rica that it's difficult to believe you are in the same country.

The Lake Arenal district is in the upper end of the same mountain chain, but that's as far as the similarity with other highland areas goes. As I understand it, the mountains dip lower at this position in the chain to form a low break or window in the Cordillera. This interruption in the mountain ridges permits a reversal of wind patterns, allowing strong easterly winds to bring moist air off the Caribbean with an abundance of rain. There is no such thing as a dry season in the Arenal area; it's a year-round wonderland of greenness and lush vegetation. When I asked one longtime resident how much it rained, she replied, "On average, about fourteen months out of the year."

Before the government started work to build a dam to create the wonderfully scenic lake, few people lived here. The project required several thousand workers and support people and sixteen years to complete. Roads were cut into the area, opening it up to Costa Rican settlers who started farms and small villages. After the lake was created, many workers elected

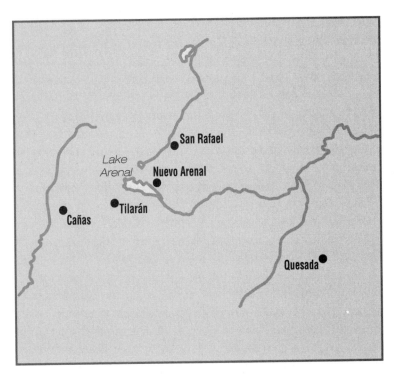

to stay on in the company housing that was built during the construction stages. The population here is still scanty, but it is growing daily, particularly in the numbers of foreigners who have "discovered" Lake Arenal.

To get there via paved road, the quickest way is by turning off the Pan-American Highway at Cañas, an extremely hot and dusty place during the dry season. Were it not for the ample irrigation water coming from Lake Arenal, Cañas would be more like a desert than a rich agricultural region. An air-conditioned auto and lightweight clothing are necessities here. Yet just 18 kilometers away by a tortuously winding road, the air conditioner is shut off and car windows rolled down to take advantage of the delightful fresh air.

Tilarán

By the time you reach the little town of Tilarán, only 23 kilometers from Cañas, a sweater might feel comfortable when the sky happens to be overcast. The countryside changes from pool-table-flat to steep-sided hills; colors change from dusty dry to emerald green. The road climbs gently now, as vegetation seems to become fresher with every curve, past fat cattle grazing fetlock-deep in richly grassed pastures and—where land hasn't been cleared for cattle or agriculture—some astonishingly heavy stands of tropical forest. Just about every imaginable kind of tropical tree or crop thrives here, from bananas to macadamia nuts.

A surprisingly nontropical-looking town—with wide streets, neatly maintained homes, and prosperous businesses—Tilarán has become the home base of a number of expatriates. The climate is temperate and springlike, due to a continuous eastern wind that drops moisture on Tilarán even during the dry season. This keeps the town green year-round, but with less moisture and wind velocity than are found at nearby Arenal. Local residents publish their own newspaper, partly in English, which promotes ecology and recycling projects for the nation.

A few miles east of Tilarán, the view of Lake Arenal bursts upon you, one of the prettiest lakes in the world. The fact that it is artificial fades in importance when the overall effect is considered. Windsurfers claim this is the second best place in all the world to enjoy their sport. What the first place is for windsurfers, I don't know, but it surely can't be any more beautiful than Lake Arenal.

Almost all residents in this area live on or near the drive that skirts Lake Arenal. The paved portion of the road has a scattering of European-type homes, chalets, and an occasional commercial unit such as a *pulpería*, those community store-tavern combinations so common in rural Costa Rica. Many homes are obviously recently constructed, giving evidence of their newness in a developing region.

This area somehow doesn't seem like Costa Rica. Were it not for the colorful bougainvilleas, flowering oaks, and luscious yellow Cortez trees, this countryside would look like an exaggerated version of the Tennessee or Kentucky hill country, or perhaps the lower elevations of Switzerland in the summer. Of course, the banana plants and broad-leaved philodendrons quickly dispel this notion.

Several neat, prosperous-looking villages are spaced along the highway between Tilarán and Arenal. The road has a surprisingly good paved surface. A few miles east of the town of Arenal, however, the road turns into graded clay and occasional pavement—a vast improvement compared to a few years ago. Only a few short stretches of the road remind drivers of the astonishing potholes the size of bathtubs that used to make the route a nightmare. Today it's entirely passable in an ordinary rental car from Tilarán to the Arenal Volcano and beyond.

Nuevo Arenal

The town on the lake is called Nuevo Arenal or, quite often, simply Arenal. This is a surprisingly prosperous-looking place, with neat little houses interspersed with expensive-looking ones. The town sits high on the sloping bank of Lake Arenal, and most homes and businesses are situated with a lake view in mind. Streets are well paved, and more are in the process of being paved in anticipation of a population explosion. Parts of town have an oddly unfinished look, as newly paved streets and vacant lots mix with an occasional house. The center of town has the inevitable soccer field with spectator benches curiously pointed toward the street, away from the field, as if the soccer team is so bad that locals would rather watch the traffic, scarce as it is.

Arenal obviously was a development planned by the government during the dam's construction phase. Many of today's homes here are left over from that era. Unlike the traditional Latin American residential style—built close together and against the sidewalk to allocate space for interior patios—some Arenal homes have real lawns, reminiscent of small-town USA. This adds to Arenal's strange, non–Latin American look.

Because of the area's beauty, the temperate-tropical combination climate, and the low cost of real estate, the Lake Arenal region is undergoing a buying frenzy. Buyers from Canada, the United States, and Europe are furtively looking at property and investing. Germans, Swiss, and Italians appear to be the biggest sharks, biting off chunks of the land as quickly as they can. They try not to appear eager as they snap up bargains, and they do their best to keep this place a secret, lest hordes of other foreigners descend upon paradise and ruin their plans of being the only ones there.

It's not surprising that prices are going up on property around Arenal. It's a very desirable area. Still, it's hard to conceive that inflation could be anything like that along the Pacific beaches. Another favorable circumstance: Since this is lakefront property, it doesn't fall under the complicated and restrictive laws that regulate ownership and construction on beachfront parcels. Here waterfront property is owned outright instead of leasing it from the municipality. However, be aware that the water level in the lake fluctuates from dry season to wet season, as water is drawn off for irrigation and hydroelectric power. Your waterfront lot could end up with a broad frontage of dry land in the dry season.

Arenal Volcano and Fortuna

No trip to Costa Rica can be considered complete until you've visited the Arenal Volcano. Active continuously over several centuries, the volcano's northern slope suddenly exploded about eighteen years ago, destroying a village and killing more than sixty people. (A geologist had tried to warn them of an impending eruption, but nobody believed him.) The nearest and best place to observe the activity is in the hot pools of Tabacón, a resort wedged into a steaming-hot river canyon at the volcano's base. You can sit on underwater stools by the bar and sip piña coladas while you listen to the thunderlike explosions accompanied by puffs of smoke and red-hot boulders coughing from the volcano's vent.

The volcano has done marvels for tourism hereabouts. The nearby town of Fortuna has become prosperous, serving the needs of the hordes of sightseers. New hotels, restaurants, and stores are appearing each season. Fortuna is an exceptionally neat and pleasant community, one that could well make a good place for retirement. With a new road going through San Ramón, San José is only a two-and-a-half-hour driving time. Surprisingly, not many North Americans had settled in Fortuna at the time of our last visit. However, this could be a place for you to look at—should you like a quiet, neat town with great potential and friendly Tico neighbors.

THE CARIBBEAN COAST

The same mountain chain that creates the delightful weather in Costa Rica's highlands further separates the country into eastern and western tropical zones. Because of this separation the Caribbean and the Pacific zones have distinct personalities. Not only are the differences in weather patterns and varieties of animal, plant, and marine life, but marked cultural dissimilarities exist as well. The Caribbean is Jamaican/African; the Pacific is Latin/European.

The word *tropics* implies long stretches of deserted beaches, with thick jungle hovering at the edge of the sand. It means monkeys jostling branches in the strangler fig trees while parrots, macaws, and 1,000 other birds screech, twitter, and sing lyrically in the sunset. Costa Rica's tropics have all of this and much more.

The Caribbean Coast has two distinct regions. Its southern portion, which is lightly populated, reflects Jamaican and African influences, blended with Costa Rican and Spanish personalities. The northern half of the coast is almost uninhabited, visited mostly by fishing fanatics, tourists, and ecology students. (Incidentally, Costa Ricans usually refer to this coast as the "Atlantic" rather than the "Caribbean.")

The northern inland lagoons and waterways are famous for world-class fishing of all kinds. Record-size tarpon and snook are routinely hooked in these scenic jungle rivers and inlets. The best snook angling is usually from the shore, around river mouths, with twenty- to thirty-pounders not uncommon. Fishermen also bring in jacks, mackerel, barracuda, snapper, and other species when fishing the Caribbean Coast. While waiting for exciting action, you are treated to the sight of monkeys frolicking in the trees, an occasional parrot or toucan darting among the branches, and sometimes a crocodile lurking along the shoreline. The Tortuguero area is known as an important nesting place of the endangered green sea turtle.

No roads enter this northern region; the only way to get here is by airplane or motor launch. My belief is that the area is far too isolated and the climate too humid for development other than ecotourism projects.

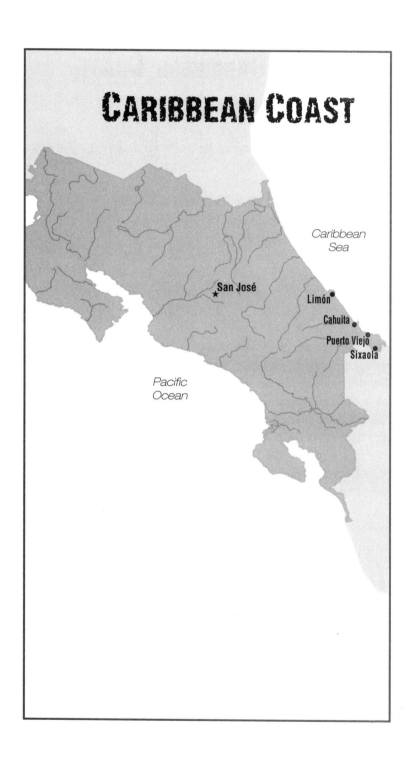

CARIBBEAN COAST

Caribbean Sea

★ San José

Limón

Cahuita

Puerto Viejo

Sixaola

Pacific Ocean

Limón Coast

The southern Caribbean Coast attracts surfers, snorkelers, and reggae enthusiasts, as well as ordinary tourists and ecology buffs, who want to savor the unique tropical environment. Weather patterns here are unpredictable, with no sharp distinction between winter and summer. Rain can fall at any time and usually does. Winds often blow down from the North, sometimes causing the Caribbean Coast to duplicate Miami's weather. The plus side of the Caribbean weather is that things stay green and lush year-round, unlike on the Pacific Coast, where it seldom rains between December and May. The downside is that this weather is always more humid, and insects tend to grow healthy and robust on this edge of the continent.

The city of Limón, a two-and-a-half-hour drive from San José, is where Columbus sighted the American mainland for the first time, back in 1502. Apparently, he thought it was another island and didn't bother going ashore himself. At best, Limón has always been a ramshackle affair—a tropical banana port, too large to have the charm of a village, yet too small to offer the amenities of a real city. To make matters worse, Limón still hasn't completely recovered from the big earthquake of 1991. Several damaged buildings are simply being ignored and probably never will be repaired. To be truthful, many of Limón's buildings look ready to fall, should someone slam the door too hard.

Having exposed my bias against Limón, I must point out that there are those who disagree with me. A number of North Americans who reside in the community testify to the charm and friendliness of their African/Jamaican neighbors. Racial tensions, resentment, and animosity that are so common in some U.S. cities are virtually unknown here. The social atmosphere here is relaxed, friendly, and neighborly. In fact, Costa Rican race relations and attitudes toward citizens of color are very different from those in many other parts of the world. Because people in Limón speak perfect Spanish as well as English with a British Jamaican accent, those with education are much in demand in the business world. They often find positions as supervisors or managers. They can communicate with London, New York, or Geneva (English being the lingua franca of business today), and they can deal with North Americans and Europeans who speak very little Spanish.

Cahuita and Puerto Viejo

To find real charm along this shore, you must travel farther south along the mostly paved highway that heads for the Panamanian border at Sixaola. As is the case all along the Caribbean shores, from Belize to Panama, many inhabitants are descendants of ex-slaves from the island of Jamaica. Their ancestors came to Costa Rica in the latter 1800s, as construction workers on the railroad from Limón to San José. Isolated from the European culture of the Meseta Central—partly because of the difficulty in traveling between the areas and partly because of malaria and yellow fever quarantines—the coastal black people retained their unique Afro-Carribe culture, a combination of British Jamaica, Spanish Costa Rica, and deepest Africa.

Because English is the area's first language (sometimes spoken with a delightful Jamaican patois), this area is favored by tourists and visitors who don't want to bother learning another language during their stay. The genuine lack of racial tension here is refreshing for those of us who have been used to the self-imposed social barriers and chasms of hostility that separate black from white in the United States. I personally feel welcome here and enjoy basking in the warmth of genuine hospitality.

From San José three and a half hours of scenic driving brings you to the village of Cahuita. (It's about four hours by bus.) The village has a picture-book quality in its tropical Afro-Caribbean setting. Many houses stand on stilts to discourage insects; some buildings are painted with bright, contrasting pigments similar to the flamboyant styles of Jamaica. Slender women and girls, dressed colorfully, carry bundles on their heads with grace and enviable posture. It's easy to imagine you are in an African seashore village.

The main road follows the shore, past black sand beaches and coral reefs to the north, and past more coral and beaches of yellow sand to the south. Along the yellow sand beach is Cahuita National Park, a 13-kilometer stretch of jungle complete with howler monkeys (which the Costa Ricans call *congos*), feisty parrots, and wildlife of all descriptions. A foot trail parallels the beach through a thick tangle of tropical trees, vines, and orchids. Butterflies, orange and purple land crabs, and iguanas keep you company on the hike.

Many North Americans and Europeans live here year-round, some operating successful businesses. Others regularly arrive in November and head home by May. I had the good fortune to meet a young California couple who invited me to visit their winter quarters in Cahuita. They lived in a picturesque, thatch-roofed cabin perched next to a coral reef and shaded by graceful coconut trees. Their house was very rustic, with minimal furniture, but they enjoyed their winter home immensely. The surf washed at their front door, spilling into a small depression of smooth black rocks where their children played, as if in their own private saltwater swimming pool.

About four years ago Cahuita experienced a few headline-grabbing crimes. One was particularly upsetting, with an attempted holdup ending with a tourist's death. Apparently, the gunman didn't intend to kill anyone, but angry because the auto wouldn't stop, he fired at the fleeing tourists and inflicted a fatal wound. Although isolated incidents like this happen anywhere in the world, the news devastated Cahuita's tourist business. To restore the town's reputation as a safe and friendly place to visit, local citizens formed the Cahuita Security Committee. The goal is to prevent crime, rather than deal with a problem after it has happened. The committee establishes a round-the-clock checkpoint between Cahuita and Limón during celebrations that attract throngs of tourists into the area. The committee members work with the police to patrol the beaches. They not only work with law enforcement but also check on the police to make sure they're doing their job. This has had a very positive effect on the tourist business and upon visitors' confidence in their personal safety here.

The Limón Coast is particularly attractive for the younger, more active expatriates. Special emphasis is placed on youthful activities, with reggae music thumping loudly from tropical bars and with surfboards, snorkel gear, and brief swimsuits the order of the day.

The village of Puerto Viejo is 16 kilometers south of Cahuita by road, and somewhat less by the beach trail. To make matters a bit confusing, there are two Costa Rican places called Puerto Viejo. The one here is formally called Puerto Viejo de Limón, and the other is a small river town in the northeast, near La Selva Reserve: Puerto Viejo de Sarapiquí. The Puerto Viejo on the Limón Coast used to be much more sleepy than its sister village of Cahuita. Things have changed, with surfers, Rastafarians, and tourists of all descriptions thronging through the town.

A problem for those planning on buying property as absentee owners: This region is susceptible to organized squatter activities. A friend told of losing about a third of his land when he neglected to watch over it for several years. He thought he was safe because he had hired a guard to watch over it. Only when it was too late did he discover that the guard was one of the squatters. So if you decide to own property here, be sure to keep your eye on it and remove *precaistas* before they establish rights. (See Chapter 9 for preventive measures.)

People who love Cahuita and Puerto Viejo will tell you that the rest of Costa Rica is too tame for them. They prefer this movie-set tropical setting—romantic, picturesque, and inexpensive. One bar in the very center of Cahuita features on its front porch extraordinarily powerful loudspeakers that blare Jamaican rock music day and night. The volume is such that it rattles windows a block away and peels the paint off passing automobiles. I love to visit here, but for long-term living in the tropics, my personal preference would be the Pacific Coast. It's my age I suppose.

THE PACIFIC COAST

This side of the country is characterized by dry winters, regular surf from the open ocean, and a much larger population of foreigners. Although most come from North America, a considerable number of Europeans are moving into the area. Many come from Germany, Switzerland, and Italy; other nationalities are well represented as well. Some expatriates operate successful hotels, restaurants, and other tourist-oriented ventures that the business-friendly Costa Rican government makes possible.

The West Coast can be divided into three basic geographic sections: the Guanacaste-Nicoya Peninsula area in the north, the beaches from Jacó to Uvita in the center, and the Golfo Dulce–Osa Peninsula area to the south. Each area has its boosters who will assure you that there is no place in all of Central America as nice as their favorite location. I've seen them all, and I can say that making a choice among them would be difficult indeed.

A nice feature of all the tropical beach areas is that they are accessible from the Meseta Central, within a few hours' drive by bus or automobile, and almost no time at all by airplane. Some locations require longer driving times than others, but as pavement replaces gravel roads, travel times will decrease.

Certain areas are highly developed, focusing on tourism, with discos, restaurants, and boutiques as well as expensive hotels and homes. Other places are oriented toward permanent and semipermanent residents, especially retirees. Still other locations are almost totally deserted, offering no facilities other than what you carry with you. Bring camping equipment if you care to; camping is permitted on all of Costa Rica's beaches except for parks and residential areas. The law considers the first 50 meters of beachland public property. Costa Ricans take full advantage of camping, and during the traditional summer vacation period (January and February), you'll see a multitude of tents lining the beaches, as Tico families enjoy economical vacations. Many foreign tourists and some residents enjoy camping as well. But they stress that you must be careful about leaving valuable belongings in a tent while swimming or visiting a nearby village for supplies. That's probably good advice for beach camping anywhere in the world. (I wouldn't know. My wife and I prefer a comfortable bedroom to a sleeping bag on the ground.)

Eastward from the ocean's surf, rolling hills of forest and farmland spread inland and up the mountain slopes, becoming steeper and more picturesque with each kilometer. Much of this land is wilderness, traversed by occasional dirt roads that become quagmires in the rainy season. Despite isolation and transportation difficulties, foreigners find these rustic sections exceptionally desirable places to live. As the government gradually paves the roads along the coast and into the interior, more and more settlers will surely swell the ranks of North Americans and Europeans who live here and operate businesses. With easy access property values ought to increase dramatically.

Guanacaste's Pacific Coast

A number of important beach locations on the North Coast attract Costa Ricans and foreigners alike for vacations, retirement, or business opportunities. These beaches are easily reached from San José in three to

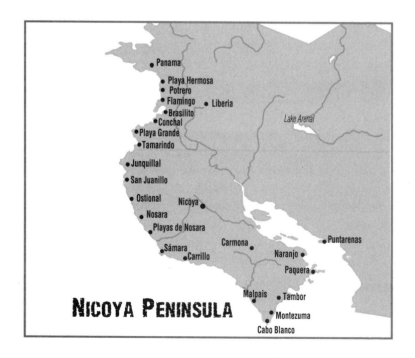

five hours by car. The main highway is paved and in generally good condition (if you discount occasional potholes) but can be agonizingly slow when you are stacked up behind a string of slow trucks on their way to or from the Pacific docks. One problem with the Pan-American Highway from San José to the Pacific Coast: They've recently placed an excellent asphalt top on the road, but shoulders haven't been added to the sides of the pavement. The result is a sharp dropoff that could be very dangerous. This is slowly being remedied, but until the job is finished, be careful not to drift to the edge of the pavement. Don't get in a hurry. Relax, go with the flow, and enjoy the sights and the ever-changing scenery from the Meseta Central to the Pacific Coast.

Rainfall is lower here than anywhere else in the country. Unlike most of Costa Rica, here the dry season is truly dry, with almost no rain falling during December, January, and February. Grass turns parched and yellow; some trees lose their leaves, often replacing them with a gorgeous display of colorful blossoms. Around homes or along inhabited beaches, you'll see more evergreen, leafy trees because they've been deliberately planted.

Playas del Coco Area

A quickly developing complex of *playas* (beaches) begins at Playa Hermosa and Playa Panama, stretching south through Playas del Coco and ending at Playa Ocotal. A nice beach in this complex and one with development potential is Playa Hermosa. *Hermosa* means "beautiful" in Spanish, and Playa Hermosa lives up to its name. This is a lovely place, with a curving shoreline of clean sand and a peninsula that shields it from the open ocean and dangerous riptides.

Development in Hermosa lags behind that in nearby Playas del Coco, the most commercially developed of these beach communities. Since the pavement ends in the center of El Coco, tourists tend to stay here rather than braving annoying stretches of washboard gravel roads to get to nearby beaches. In contrast with neighboring communities, which are sleepy and tranquil, in Playas del Coco the restaurants, bars, and discos stay open late on weekends, with happy people singing and shouting in exuberance all night long. (At least it seemed that way to me one weekend when I was trying to catch up on my sleep!)

Playas del Coco is a fun place to be, with potential for investment opportunities. Numerous North Americans have settled in Playas del Coco, some operating viable businesses, others enjoying ocean fishing and the beaches. But for retirement or long-term vacations, I might choose one of the quieter, nearby places. A number of foreigners own homes along the fringes of the less populated beaches. I understand that many North American families live in Hermosa Beach and more are in the planning stages of building. Italians and Germans are represented here as well.

One resident, a retired air force sergeant, related his reasons for settling here. First, he bought ten acres (by mail) before he retired from the military. Then before he had the chance to visit the property, he received a letter offering to trade the ten acres for one and one half acres of jojoba bean property. This seemed to be a good deal, so he signed the papers for a trade—again, all by mail. When he finally retired and arrived in Costa Rica to claim his jojoba bean plantation, he discovered that jojoba beans don't grow in this area, and furthermore, the property was not only inaccessible by automobile but had a Nicaraguan family living on it who were not inclined to move simply because the owner wanted them to. While he was looking for a way to visit his jojoba bean farm, he fell in love with a Costa Rican lady and got married. He forgot about his agricultural fiasco and settled down in his wife's village. "Now I have a seven-year-old daughter, a house in a village where I am the only Gringo, and I have a good life. My pension is only $855 a month, but I live like a king." He took a part-time job at a tourist hotel as night watchman to supplement his pension. "The only thing I don't like about being a night watchman," he said plaintively, "is weekends, when guests party all night; they make so much noise I can't sleep." He was right; they kept me awake too.

There can be no question about Coco's potential for business, retirement, or long-term living. Several very successful, American-owned enterprises operate here, and more are on the way. But if I don't sound particularly enthusiastic about the place, it's probably because this is where I locked my keys in my rental car and struggled for two hours in the hot sun before figuring out a way to get inside without breaking a window. A good car thief could have done it in less than twenty seconds. (One of the most horrible sights in the world is a set of ignition keys hanging in a locked rental car.)

A few kilometers to the south is Playa Ocotal, a place that maintains a village atmosphere despite also having a deluxe tourist resort. The accommodations are tasteful, blending in with the natural surroundings. The village is on the shore of Bahía Pez Vela (Sailfish Bay), and the fishing is said to live up to the name. At the time of my last visit (spring 1998), a noticeable increase in housing was making this a viable retirement option.

Flamingo Beach

The next beach complex is just a few kilometers south and is probably the most popular of all the Pacific Coast. New paved roads have opened the area to increased settlement. This array of beaches starts with Playa Pan de Azucar and continues south to Playa Tamarindo, including the beaches of La Penca, Potrero, Flamingo, Brasilito, Conchal, Playa Grande, Tamarindo, and Langosta.

By far the prettiest beach is Playa Flamingo. A wide, curving stretch of white sand, with startling blue waves that turn to whitecapped rollers before crashing loudly against the shore, creates one of the prettiest scenes imaginable. Hotels here cater to affluent tourists who can afford to fly in from San José and spend $150 a day for rooms. Tourists on ordinary budgets will find few (if any) reasonably priced rooms. Ongoing building activity may change all this.

As you might imagine, foreigners have taken over this beach and have built some very spiffy places. I consider Flamingo the "Cadillac" of Costa Rican beach communities. The hillsides display sumptuous homes, set in tropical landscaping and overlooking a gorgeous beach view. The scene is reminiscent of Acapulco many years ago when it was the playground of the Hollywood and European jet set. Needless to say, Flamingo is not the place to look for inexpensive ocean-view lots!

Some private homes offer rooms for rent and probably do well, for there were absolutely no vacancies in town when I last visited here. Most of the nondeveloped beachfront is also owned by foreigners. However, local authorities have done well in keeping the first 50 meters of beach open, affording the public unlimited access.

The beach adjacent to Flamingo is Brasilito. Instead of having a tourist resort atmosphere, the village of Brasilito is more like a typical Costa Rican pueblo—complete with a soccer field, small bars, and restaurants. This a "bedroom community" for workers employed by affluent residents and businesses in Flamingo. It's also an inexpensive place for Ticos and residents on a budget to find an inexpensive *cabina* or a room and enjoy the beach. The beach isn't bad at all; I'm surprised there isn't more commercial development and foreign settlers. For a beach community, property is reasonably priced.

The next village is at Playa Conchal. The Spanish word *Conchal* refers to the shells on the beach. In fact, the entire beach is composed of tiny, water-worn shells instead of sand. This area has attracted numerous expatriates in the past few years. Although the place is still somewhat quiet and undeveloped, a rumored 5,000-room resort could change all that.

About 2 kilometers north of Flamingo, the village of Potrero has a growing population of foreign residents. They're building along the beach, toward Flamingo, eventually to become an integral part of one community. The village itself is much more laid-back and relaxed than Flamingo, with some residents' homes built on the hillside overlooking Potrero's exceptionally gentle beach.

Turtle Beaches

An excellent example of how tourism and conservation can work hand in hand is found south of the Flamingo Beach complex. Starting at Playa Grande and continuing south to Playa Tamarindo, a broad, sandy beach serves as nesting grounds for endangered leatherback turtles. It used to be that local residents awaited the arrival of these huge, prehistoric survivors and collected the eggs in buckets as they were being deposited, selling the harvest to bars and restaurants all over the country.

Alarmed by the possibility of the turtles' extinction, the Costa Rican government instituted a model conservation program. Local people are enlisted to help protect the nesting grounds. Guarding the beaches and guiding tourists through the nesting grounds put local people to work. Hotels and restaurants have opened to accommodate the ever-increasing number of tourists. Jobs are created for even more local residents. This boom has only begun; future development seems inevitable.

Conservationists have expressed mixed feelings about this program. While they praise the protection of the nesting grounds, they point out that the extra tourist foot traffic causes damage by visitors inadvertently stepping on the hatchlings. On the other hand, the number of baby turtles killed in this manner is nothing when compared with the unborn ones that used to end up as a tasty *boca* in some San José bar.

Playa Grande

Turtles need a wide, sandy beach with ample portions not touched by high tide; Playa Grande fills these requirements admirably. It's long and unpopulated, with few human footprints to disturb the solitude. A few years ago only a handful of homes and one or two tiny motels were to be found near the beach's access roads. Today the development is rapid. As part of the Tamarindo Refuge, the area will always be somewhat restricted in tourist development, even though the region's natural beauty and wildness is bound to attract even more people in the future.

I looked at several developments here, most catering to luxury homes, on beachfront lots as well as away from the ocean. The cost of land in the spiffy developments was surprisingly expensive, particularly right on the beach. However, the vast majority of Playa Grande's land is undeveloped and presumably far less expensive. It has a tremendously long way to go before it could approach being "crowded." Services—such as grocery shopping, hardware stores, and doctors—require a long drive.

One place I looked at was a large, tastefully constructed home with a neatly manicured lawn ending at a beach wall marking the 50-meter boundary. The owner half-apologized for the home's isolation and lack of anything to do, adding, "The hope of this little community is that things won't change. What we offer here is location, nothing else." He indicated the broad expanse of beach visible through a stand of coconut trees and said, "The whole idea here is to fit into the ecology without disturbing things, particularly not the nesting turtles and their life cycle." The house's window frames were made of wood instead of the more practical aluminum, "because metal frames reflect moonlight and confuse the hatchling leatherbacks. We don't allow any lights from our homes to escape at night. For bright lights and nightlife, you have to go to Tamarindo." Since my writing of these lines, several bars and restaurants have opened near Playa Grande, and a couple of housing developments are under way. But Playa Grande is still a very quiet place to live.

Playa Tamarindo

Tamarindo Beach begins where Playa Grande ends, a picturesque estuary separating the two. Tamarindo is where leatherback-turtle-watchers find hotels. Launches begin ferrying passengers across the estuary around midnight. Visitors tiptoe quietly along the beach and pause to observe the huge turtles as they awkwardly pull themselves up on the beach to bury their eggs 6 feet deep in the sand. This is an unforgettable sight; some of these turtles are more than 12 feet across and weigh up to 1,500 pounds! The one I watched laying eggs must have been a pygmy; she was barely 8 feet wide. Our guide claimed that during the peak of the season, as many as 350 turtles can be on the beach in a single night.

The town of Tamarindo is a textbook example of foreign development of a Costa Rican beach village. Almost every business—restaurants, hotels, shops, bars, and so forth—appears to be owned by Canadians, Americans, Italians, or Swiss. The influx of foreign money and the resulting buying frenzy have pushed the price of most properties into the range of the ridiculous. According to local Ticos, the asking price for a lot (not a hectare, but a quarter-acre lot) can top $50,000! There seems to be no end to the buying and selling, constantly jacking up prices.

The emphasis here in Tamarindo is strictly on foreign tourism. I find this a little disturbing; native Costa Ricans are being left out of the picture. Few Tico families can afford to pay the $60 a night and up that hotels demand, and the price of real estate makes property ownership impossible. Several local people expressed a concern over this trend, saying, "We keep selling our land and moving farther back into the hills. We end up working for foreigners on land we once owned. Before long we won't be able to afford to live in our own village anymore!"

Several real estate developments are either under way or completed in this area, plus many private houses and building lots are for sale. The more desirable places are some distance from the hustle and bustle of Tamarindo's tourist-centered businesses. Although property prices seem high here, my guess is that property here might have even more appreciation left in it. Every time I visit here, Tamarindo gets bigger.

Playa Junquillal

South of Tamarindo the coast seems to be rather unpopulated by foreigners and Ticos alike. This is partially due to the seasonal condition of the dirt roads along the coast. Since most residents believe that a paved road will not be far in the future, this area might have potential for development. A series of long beaches front the Pacific along this coast, some with tiny villages, others almost unpopulated. Among the beaches are Playa Avellana, Playa Negra, Playa Junquillal, and Playa Lagarto. These beaches are graced by large waves rolling in from the open Pacific and are very picturesque. Since I'm not an expert swimmer and know little about ocean currents, undertow, and riptides, I can't vouch for the safety of these beaches. You'll need to consult local authorities on the subject. You wouldn't want to build a home on a beach where you can't swim.

One village I visited in 1998, Junquillal, seems to be in the early stages of a vigorous foreign development. The village has several new businesses and new residents, almost all of them from Italy. One small hotel is owned by several Gringo couples. Then a few kilometers from the village center, a couple of elaborate residential developments are being purchased exclusively by Canadians and Americans. Construction quality is tops, with all amenities, and prices fit the occasion. Since there is such a small population here, shopping and other services are about forty-five minutes away.

Beaches of Nosara

About 80 kilometers south of the Tamarindo-Flamingo region is an area with a different developmental emphasis: the Beaches of Nosara. Starting at the Nosara River, three lovely beaches and a wildlife reserve extend south—from Playa Nosara and Playa Pelada to Playa Guiones. Nosara is an experiment in different concepts of foreign development. The emphasis here is on private homes and pristine beaches rather than tourism and commercial enterprise. Residents here have a militant organization of property owners and have so far successfully kept this part of the coast residential and natural. Along more than 5 miles of beaches, only one small restaurant is located right on the beach. As you stroll the beach, you'll see natural vegetation, trees, and mangrove along the edge of the sand—no discos, fast-food places, miniature golf courses, or any other evidence of higher culture. Just beach and jungle.

It all began about twenty-five years ago, when a farsighted American investor purchased a huge tract of beachfront and decided to develop the property in such a way as to preserve its natural beauty and wildlife resources. He did a marvelous job, developing each lot with its own part of the wilderness. Almost all buyers were from the United States or Canada; they loved the isolation and the idea of preserving beaches, forest, and animals.

Things were going well until a few years later, when the original developer unexpectedly dropped out of the picture. Residents feared the area could turn commercial like Tamarindo or Sámara (farther to the south), so they formed a property owners' association, totally committed to protecting their unique environment. To forestall commercial development, residents dedicated the entire beachfront to the government as a wildlife and nature reserve. The association provides housing and pays the salary for a government ranger to keep an eye on forest and wildlife conservation. It has spent a good deal of money for legal fees, even taking a case to the Supreme Court, in an effort to keep large developers from turning Nosara into a new Miami Beach. So far the association has been successful, limiting new business to small, low-impact, family-operated enterprises. However, Nosara isn't unfriendly to tourists. On the contrary, the community welcomes them and is happy to see tourists patronize the many small hotels and restaurants that are located a few hundred meters from the beach. Consequently, Beaches of Nosara draws a different type of tourist: one who appreciates quiet, uncrowded, and natural beaches and who doesn't require discos, T-shirt emporiums, or beachfront pizza parlors to keep him- or herself amused.

"One major problem we have is that newcomers aren't as ecologically conscious as the original owners," said Michael Sandwig, the association manager. "Over the past twenty years, many of the original owners have died, grown old, or lost interest. So we try to educate newcomers about the treasures we have here, about the importance of not cutting down the trees or destroying our animals' habitat." He explained how the monkeys have regular "trails" through the treetops that they use daily to go from one feeding area to another. When the trail is broken by clearing some of the trees, the monkeys are forced to move away.

Because development in Nosara is still in its infancy, property prices haven't skyrocketed as they have in Tamarindo Beach and other places along the coast. At any given time about fifty lots are up for resale, as are many homes. But as with all prices along the Pacific Coast, asking prices are climbing steadily. View lots start at $40,000; lots without views but close to the beach begin at $15,000. Several local contractors build quality homes at reasonable prices.

The gravel/dirt roads around here make access to medical care a bit difficult; the nearest hospital is in Nicoya, an hour and fifteen minutes away. However, an emergency Cruz Roja station in the village of Nosara has a four-wheel-drive ambulance ready for the trip to the hospital in Nicoya. The exciting news here is that the government has set aside $833,000 to build a comprehensive health center soon. Until then a flight to major San José hospitals takes twenty minutes from the local airstrip. However, at the moment the airport here is closed, because too many cows like to wander about the airstrip. The government promises to fence off the facility and open the field to air transport sometime in late 1998.

It's interesting to compare this area with the resort area of Sámara, just 25 kilometers to the south. There the natural vegetation has been stripped away to make room for commercial projects. What is left is burned off every dry season to make room for new plant cover the following rainy season. Native plants, those specially adapted to this climate, no longer exist; they've been crowded out by plants whose natural winter state is to lie dormant or by those whose seeds resist fire. None of this is to say that Sámara isn't a beautiful place—with its gorgeous beach, it can't miss—but it's different from Nosara, a contrast in attitudes toward conservation, a contrast in development styles.

In Nosara tall native trees and shrubbery shade the ground helping to conserve water during the dry season. This keeps vegetation greener year-round. Unlike Playa Sámara or Tamarindo, Nosara is covered with native grasses, bushes, and vines, all uniquely adapted and suited to this environment.

North of Nosara several small-scale developments are under way near the town of San Juanillo, an isolated area with a gorgeous beach and protected cove. As with the other beach communities along the Pacific Coast, the major obstacle to full-scale development is the lack of a paved coastal highway. Driving can be slow along the bumpy gravel and dirt roads, particularly during the rainy season. The government has plans to pave the main road, but when that will happen is a big question—estimates run between two and five years, and never.

Sámara and Carrillo

When the government manages to build a bridge across the Tempisque River to replace the bottleneck ferry, this central Nicoya Peninsula area will be an hour closer to the Meseta Central. When this happens, I expect the beach communities here to boom. The last of the easily accessible beaches along this stretch of coast are the twin bays of Sámara and Carrillo. Each curves in a semicircle of magnificent white sand beach, backed by steep hills that provide breathtaking vistas of the coast. Playa Sámara is well developed, with numerous small hotels, restaurants, and other tourist-oriented businesses. The recently completed pavement makes visiting here a relatively simple matter, compared with the old gravel and mud road that previously accessed the local beaches.

For some reason, other than business owners the number of foreign residents in the area is not as large as one might expect. Possibly Sámara's bustling commercial atmosphere has something to do with this, but Puerto Carrillo has even fewer foreigners living there. This is certain to change, for Playa Carrillo is one of the most beautiful beaches in a country of lovely beaches. I have a friend who claims, "Puerto Carrillo has the best and safest beach between Los Angeles and Tierra del Fuego." Development here has scarcely scratched the surface of its full potential. Almost the entire beach is flanked by a wide road, fringed with coconut palms, and freely accessible to all. Except at the southern end, almost no development of any kind mars the unblemished shoreline. As in Sámara, several hillside developments offer view lots that suggest future appreciation.

An item of interest about Carrillo: About 1 kilometer south of the airstrip here is a bridge over a small river where two large crocodiles lurk. Local residents regularly feed them by throwing frozen chicken carcasses—tied with nylon line—into the river. They then troll the tasty morsels toward the bridge to lure the monsters from their hiding places. Although the river isn't posted against swimming or wading, I would highly recommend that you refrain from this activity. The crocodiles will disagree with this advice.

Cabo Blanco

On the southern tip of the Nicoya Peninsula, a string of beaches with tremendous potential are undergoing development. The beaches run from Naranjo, on the Gulf of Nicoya side, to Cabo Blanco, at the very tip of the peninsula, and then up along the coast via unpassable roads, toward Puerto Carrillo. Most investors agree that the developmental potential between Cabo Velas and Cabo Blanco is among the best in the country. It all depends upon when (and if) the roads will be made passable.

Getting to this area from the northern part of the peninsula has always been a problem. The paved highway ends abruptly at the little town of Carmona, presenting about a 30-kilometer stretch of dirt road to the coast. The road paralleling the Pacific Coast dwindles to a trail from time to time, and you have to ford several good-size streams. Even rugged four-wheel-drives avoid the coastal route. An easier way is to take a ferry from Puntarenas to Playa Naranjo or Paquera, which shortens the drive considerably.

Conditions are changing. For better or worse, progress arrived on the southern peninsula in the form of a huge construction project—a 1,500-room hotel—at Playa Tambor. To encourage the development, the Costa Rican government agreed to install a new ferry terminal to bring tourists from Puntarenas, to pave the road to the hotel, and to provide housing for construction workers who are building the project and who later will be employed by the resort.

I say "for better or worse" because construction crews immediately began filling in the mangrove wildlife preserves and leveling a mountain-top. Ecologists claim the builders are destroying the natural wonderland that they came to exploit. At the time of this writing, half-hearted legal proceedings are under way against the project, and complaints have been lodged against local authorities for not enforcing regulations more strictly.

Regardless of whether the Tambor project is successful, the rest of the area is ready for less ambitious development. Costa Rica doesn't have more enthusiastic or optimistic supporters than those property owners on this part of the Nicoya Peninsula. The communities of Montezuma and Malpaís are growing and bringing in foreign residents at a respectable clip. I feel it's worth a trip here for the prospective property buyer.

Mid-Pacific Coast

If there is any place in Costa Rica that's bound to bloom with foreign investors and retirees, it would have to be that stretch of beachfront from Jacó to Dominical.

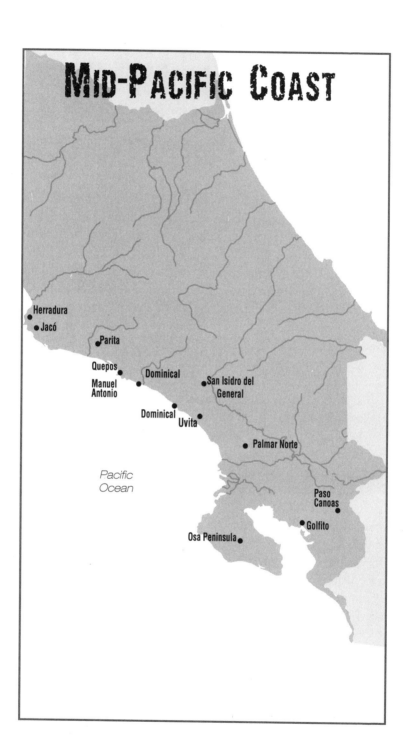

Although pretty beaches line both sides of Costa Rica, these are particularly accessible for residents of the populous Meseta Central. A short drive or bus ride makes this coast practical for overnight sojourns. A weekend home here is convenient and usable by family and friends, whereas one that requires a five-hour drive over horrible roads might sit vacant most of the year. When the main route has been paved and time-saving shortcuts completed, a drive from Escazú or other suburbs will take as little as an hour to Jacó, or two hours to Dominical.

Playa Jacó and Playa Herradura

Because they are the easiest to reach from the San José area, the most popular places for ocean swimming and weekends at the beach are at Jacó and Herradura. It's entirely possible to drive down in the morning, enjoy the surf, and be home for supper. The town of Jacó is more popular with fun-loving tourists than with foreign residents seeking peace and quiet in a beach town. This fun-and-games atmosphere is Jacó's downfall. It's full of youngsters from San José who come here for the all-night discos, parties on the beach, and general hell-raising. Some North Americans live in Jacó, mostly for business reasons, but more live nearby in the hills overlooking the ocean or in places like nearby Playa Herradura.

Playa Herradura is smaller than Jacó, enjoys gentler surf, and has more shade trees. At the moment Herradura offers economical tourist hotels and weekend homes for highland residents, both Ticos and Gringos. But the town extends a promise of better things to come. For a beachfront community Playa Herradura boasts property that is reasonable—at least compared with prices at Jacó or Manuel Antonio. Many building lots can be found within walking distance of the beach, and construction is booming. An upscale development known as Los Sueños, by the Braemar Group of Southern California, is under way at Playa Herradura. With its large-scale marina, luxury homes, and condos, Los Sueños will raise the general tone of Herradura and bring in more development.

Manuel Antonio

It was the middle of February, and we were sitting with a group of friends in a restaurant overlooking the Pacific. A long, palm-fringed beach stretched out into the distance as far as we could see. Behind us loomed mountains covered with rain forest, sweeping down to accent the beach with its azure-blue water and sparkling surf. The sun was at its zenith, beating directly down with dazzling strength. Two members of our group were complaining about the heat. We consulted a thermometer and found that the temperature was eighty-five degrees. Suddenly they broke into laughter as they realized that Baltimore, their home town, was buried under four inches of sleet and snow. Two weeks of Costa Rica's idyllic weather had turned them into indignant complainers over an ordinary 85-degree day at the beach! We all ordered a cold beer served over ice cubes (a Costa Rica tradition) and looked out over the panorama with renewed appreciation for where we were: Costa Rica's famous Playa Manuel Antonio.

What kind of name is that for a beach? According to legend, a husband, worried about his pregnant wife, placed her in a dugout canoe and headed north for Puntarenas, hoping to find a doctor to deliver the baby. But before they could go very far, the wife went into labor and they paddled ashore to camp in the shelter of a gentle beach cove. His wife gave birth to a healthy child, whom they named Manuel Antonio; the beach has been called that ever since. Travelers who have visited beaches all over the world swear that Manuel Antonio is the most beautiful of all.

The coastline north of Manuel Antonio is a long shore of golden sand that catches the full force of the Pacific's waves as they roll in from China. Then at Manuel Antonio Park, a narrow peninsula juts out into the ocean, curving about to form two protected coves on either side of the land. Here the waves suddenly become gentle, a place where you can float on your back for an hour without worrying about getting surf in your face. You'll often find a sailboat or two anchored here, gently swaying, resting on the way to the Panama Canal or the big voyage north to Acapulco.

Originally United Fruit Company banana property, the area was made into a national park in 1972 with almost 700 hectares of land, partially expropriated, partially donated. The park contains three beaches, each with its own character. The first is Playa Espadilla Norte, which sees occasional riptides—although many people swim here anyway. Next is Playa Espadilla Sur and then Playa Manuel Antonio, both quite safe for swimming and snorkeling. From the beginning the emphasis has been on preserving the natural beauty and protecting wildlife. Whiteface capuchin monkeys frolic in the trees, competing with arboreal iguanas for food. A tropical storm in 1993 ripped up some of the trees, causing the sloth population to go elsewhere, but other than that the damage was minimal.

One of the earlier tourist developments, Manuel Antonio soon became a popular place for retirement and vacation homes, hotels, and restaurants. To protect the area from total development, the government demands that new construction be connected with tourism in some manner. Buildings cannot be more than stories high and must provide a minimum of three times the square footage of green space for each foot of building. To satisfy the requirement that development be tourist-related, several North Americans have built homes with rooms or apartments that can be rented out to tourists; they keep part of the house as living quarters.

Since Manuel Antonio's fame makes it an almost obligatory part of a tourist's itinerary, a bed-and-breakfast or room rentals can be a very viable business. Rooms are likely to be rented solidly through the summer (December, January, and February) and to have low vacancy rates during the rest of the year. During a recent trip we rented an apartment from a lady who came from Florida eighteen years ago to build a small house for herself. She added a couple of rooms for extra income during the tourist season. As the volume of tourism during the off season increased, she added more rooms, until she now has a pleasant ten-room hotel plus two apartments across the road, all with a splendid view of the ocean. "I hadn't considered becoming a hotel owner when I came here," she explained. "It just happened to work out that way."

The biggest hindrance to optimum development at Manuel Antonio is the present condition of the highway. The stretch north to Parrita is 25 kilometers of teeth-rattling gravel and washboard. The next 50 kilometers north to Jacó Beach is paved, but with some of the deepest craters this side of the moon. Purists might think this is a fine arrangement; it keeps people away. But local residents are so highly incensed at their isolation that they staged a strike in 1993, preventing tourists from entering or leaving Quepos until the government agreed to begin long-overdue road repairs. It must not have been an election year, because last time I traveled the road, it was little improved. When (and if) smooth pavement reaches Manuel Antonio, the retiree-investor may expect gratifying appreciation on investments. On the other hand, we'd all hate to see such a lovely setting marred by a Miami Beach type of development.

Any North American thinking about investing in Manuel Antonio (or anywhere else in Costa Rica, for that matter) would be well advised to speak with Roger Connor, affectionately known as Don Rogelio by local residents. His development, the Plinio Hotel and Restaurant, could be considered a model for nonobtrusive construction in ecologically sensitive areas. Buildings cling to the side of the hill, with minimal disruption of the forest and accompanying wildlife. Nature trails wind several kilometers through Roger's twenty acres and adjacent lands to give guests an in-depth appreciation of the area. Don Rogelio's place is on the Manuel Antonio road, near Quepos.

Dominical

South of Quepos and Manuel Antonio, along the 45-kilometer stretch of gravel road to Dominical, you'll find occasional roads leading to the beach. We've found a few small hotels along this part of the coast, but for the most part this country is either palm-oil plantations or flat farming land. Yet starting with the village of Dominical south, this part of the coast could turn out to be another of those "undiscovered" places with potential for retirement and/or investment.

Plans are in the works to complete the pavement from Jacó Beach all the way to Palmar Norte, thus opening this section to traffic from three directions. This route will take considerable pressure off the present Pan-American Highway as well as open the region to tourism and development. Buses travel this route now, and it's not a bad drive in a rental car; the road bed is often graded, and it goes through level country.

Once paved roads are in place, you are going to see a steady stream of traffic cruising along the beach—tourists looking for rooms and retirees buying property. The village of Dominical and its surrounding communities can't help but flourish. As you might guess, many foreign residents prefer things the way they are; they dread the thought of developments and tourists destroying the peace and tranquillity that have been theirs for so long. But road crews are already at work; it is too late for anything but anguish. As one man said, "It will seem funny to think that in a few years we'll be looking back fondly to the time when there were no traffic lights here."

If you want to drive on pavement all the way to Dominical, travel south on the Pan-American Highway and turn toward the Pacific at San

Isidro del General, then just follow the signs through town. Because of San Isidro's system of one-way streets, you may have to ask directions by pointing in whichever direction you are going and asking "Dominical?" Someone will steer you right.

In its own way, this road is one of the more scenic in all of Costa Rica. The narrow pavement traverses rich farming country, up somewhat steep grades, running along ridges with breathtaking views on both sides of the road, looking into deep valleys where the farmhouses are so distant that they seem like toys. Even during the dry season, the countryside is lushly green, plants heavy with foliage and banana trees shading the roadside. Although the drive is less than 25 miles, it takes about forty-five minutes. That's the way it should be, because the scenery is so spectacular that you might miss something if you could whiz along at 100 kilometers-per-hour. Also, the pavement has a way of disappearing from time to time, turning into stretches of gravel road where construction crews are still at work. The problem is not serious; just slow down and relax.

The paved highway ends at the gravel and cobblestone coastal road at the Barú River, a picturesque mountain stream that empties into a lagoon at this point. A turn to the left, over the river's new cement bridge, and you find Dominical. Take the first right turn past the bridge. This is not a town—even though it may appear as such on the map—it's a collection of *cabinas,* private homes, and a handful of restaurants, sometimes almost hidden behind tropical vegetation.

Dominical's main street (there are only a couple of streets here) follows the river past several rental cabins and businesses. It ends at the beach, where another road follows the shore down to Punta Banda, also known as Roque Azul. Camping beneath a grove of shade trees is free on the edge of the broad, sandy beach of Playa Dominical. Restrooms and showers are strategically spaced along the beach. For the most part, campers are Tico families and backpackers, but all are welcome.

The surf is spectacular, booming in on the sand and making swimming occasionally hazardous, with riptides to harass those not used to handling them. "You usually don't realize what is happening," said Richard Dale, a longtime resident here and the owner of the *cabinas* on the river where we were staying. "It seems as if you are staying still in the water, but the beach is moving away from you. We lose a couple of tourists every year to these tides, and it isn't necessary. Instead of frantically trying to swim against the current, the best thing to do is relax and leisurely swim parallel to the beach, until the shore stops moving away. The current is only a few feet wide. Then work your way back to shore, pausing to float on your back and rest. The water is so warm and so salty that you can float all day long and never get tired. There is no reason for anyone to drown in a riptide."

Serenity and calm at Playa Dominical and Playa Barú make this a great place to spend the winter, away from the ice and snow of northern climes. Many people do just that. Prices are particularly affordable if one doesn't need an ocean view. A visitor from the Yukon, a man who has been coming here for several years, was very excited as he described the house he was buying in a nearby village. It was a brand-new, two-bedroom place on three hectares of land. "To make sure everything is all right, I agreed to rent it for two months," he said. "At the end of that time, if the house is satisfactory, I'll go ahead and buy it."

Several local businesses are owned by North Americans. A deep-sea diver from Rhode Island, who worked and traveled all over the world, decided Dominical was the place to settle down. He set to work building a combination bakery, deli, and coffee shop, which turned out to be a success with Ticos and Gringos alike. It's called the Deli del Río and is known for brick-oven pizzas, turning out forty to fifty a night.

Next door is the Auberge Willdale, a small motel owned and operated by Richard and Ann Dale and their son Will. In their absence the business is managed by Joe Goodman, a resident massage therapist who has lived in Costa Rica for twenty-five years. A Californian from San Clemente bought a restaurant-bar and named it the San Clemente, after his hometown; he also has a set of *cabinas* near the beach called San Clemente. Two couples—one from Brazil, the other from Italy—built an impressive structure that houses a store, a real estate office, a salad and juice bar, and one of the finest restaurants I've encountered in Costa Rica. (Normally this book doesn't recommend restaurants, but this one, the Manigordo, is special, with a combination of Italian and Brazilian cuisine.)

Every night a couple of bar-restaurants break the tranquillity with loud stereo music as they try to attract customers. Since local surfing is reputed to be the second best in Costa Rica, there are always a few sunburned, salt-soaked revelers to join the more sedate patrons of these "nightclubs" in hoisting a cold *cerveza*. The music doesn't last long, however, since early-to-bed is the norm here.

A couple of retired North Americans expressed surprise that Dominical hasn't attracted a larger retirement community. "The views from here south to Escaleras and beyond are spectacular," said one.

Dominical and surrounding villages sit right on the water's edge, and rainfall is about the same as in other coastal towns to the north or the south. Logically, Dominical's climate should also be similar: hot days and warm evenings. But this is not exactly the case. Mornings and evenings are much cooler, and even during the middle of the day, pleasant breezes come in from across the ocean. At night temperatures drop into a delightful range, making it possible to sleep without an air conditioner.

Don't misunderstand, the climate here isn't like that of the Meseta Central, but it is noticeably cooler here than in many other parts of the coast. This is due to an odd juxtaposition of geographic features. Not far from the beach, mountain slopes start climbing sharply from the flat shelf of land that borders the ocean. They swoop higher and higher until they reach Costa Rica's highest point: Chirripó Peak. During daylight hours the sun beats down on that narrow strip of land between the ocean and the mountain slopes, heating the air, causing it to rise. As the warm air flows upward along the mountain's face, cooler air is continuously pulled in from the ocean. Then in the evening, when the sun's heating action stops, cool air from the high peaks descends (cool being heavier than warm), reversing the direction of the breeze and pushing the humid, muggy air out to sea.

Uvita

South of Dominical, as far as the village of Uvita (18 kilometers distant), numerous beaches face the ocean, some with houses or tiny farms, places that will someday become villages. One of the prettiest on this part of the coast is called Punta Dominical. A high point juts out into the ocean, with cliffs and surf reminiscent of California's Big Sur or Spain's Costa Brava. Below a small hotel cliffs and rocks catch the full force of the ocean's strength as waves crash and send cascades of white foam flying high in the air.

Most property along this coast seems to be owned exclusively by foreigners, many of whom don't appear to be particularly eager to sell and, when they do, not at bargain prices. Occasionally a beachfront property can be found but at highly inflated prices. Affordable property is found away from the beach, where Ticos have land for sale. I looked at one parcel in Uvita, about 1 kilometer from the beach, five hectares (twelve acres) of land with a comfortable house for half of what it would cost near Dominical. There were many fruit trees and enough pasture for keeping a horse or two. (By the way, horses are a very practical form of transportation, with the roads in their present condition.)

A longtime resident named Lillian said, "We looked all over Costa Rica before settling on Uvita. We found a ten-hectare plot up on the mountainside. Not only do we have a gorgeous view, but there are six beautiful waterfalls on the property. For me it's like having my own national park." She added, "We are holding it in trust for our two granddaughters, as a future for them."

A difficulty with a small community like Uvita is that there aren't enough residents to form a central community organization. Local people hold informal meetings, but not enough attend to get much done. Most foreign-owned land is in the hands of absentee owners, with nothing built on the properties. Nowadays the road south connects with paved roads at Palmar, on the Pan-American Highway. As the road improves and eventually becomes paved, property values should soar and even more property will become available for development. When this happens, a property owners' association would be a logical move.

Finally, one problem with isolated areas like Dominical or Uvita is the lack of sophisticated medical care. Often a resident doctor in the village can handle emergencies, but for serious problems the nearest emergency clinic in this region is in Platanillo, about 13 kilometers from Dominical, or the hospital in San Isidro, some 45 kilometers distant. Uvita's medical needs are taken care of in Palmar Norte.

This problem of medical care was brought home to me on a recent trip. As I was driving from Dominical to San Isidro, a campesino ran out into the road and flagged me down. His hand was bleeding from an accident, and he needed to get to the hospital. I had to act as an ambulance driver, not knowing whether to go top speed and risk killing us both or to slow down while my patient bled to death. He was the calm one, as he insisted on trying to show me his wound and describing in minute detail what had happened. Fortunately, we both lived.

Golfito Area

For years I had heard people speak of Golfito and the Osa Peninsula. The area sounded like a place of adventure—panning for gold in forest streams, fishing for trophy sailfish, or hiking rain-forest trails. In order to complete research for this book, I resolved to spend some time around Golfito to collect information. But when I asked folks around San José, who either owned property or regularly visited here, I found their answers short and vague, always skirting the subject as if trying to draw my attention elsewhere. When I spoke with a man who owned property on Zancudo Beach, his face burned angrily as he said, "Zancudo is my special place, and I don't want any damned travel writers drawing attention to it! It would destroy things for all of us!"

Obviously, our interview was over, but now I knew I had to go! I rented a car and was soon on my way to Golfito, the jumping-off place for the Pavones–Zancudo Beach areas. The drive south on the Pan-American Highway is gorgeous. One unbelievable view after another invites a pause wherever the car can be parked safely off the pavement. Ordinarily, the trip takes six hours, but by the time I stopped several times to sample pork *chicharones,* marvel over the views, and take a nap in the shade of a banana tree, the trip stretched into an eight-hour day. If and when truck traffic is diverted along the proposed new coastal highway, you'll be able to make the trip in five hours.

Golfito is an often neglected part of Costa Rica, with scanty information provided by most tourist guides. The town began its existence as a banana port for United Fruit Company but was abandoned when the company decided that the operation had become unprofitable. When it was a banana port, there was no incentive to develop it as a tourist attraction, although today the area is trying hard to do so.

Sitting on a bay of Golfo Dulce, Golfito's water scene is absolutely gorgeous, reminiscent of the San Juan Islands in Puget Sound. The coastline and islands jut steeply from the water, green and matted with trees, vines, and thick brush. The water is so calm at times that it is hard to realize that this is not a lake but a protected little bay of the Pacific Ocean. From the slope a rain forest watches over the town as fishing boats ply the calm waters of the Golfo Dulce. During the town's banana-shipping days, the company wisely kept these mountain slopes as a wildlife preserve and watershed, ensuring Golfito a relatively pure water supply.

The town itself can hardly be described as anything but picturesque. It looks like a cliché movie set of a banana-shipping port. Just a few blocks wide, the town follows the water's edge, with some houses actually standing over the water on stilts, others clinging to the cliffs and hanging out into empty space. A couple of excellent hotels accommodate the growing number of curious tourists, but most lodgings are rather rustic.

A surprising number of North Americans live in or around Golfito. One place to meet them is at Louis Brenis Restaurant, which sits across from *la bomba* (the gasoline station). The Costa Rica Surf bar is another local Gringo hangout. The main commercial street, looking ramshackle, climbs a hill paralleling the highway and waterfront. Foreign residents patronize a couple of open-air restaurants here, as well as hardware stores, shops selling tackle and boating supplies, and several red-light bars.

Because of special circumstances, some of Costa Rica's better property bargains can be found around Golfito. A local resident explained, "When the United Fruit Company pulled out, it left us without our biggest employer." Workers started moving away, selling property for what they could. Next a disease called the "Panamanian Blight" hit the cacao crop, which was the second line of defense for farmers here.

Property became difficult to dispose of. Sellers were plentiful, but buyers scarce. This buyer's-market situation is still in effect to some extent, but demand by foreign purchasers continually pushes beach property prices upward.

The government is working hard to find a solution, trying to attract new businesses to fill the niche that United Fruit left when it abandoned the economy. Starting new types of agriculture is not a good option, because the chemicals and pesticides used to grow bananas have made it difficult to grow anything else afterward. One project that helps local commerce is a Free Trade Zone, a special place for manufacturing and exporting by Costa Rican and foreign businesses. Those operating within the zone's coverage are exempt from some taxes and customs on importation of raw materials, components, and parts. This should attract investors who would like to take advantage of the tax breaks and the availability of good local workers.

Buses from San José take seven hours to Golfito, leaving San José from Calle 4 at Avenida 18. Spectacular scenery makes the trip enjoyable. For the impatient, daily flights, either on SANSA or Travelair, will take you there, but expect to pay a lot more than for a bus.

Playa Zancudo

Although Golfito is the central focus of the area, most North Americans do not actually live here their homes and business interests are in nearby communities or on isolated bays around the Golfo Dulce. Playa Zancudo is one community that attracts many foreigners and is especially popular with North Americans. Those who live here are more than usually convinced theirs is the best place on the entire coast.

A long, black sand beach with widely spaced homes, small hotels, and cabin rentals, Playa Zancudo is a favorite tourist and retiree development of the Golfito area. Unlike Pavones, the famous surfing beach just to the south, Zancudo's beaches are very swimmable.

Property isn't cheap here, not by any means, but it is not exorbitant either. When I was last there, the going rate for Zancudo beachfront property was around $50,000 for a 100-foot lot with a house, and $35,000 for undeveloped property—up many percentage points from my visit in the early 1990s. In the case of one property I inspected, this included a generous stretch of beachfront, with perhaps 150 feet of land between the high-tide level and the road, as well as land on the other side of the road, ending at a small river. Along the beach the usual coconut and strangler fig trees concealed the property from the view of swimmers and surfers. The rest of the property was planted in varied tropical trees, shrubs, and flowers.

Several bars and restaurants serve as social centers, with occasional weekend dances. A stop at Susy's bar-restaurant will usually find a table or two of North Americans or Europeans discussing local news and making plans for the development of their properties. Paving the road is a common topic. Those who own homes along the beach shudder in horror at the image of the throngs of tourists, property buyers, and developers a paved highway will surely bring. They feel that since they have discovered this part of Costa Rica, it is rightly theirs, and it would be downright rude for others to crowd in. On the other hand, those who have businesses, who depend on tourists and new residents to make their enterprises grow, eagerly look forward to the road and the increased prosperity it will bring.

Several folks I spoke with routinely come here for three months or longer every year. A cabin with a small kitchen, right on the beach, can often be found for as little as $350 a month during the off-season. Others are available from $500 to $900. By all means, stay for a couple of months before deciding to invest or build.

A local resident remarked, "Everyone wants to come here in the winter months [Referring to winter and summer in the North American sense.] People seem to think that summer is a total monsoon. But the weather is wonderful then. It's actually a little cooler during June, July, and August. Every morning is sunny, and at least part of the afternoon is usually rain-free. Often it doesn't rain at all." The hottest month of the year is March, according to local residents. This is just before the rainy season gets started.

Having said all of these nice things about Zancudo, I feel it's only fair to point out a possible problem with owning property here. Something that escaped my notice during previous visits is this: Zancudo Beach is actually a narrow peninsula with ocean beach on one side and a river-swamp inlet behind it. Therefore, the majority of dry land sits entirely within the 200-meter *zona maritima*. Everything seemed OK until recently, with property owners paying taxes and assessments to the municipality of Golfito. Then out of the blue, the mayor of the municipality began questioning the right of the property owners to be on Zancudo Beach. My understanding is that the dispute has been settled, but before investing any money there, speak to your lawyer as well as Zancudo residents.

Buses and stake-bed trucks bring families from nearby towns on weekends, loaded with children eager to enjoy the beach. The waves are gentle, the water warm, and kids in no danger of anything worse than sunburn. An easier way to get here is by water taxi from Golfito. Schedules vary with the tides.

The shortest way to the beach is a two-hour drive over a gravel and sometimes rocky trail. This same road splits off and goes to Zancudo's sister beach to the south, Pavones. During the rainy season this route requires a four-wheel-drive, and it's not all that great in the summer. Maps don't help much in finding either Zancudo or Pavones. I have three different maps; for all practical purposes they might as well have been of three different countries, because each has a different version of the road system, none approaching reality. It's best to stop often and make inquiries.

The road is paved from where you turn from the Golfito highway (10 kilometers from Río Claro) until you come to a quaint little ferry across the Coto River. On my last trip the old automobile engine that powers the ferry wasn't working, so they used a canoe with an outboard motor to move! If nobody's around, honk your horn, and the operators will come running. (It takes two: one to manage the ferry and one to work the canoe.)

A longer route to Zancudo—which offers much smoother roads and is easier on your rental car—takes about the same time and is usually passable during the rainy season. Follow the Pan-American Highway all the way to the border town of Canoas, then along a paved road (one side Panama, the other Costa Rica) to the town of Laurel, and from there a gravel road north to the village of Conte and on to Zancudo.

Pavones

Located in the southernmost region of Costa Rica, near the mouth of the Golfo Dulce, the last bit of Costa Rica before the coast becomes Panama, Pavones at one time attracted attention as a possible place for investment and/or residency. Reputed to have the longest surfing beach in the world, Pavones is well known among surfboard enthusiasts, who pilgrimage here from all corners of the world. Much of the land is in what appears to be primary forest, loaded with wildlife and rare plants.

At last visit I found about a dozen foreign families living along the beachfront road—mostly North Americans, mostly young (if you consider anyone under fifty-five young, as I do). Of course, surfers visit in numbers unabated, blissfully unmindful of any worldly problem that doesn't involve the height and angle of today's waves. In the local cantina waves seem to dominate most conversations. A road parallels the beach for several miles just north of Pavones, with only an occasional ranch house or cabin observable from the road or the beach. Farm clearings alternate with tracts of virgin forest, with lovely stands of native trees, tangles of vines, and a profusion of birds and animals.

The Pavones Coast is a wonderful place to visit, a great place to surf, and famous for its tropical scenery. But at this time it is a very poor choice as a place to buy property. Much of the land here has been in bitter legal dispute since 1985, and previous editions of this book warned against buying here. Investing in land that has even a shadow of legality hanging over it is a violation of our basic guidelines for Costa Rica real estate transactions. Over the years several serious incidents occurred around Pavones, resulting in the deaths of two Costa Ricans and one American. The most recent tragedy occurred in 1997. Perhaps we should look into the background of the dispute in Pavones. We may gain some insight into the questions of squatters and individual rights in general.

Today's problems can be traced back twenty-six years ago, when a wealthy Californian named Dannie Fowlie acquired extensive properties in Pavones, including some 15 miles of beach concessions. As the area's major landowner, Fowlie spent a lot of money developing the area and apparently was well liked by local Ticos and Gringos alike. He built roads, schools, churches, bridges, and airstrips, and he paid generous wages to Ticos. Then in 1985 Danny Fowlie somehow ran afoul of the law, not in Costa Rica but in California. (According to his son, Danny Fowlie, Jr., the problem was a small amount of marijuana found on his California ranch while he was living in Costa Rica.)

Danny Fowlie's sudden disappearance from the scene prompted a massive invasion of *precaistas* (squatters) on his properties and those belonging to other North Americans. The squatters' pretext was that the land wasn't legally owned, because the owner was a criminal. There can be no doubt that the incursion was well organized, that local officials sympathized with the squatters, and that the government did little to uphold the legality of registered deeds and concessions. Nevertheless, Fowlie's properties were sold to unsuspecting buyers.

Squabbling over property rights escalated into armed conflict between landowners and squatters. Both sides began carrying pistols and rifles. In a Wild West showdown between landowners and squatters, a Tico was killed by a guard protecting an American's property. Foreigners' buildings were burned in retaliation. Shots were exchanged. The government was unable, or unwilling, to find a solution. In late 1997 the battle escalated even further, when Max Dalton an American property owner, strapped on a pistol and went after some squatters who were herding cattle across his land (presumably to harass and provoke him). As so often happens when people use handguns to solve problems, tragedy followed. Max Dalton—according to friends, a gentle and non-violent human being—shot and killed one of the intruders and in turn was killed by one of the squatters. My question: Is a piece of land—no matter who legally owns it—worth two lives?

A tense atmosphere prevails today in Pavones. Local Ticos insist that it isn't anti-Gringo sentiment at all, but antilandowner, no matter what nationality. The conflicts continue with no end in sight, with squatters organized into a unionlike organization, the Costa Rican authorities unable to act, and the U.S. government demanding an end to the problem. Until things settle down, investment here is hardly recommended.

Unfortunately, the situation has discouraged tourism to the Pavones area, much to the dismay of the vast majority of Tico residents who have no stake in the dispute. A recent traveler's advisory from the U.S. State Department added to tourists' fears. But the tourists who regularly take surfing vacations in Pavones say that the Ticos there are just as gracious and friendly as anywhere else in the country. Just don't buy disputed land.

Buying Beach Property

When considering beachfront property, always bear in mind warnings about having a good lawyer and not taking sellers at face value. The pertinent legalities are discussed in detail in Chapter 18. If nothing else, remember that you don't actually own the first 200 meters of land; that belongs to the municipality. You lease it, for renewable periods, usually from five to twenty years and in some cases up to ninety-nine years. But under no circumstances should you consider buying any land that is in dispute. It's a losing proposition.

WHY CHOOSE COSTA RICA?

It's always puzzling to hear some tourists—and even an occasional resident—complain about high prices in Costa Rica. For some reason, these people assume that property, goods, and services ought to be dirt cheap in a developing Central American country like Costa Rica. They feel cheated to discover that some things cost as much here as they do back home—imported goods even more.

Not long ago we were having dinner in a local restaurant, listening to a Gringo couple at the next table complain bitterly about high Costa Rican prices. They had moved to Costa Rica three years earlier. After a long tirade I interrupted to point out, "You are drinking a bottle of beer that costs 90 cents, and you ordered a large meal that costs a little more than $3.00. What would you pay where you come from?"

"Well, those are exceptions," the lady admitted, "but, everything else is sky-high." When asked if she paid her maid or gardener more than the minimum of about $160 a month, she admitted that she did not but insisted that low wages were another exception. I finally challenged the lady and her husband to name some items that aren't imported yet are priced outrageously. After some thought she replied, "Cat food and kitty litter." Her husband triumphantly added, "Shaving cream and ball-type deodorant."

I sarcastically acknowledged that these items would indeed raise one's cost of living significantly and suggested that he try switching to underarm-type deodorant. But the sarcasm was wasted. For some people, no matter how low the price, it's still too much.

When it comes to real estate, these same people are sorely disappointed when property isn't next to free. Not long ago I was showing guests from Michigan a gorgeous beach-view lot we were considering buying. Our guests were shocked when I quoted the price. "Why, back home, we could buy a larger lot for *half* that amount!" they exclaimed. I wanted to ask whether the Michigan property had a good view of the Pacific. For sure, a California lot with a similar oceanview would command several million dollars.

Although I have a hard time imagining a quality place in the United States or Canada that makes Costa Rica look expensive, my routine reply to bargain hunters is: "If rock-bottom prices are your priority, look elsewhere." Many places in the world offer cheaper living than Costa Rica. But is the quality of life the same? Is the weather as nice? Are the people as friendly?

You're in for a disappointment if you expect to pay $3.00-a-day wages for your gardener or maid, buy gasoline at 68 cents a gallon, or purchase ocean-view property at Texas Panhandle prices. If you anticipate luxurious $10.00-a-day hotel rooms and lobster dinners for $5.00 when traveling about the country, this might be the time to return this book to your public library.

In general, I estimate that most Costa Rican prices are about one-half to two-thirds of those in most North American communities. Of course, imported goods can be twice as much, even more. The rooms in hotels that Costa Rican residents patronize usually range from $25 to $45 a night for a couple, including breakfast. These aren't luxury establishments by any definition, but they clearly offer far more than budget hotels in the United States or Canada for the same price. Backpackers are delighted to find rooms for $5.00 to $10.00, since they don't mind sharing a bath. Yes, some luxury Costa Rican hotels charge $80 to $120, but similar hotels in many parts of the United States or Canada will easily eclipse that. Restaurant meals? Go to just about any good restaurant in Costa Rica and check the menu. Few entrees are priced over $9.00. A juicy steak goes for about $6.00, and if the item exceeds $13.00, you're probably ordering lobster or jumbo shrimp. (For some reason shrimp is expensive in Costa Rica.) If you're into *tipico* Costa Rican food, you can order a *casado* for about $2.75: a huge plate of beans, rice, fried banana or yucca, salad, and your choice of chicken, fish, or a pork chop. All for less than a hamburger back home, and delicious.

Let's forget about hotel prices and restaurant costs; they don't figure heavily in most long-term residents' budgets. More important is comparing the cost of everyday living here with the lifestyle the same amount of money provides elsewhere. You would be hard-pressed to find another place with so much to offer for such a reasonable outlay. Let's start with housing prices.

In many foreign countries North American residents feel they must live in certain "safe" areas, for which they pay premium costs. Because Costa Rica is not a highly stratified society, North Americans feel comfortable living in just about any neighborhood. This translates into a wide selection of rents and housing prices. While you can pay $1,200 a month for rent in a luxury section of Escazú, you also can often find a nice place for $600 a month in the same neighborhood. For $300 you can find accommodations in a very livable area like Alajuela or San Pedro. All three locations are just a few minutes away from shopping and conveniences, and all offer quality living with superb climates. If you're content with less sumptuous digs, your rental costs can be even less. I have a friend who lives in a small house near San José that he rents for $135 a month.

Utilities, a significant part of most budgets, seem almost free in Costa Rica when compared with such costs in the United States or Canada. Our last telephone bill (with unlimited local calls) was $6.40, and that included a $1.67 long-distance call to Oregon. Water and garbage service would cost about $4.00, but they are included in our monthly condo fee. Homes on the Meseta Central have neither furnaces nor air conditioners to drain money from budgets. Electric bills for our condominium in Rohrmoser averaged $13 a month, a fifth of what we pay back in California. However, electric, water, and garbage rates vary from community to community. At our Costa Rican Pacific Coast home, electric bills are considerably more (why I don't know), and water bills are very high (because local bills include road maintenance and other services). No matter, we have friends in Missouri and Ohio who spend more to heat or cool their homes every month than most Costa Ricans earn in a month! Compare the cost of living here with that in your own hometown and then tell me Costa Rica is expensive.

Food is affordable too, with tropical fruits and veggies not only at giveaway prices but deliciously fresh. Costa Rica produces tasty grass-fed beef; a filet mignon in a San José supermarket costs about the same as round steak in a Baltimore supermarket. Some new residents here report spending a third less on their food budget than they did at home. The key is to buy local foods and avoid imported goods, which carry heavy import duties.

Property taxes are almost nothing, at least for North Americans accustomed to forking out big money for taxes. According to people I interviewed for this book, an average middle-class home—with three bedrooms and two baths—is taxed at the rate of $150 to $200 a year. Most U.S. communities collect more taxes than that every month. Tax reform laws passed in 1996 boosted some property taxes but were basically aimed at collecting from those who've evaded taxes altogether.

However, tax reform laws passed in 1997 *dropped* property taxes! (I'm almost embarrassed to report that the assessment on our two-bedroom home—a basic, nonluxurious place—dropped from more than $100 in 1997 to only $46 in 1998.)

Besides affordable housing, utilities, taxes, and food costs, what other bargains does Costa Rica offer? Oh yes—servants. A housekeeper will clean your house and wash and iron clothes for about $220 a month. That includes benefits such as Social Security and a Christmas bonus. (See Chapter 11 for further details.) We pay our gardener-handyman $1.50 an hour for part-time work, and that's well above minimum wage. We have a delightful cleaning lady who comes in one half-day each week. She washes clothes, changes bed linens, mops and disinfects floors, and waxes the veranda deck—also for $1.50 an hour. (By the way, what do you pay servants in *your* hometown?)

Is everything inexpensive in Costa Rica? Of course not. Clothing prices here will probably be the same as where you came from. Gasoline costs about the same, sometimes a little more, ranging from about $1.35 to $1.60 a gallon, depending on the current world price of crude oil and whether the government needs more tax revenue. Still, gasoline prices in Costa Rica are usually the cheapest in Central America.

Since the bulk of Costa Rica's governmental income comes from customs duties, obviously anything imported will be pricey. Cameras, TVs, electrical goods, and other imported items will cost much more because of high tariffs. Tropical countries aren't suited to wine production, so drinkable wines are imported from Chile, Europe, or California. (Chilean wines are very popular and inexpensive.) Since almost anything from Europe or North America is expensive, local consumers solve this problem simply by making do with goods made in Costa Rica or other Central American countries.

High import taxes are a way of life in almost all Latin countries. This makes automobiles *very* expensive. New-car sticker-shock will knock your socks off, with import duties of 100 percent of list price, plus sales tax. This can bring the cost of a Japanese import to about $26,000. (The same car might sell for $12,000 in Oregon!) Something with a larger price tag—say, a Mercedes that would sell for $45,000 back home—could set you back more than $100,000 in Costa Rica. At one point the government tried to do something about high automobile prices by lowering the tariff on used cars. But they were forced to restore taxes when the already overcrowded streets of San José were flooded with cheap used imports! A fact of life is that cars will probably always be expensive here. Fortunately, public transportation is excellent and inexpensive. Depending upon where you live, a family car may not be the absolute necessity that it is back home. Buses travel all over the Meseta Central, at frequent intervals, for as little as fifty colones (twenty cents), more for longer distances. Taxis are plentiful and inexpensive. Even in the country, far from city conveniences, buses and taxis are abundant. Where public transportation is all but nonexistent, the custom is for automobiles and trucks to pick up pedestrians. I've made several acquaintances that way.

Social Life

No, I've never promoted the idea of retirement in Costa Rica on the basis of cheap living. The attraction here is *quality* living: an adventurous, interesting life in a superb climate, with exotic tropical surroundings. The icing on the cake is affordable costs. When asked why they decided to live in Costa Rica, most people begin by describing the gorgeous weather and magical tropical surroundings. They'll rave on about favorite beaches, mountain retreats, and cloud forests, and eventually they'll mention the affordable cost of living. But oddly enough, when you ask them to pinpoint the most important factor in making the decision to relocate to Costa Rica, most people will agree that lovely surroundings are only part of it. There must be something else involved; after a while any pretty, exotic scenery becomes like new wallpaper: You get used to it. When you pin most people down, they'll admit, "We like the many friends we've made and our social life here."

It turns out that North Americans who live in a foreign country tend to cling together, to form close social groups, to reach out to draw newly arrived English-speakers into their midst. This is partly because they feel isolated from non-English-speaking neighbors and crave all the friends they can possibly attract. Since the pool of English-speakers is limited, each addition to their circle of friends is valuable. People with almost nothing in common—who wouldn't even nod at each other back home as they passed on the street—become great pals in a foreign setting.

I've found this to be true no matter which non-English-speaking foreign country I've researched. Expatriates in Mexico, Spain, Argentina, and Portugal affirm this close camaraderie among fellow English-speakers. Whenever I ask, people usually respond by saying, "Everyone is so friendly here! I have more friends and companions than I ever had in my hometown. There I barely knew my neighbors. My friends were mostly people I worked with." Only as an afterthought do they mention the exotic surroundings or affordable costs. Friendship and social activities almost always head the list of advantages of living in Costa Rica.

Think about it: Let's say you're moving from Syracuse to Scottsdale. You'll enter the neighborhood as total strangers. If you want friends, you must start over. That's not easy; it takes a certain personality type to successfully cultivate a compatible circle of friends from a field of aloof strangers, and it takes a certain amount of exposure (parties, social events, and so forth). In Costa Rica you'll be sought after.

This doesn't mean that you don't have to work at making friends in Costa Rica. You must go halfway. If you wait for expatriates to knock down your door and drag you out to dinner, you may give the impression of wanting to be a hermit.

It's wonderful to make friends with fellow countrymen, but what about making friends with Ticos? That's another bonus of living here: Ticos are also friendly and approachable. As you travel through Central America, or any other Latin country for that matter, you'll note definite national personalities. I see Mexico and Chile, for example, as having introspective, formal, and quiet personalities. Other countries, such as Costa Rica and Argentina, exhibit gregarious, exuberant faces to the cosmos; smiles and jokes are the order of the day.

Also, Ticos have a strong sense of equality. Social classes aren't well defined, because there isn't a wide gap between rich, middle class, and poor. Instead of meeting foreigners with an awestruck bowing of the head—as is the custom in many Latin America countries—Ticos look strangers in the eye, shake hands, and maybe even invite the stranger to visit their homes. That would seldom happen in other foreign countries—probably not in your hometown either.

Even if your Spanish is far from fluent, communication flows. Most Ticos have learned about as much English as you've learned Spanish. So all sides have lots of fun talking, learning new phrases in the other's language, and becoming friends. Making friends among the Tico community is rewarding; however, you should resist the temptation of moving to a totally "non-Gringo" community, away from other English-speaking neighbors. Most Gringos need a circle of English-speakers to round out their lives. They find that even though communication with Ticos is good, many common elements of understanding are lacking. After a while there's a craving to talk politics, to discuss movies, or to reminisce over the "good old days." You'll receive blank stares from your Tico friends when you start speculating about the Chicago Cubs' chances for the pennant or whether Senator Phoghorn can be reelected. In short, the average newcomer to Costa Rica needs both Gringo and Tico friends. Happily, this is possible! Newcomers are attacked with aggressive friendliness.

Clubs and Activities

There's no excuse for being lonely in Costa Rica—there's too much to do, too many people to meet, too many places to go. Take some Spanish classes, attend a meeting of Republicans Abroad or Democrats Abroad, do some volunteer work, learn to play tennis or bridge. You'll meet more friends than you've dreamed of, and you'll live the rich life you moved to Costa Rica to find.

The biggest mistake some make is not keeping active. Some newcomers will take a drink or two when things get too quiet for them; next thing they know, they're drinking too much. If you haven't already acquired interests to keep you busy in your new location, open the *Tico Times* to the Club Directory section and look at the broad range of invitations. (If you can't find a group of friends who are involved in your favorite activity, chances are, your favorite activity is illegal or immoral!) Volunteer work is another satisfying way to make friends and become involved in fun activities; this can be much more satisfying than sitting around a bar talking to losers until closing time.

An excellent example of a volunteer project, and one in which my wife and I are currently involved, is the establishment of a library in a village in Guanacaste. Local expatriates contributed funds to purchase several shelves of reference material as well as books that are fun to read for adults and that will enhance the local children's interest in education. When enough money was donated, we expanded the library by renting a building separate from the school and opened the facility to adults as well as children. We now have art programs for children, four computers for teaching marketable skills to teenagers and adults, and fiction and nonfiction shelves in both Spanish and English for Gringos and Ticos. Just a slight exposure to worthwhile projects like this increases one's social circle immensely

Latin Lovers

Single women visitors find that Costa Rican men tend to fancy themselves as prototypes of the "Latin lover." It's as a Brazilian friend once explained: "When I was young, my father one day took me aside to tell me the facts of life. He said to me, 'My son, in this world you must understand one thing. You cannot expect to go to bed with every woman you meet. But, of course, you must at least *try!*' "

That's the essence of a "Latin lover." This attitude often is expressed in the form of *piropos,* or flirtatious, double-entendre remarks emitted as a lady strolls past a group of Latin lovers on a street corner. The remarks are intended to be humorous asides to draw laughs and approval from the man's companions. The woman isn't expected to respond. Unlike the situation in some countries, the remarks here are rarely blatantly offensive, so a lady can safely smile as she continues on her way. Costa Rican ladies take it all in stride, either pretending they heard nothing or smiling if the *piropo* was particularly flattering. But American women, unused to this unwanted attention, sometimes take offense. Showing anger is a mistake, because your indignation simply amuses the offender and the bystanders. Although you may disapprove of this social absurdity, *piropos* are a fact of life in Costa Rica. When you, as an outsider, single-handedly try to change cultural behavior, you could end up making a fool of yourself. If you absolutely cannot ignore the remark, a simple curling of the lip as an expression of disgust, as you continue on your way, is ample. You've put him down as repugnant instead of being clever enough to get under your skin.

It's perfectly acceptable for single women to enter higher-class bars, restaurants, or nightclubs. Here they'll rarely be bothered by *piropos,* because this behavior is suitable only for street corners, and most bartenders won't stand for it. But since the bar will be full of "Latin lovers," you can be sure that before too long some feisty man will be testing his luck and charm by professing his undying love. Curiously, according to the foreign ladies I've talked to, every one of the men who tried to date them in bars was either "single" or "divorced." Now, isn't that convenient? The fact is, while divorce in Costa Rica is not common, a married man pretending he's single or divorced is quite common!

Women who find that rare, single, and marriageable male: Before you consider marriage, check out your intended rather closely. Remember that the custom of having a mistress is a socially accepted custom here, as in most other Latin countries. If this bothers you, make it crystal-clear to him what you expect out of the relationship.

What About Single Men?

"After the divorce, the first thing I thought about was coming here to get away for a while. There's something romantic about the name 'Costa Rica,' and I needed something to cheer me up after all my problems. I just knew this would be a great adventure." This was a typical reply when I would ask a single man why he was visiting here. A common follow-up statement was, "Actually, I planned to stay only for one month, but before I knew it, I met this pretty young lady, and now I'm married again!"

I've known a dozen or more fellow countrymen who married Costa Rican women, but just a few American women who married Costa Rican men. Why? I asked an ex–New Jerseyite who married a Tica lady almost five ago. "Why?" he responded. "Because Costa Rica women are different in many ways. It's not just that they are pretty and young—that's not what it's all about. We come here looking for something we think we lost somewhere back along the years. What we find is a pretty young thing who treats us as if we were special and were twenty years younger. They don't nag or complain if we're not perfect. In my case, I found a nice-looking woman who does whatever she can to make me feel at home and wanted."

What's the downside of this kind of relationship? It is often expected that the new groom will provide not only for his new wife and, often, her children from her first marriage, but for his wife's family as well. Thus, when Mami needs a new refrigerator or when Papi wants new false teeth, the husband is expected to pay for it.

Single North Americans tend to congregate in an area I call Gringo Gulch, around the odd-numbered Avenidas and odd-numbered Calles, on the edge of downtown San José, where several inexpensive hotels and singles bars attract a large number of male fugitives from the northern climes. They hang out in small bars, where they console each other over bottles of Pilsen beer, or they visit spacious, romantic nightclubs. Many North American habitués of Gringo Gulch are divorced, widowed, or confirmed bachelors. The majority are of Social Security age, looking for that one last go-round. Surprisingly enough, some actually find it. Many ladies in these bars aren't hookers (prostitution, however, is legal in Costa Rica, with women undergoing mandatory testing on a regular basis), they're really hoping to meet a financially fixed foreigner to marry, someone to take them away from all this. An older Gringo with a decent pension will do just fine.

One word of caution to would-be Don Juans: Be cautious after dark, and especially avoid the *zona roja* (red-light zone) in the opposite corner of downtown as it gets later in the evening. Some street girls here are fairly good thieves. Your wallet can disappear quickly while you are basking in sweet talk from a pretty young thing. Their scam is pretending to be overwhelmed by a man's sex appeal. Look, if a sixty-year-old thinks his sex appeal is so overwhelming to a young Tica, maybe he deserves to be scammed. Most habitutés of Gringo Gulch are transient and ephemeral. Within a few weeks they either move on to discover the real Costa Rica or return home with exaggerated tales of their sex lives in Gringo Gulch.

Gambling Casinos

For those addicted to the sound of a roulette ball bouncing along the wheel or to the riffling sound of cards being shuffled, you'll find no lack of action in Costa Rica. Most gambling casinos are in the San José area, with casinos in hotel lobbies. Sometimes it seems like a miniature Las Vegas. Occasionally, gambling casinos are found upstairs over nightclubs or restaurants.

While I sometimes like to gamble, I also like to have a chance of winning. I have the distinct feeling that gaming in the average Costa Rican casino is not really gambling but merely donating to the profitability of the establishment. House rules make it highly unlikely that you will break even, much less win. The games aren't standard ones that can be easily understood—even though they seem similar to poker or blackjack. Play is similar to that at Las Vegas or Reno, but the rules and payoffs are different, sometimes confusing, stacking the odds in favor of the house.

Another disquieting thing about gambling in Costa Rica is that there is almost no government regulation, as there is in Las Vegas or Atlantic City. I doubt very much if the house cheats. It doesn't have to cheat, since the odds are so much in its favor, but there is little or nothing to prevent cheating from happening.

Living in Costa Rica

A longtime resident once said, "I don't consider Costa Rica a Third World nation. I'd call it a 'Second World' nation—if there were such a thing. After all, it's a place where you can drink the water and eat the food, where your conscience isn't continually assaulted by beggars and abject poverty. Furthermore, it's a place where the government isn't run by a bunch of military thugs." For these reasons North Americans find adjusting to Costa Rican everyday living conditions rather easy. Of course, there are differences in lifestyles, but instead of being traumatic, in most instances the variations are charming.

Whether you thoroughly enjoy living in Costa Rica, however, depends on your approach to life. If you expect people to conform to your ideals, if you want conditions to be exactly as they are in your hometown—you are bound to be disappointed. Costa Rica is, after all, a foreign country, and that's exactly why most of us choose to live here. In this chapter we'll look at some everyday living conditions that make Costa Rica different.

Latin American Time

A difficult notion to understand is the way Latin Americans view time. When one is invited to a social event in the United States or Canada, it's considered ill-mannered to arrive late. Not so in most parts of Latin America. Should you receive an invitation for dinner, say, at 7:00 P.M. and actually arrive at that time, you are likely to embarrass the hosts. She is probably in the shower, and he still at the office. Guests are expected to arrive late. It doesn't matter, because the 7:00 P.M. dinner isn't served until 8:00 or 9:00 P.M. anyway. When keeping appointments with businesspeople, you can arrive at the office a few minutes late without worrying about it. You'll have time to catch up with the latest goings-on in the world by reading *Newsweek* and *La Nación* while waiting for your appointment. Still, even after several decades of exposure to Latin American time, I've never understood it, nor will I ever. When invited for a social gathering at 8:00 P.M., I always ask, "Is that eight o'clock Tico time or eight o'clock Gringo time?" The reply is usually a grin and, "Better make that nine o'clock." Most

Costa Ricans share this cavalier view of time—however, not to the extremes found in Mexico or Argentina.

On the other hand, my personal experience with my Costa Rican employees is that they're usually on time. I'm always surprised to see them arrive at my house early, start to work on time, and—after a morning and afternoon break—go home on time. Maybe this is because I pay more than the going wage scales, but I suspect that the Costa Rican work ethic is unusually positive, at least for Latin America.

Courtesy and Custom

Costa Rican social behavior is a curious mixture of Old World, European formality and a special Tico style of relaxed interaction. You shake hands politely when being introduced or when meeting an acquaintance on the street, women as well as men. Women may also greet other women friends with a kiss on the cheek; with close friends a lady may do the same with a man, but only if they know each other well. Exaggerated hugging and kissing—common in the United States—is not approved of here. Men, when greeting truly close friends, will give an *abrazo*—a quick hug and pat on the back—or perhaps lightly clasp the friend's wrist or forearm instead of shaking hands.

"Getting down to business," as we North Americans are apt to do, without any preliminary greeting and small talk is considered somewhat rude in Costa Rica, but not terribly so. Costa Ricans know how we North Americans are, so they never make a big deal out of it; they realize that "business" is the custom in our countries. To be polite, you might spend a few moments inquiring about someone's children or spouse, or perhaps give a compliment about the person's clothing, the weather, or anything else you might think to say before talking business. Doing so gets things off to a smoother start.

Costa Ricans have a delightful habit of issuing off-the-cuff invitations to visit them at their homes, for dinner or for cocktails, but you should always wait for the invitation and not just drop in. An exception to this is when someone moves into the neighborhood or when you move into a new home. Then it's considered polite to knock on the door and introduce yourself. When invited to someone's house for the first time, it's customary to bring flowers or some small gift.

A crucial point to remember: In social or business transactions, Ticos just cannot handle confrontation. Unlike the people of some countries—where arguing, shouting, and mock displays of anger or emotion are the accepted norm—Costa Ricans are appalled at such behavior. It's considered not only rude but also humiliating and degrading. Confrontation is foreign to the culture.

I know a New Yorker who lost an excellent gardener when his Gringo temper flared momentarily. Chuck's employee had planted some flowers in the wrong place. As usual when making a point, Chuck raised his voice and waved his hands in the air to signify his displeasure: "No, no! Not here! I wanted them over *there!*" The astonished gardener loaded his tools in his wheelbarrow and left the property, never to return, despite pleas from the homeowner's wife, who tried to explain, "That's just Chuck's way—he doesn't mean anything by shouting."

The Post Office

Although Costa Rican mail service is pretty good when compared with that in some Latin American countries, it's hardly up to the standards we expect at home (such as they are). In a country where streets rarely have names and houses lack street numbers, home mail delivery can hardly be expected to be reliable. I waited six months in vain for my first bank checking account statements. Then one day out of the blue, they all appeared at the same time. Instead of complaining, I was astonished that the mail carrier actually found my house. The address on the envelopes read, "300 meters north from Amistad Park, 100 meters to the east, and 25 meters to the south." (But which house?) The poor guy probably carried these bank statements with him every day for months, just in case he deciphered those directions and figured out which house I lived in. Unfortunately, the statements arrived after we'd sold the house and closed our checking account—having decided that having a checking account wasn't all that convenient.

That's why most folks rely on post office boxes, known as *apartados*. This means a trip to the post office every couple of days, but at least you are fairly certain your mail will be waiting for you. My post office box in the village near our Guanacaste home costs $7.50 a year. I understand the cost is considerably higher at the downtown San José post office.

For the past couple of years, there's been a problem with mail being stolen by employees within the post office system. My impression is that most thefts occur in the main post office in San José rather than in the smaller substations around the country. Postal officials are working on the problem, and they seem to have stopped most of the thefts. At least, newspapers haven't reported recent problems with mail, and our letters have been getting through OK. But never send cash. It's preferable to send checks or postal money orders via certified mail, which seems to get through OK. The substation holds a certified letter until the recipient identifies her- or himself and signs for it.

Airmail between Costa Rica and the United States or Canada involves ten days each way. That means at best a twenty-day turnaround between the time you send a letter and the time you receive the reply. A practical way to avoid this delay is by fax machine. Seems like everybody's got 'em here. A fax to or from the United States or Canada costs about $1.65, but the turnaround for an important letter or document is a matter of minutes instead of weeks.

Internet service is also available in Costa Rica, with the government hookup costing between $15 and $25, depending on the hours you want to use. At this time the government agency Radiográfica Costarricense (RACSA) is the only provider allowed. For $15.00 you get five hours with extra time at $5.00 an hour; $25.00 buys twenty-five hours and extra hours for $1.00 an hour. Hookup fees are about $40 for residents and $80 for nonresidents and include the first month's service. You can pay automatically by credit card, and you can suspend the service while out of the country by notifying RACSA a week in advance. Once you are connected, your Internet e-mail messages zip off anywhere in the world for next to nothing. RACSA offices are located in downtown San José, near the old U.S. Embassy building; the phone number is (506) 287–0463.

Another way to beat the system is with one of several Miami–San José Post Office box services that offer same-day delivery by air courier to and from Costa Rica. One I'm familiar with, a company called Star Box, charges $22.00 for up to five kilos of mail, magazines, catalogs, samples, and so on, with $3.25 for each kilo thereafter. Call (506) 221–9029 in San José, or write Star Box, 5177 Northwest Seventy-fourth Avenue, Miami, FL 33166. Other similar services are AAA Express, (506) 233–4993; Aero Casillas, (506) 255–4567; and Interlink, (506) 232–2544. Ask your neighbors for recommendations.

Telephone Service

As in most Latin countries, there is a waiting list for new telephone installations, and in some isolated areas of the country, the wait is measured in years; only a limited number of radiophones are available. Should you be impatient for a telephone, you might check the classified ads in *La Nación* for people who want to sell their phone lines.

Cellular phones are invading the country, and more are on the way; that should help out-of-the-way places, where phone lines are scarce or impossible. You can call (506) 257–2527 to see about one from the government phone company. An American enterprise, Millicom, tried to obtain franchises to install its equipment, but the request was denied. The government is determined to maintain its monopoly over communications. A big problem with cellular phones in some areas is that reception is often so bad that you have to drive to a hilltop to send or receive a call.

Making a pay-telephone call in a foreign country can be difficult and frustrating. You don't know how many coins to use, what kind to use, or when to drop in the money. The apparatus often makes strange noises: whoops, wails, and whistles, all having meaning to someone who knows the system but a total mystery to those of us who don't. Sometimes after you finally get through to your party, the call terminates before you can begin talking.

Thankfully, Costa Rica's phone system isn't at all difficult to use, and it is surprisingly efficient, even though it does send out mysterious signals at times. Phone calls to anywhere in the country go through very quickly. Even when you are dialing from a tiny village from one end of Costa Rica to the other, connections are usually as clear as if it were just across the street. Tolls are surprisingly low. A five-colón piece (about two cents) will place a call anywhere in the country. The length of time allowed for a five-colón coin depends upon the distance, but the time allocated per coin is always generous. Public pay phones operate differently from those we are used to; they have a kind of rack at the top where coins go. To make a call, you line some coins in this rack—more if you are making a long call or a long-distance call—and then start punching in your number as soon as you receive a high-pitched tone that indicates the phone is ready. When your party answers, the phone automatically swallows a coin, permitting the other coins to roll down and be in position to drop if you go over the limit for that particular coin.

To reach an AT&T international operator, you dial 0–800–0114–114, no coin needed. MCI is 0–800–012–2222; Sprint is 0–800–013–0123; Canada Bell is 0–800–015–1162; information is 113. An English-speaking operator will accept your credit card number or place the call collect. Compared with phone service in other countries, where it takes hours of waiting around a telephone office to get a call through, this is a miracle. If you have a phone in your home, direct dialing is not only easy but also the most inexpensive way to place an international call. The telephone directory lists codes for each country. You dial the country code, wait for the connection, and then dial the number you wish to reach. For example, to dial the United States from Costa Rica, first dial 001. To call Costa Rica from the United States, the prefix is 011.

Emergency calls can be made by dialing 911—just as you do back home. The fire department is 118; highway police, 117; the Guardia Civil, 127; and an ambulance (Cruz Roja), 128. To report a problem with your telephone, dial 119. For electrical problems dial 126; for water problems, 223–5555. To receive or send Western Union money orders, go to the office at Calle 9, between Avenida 2 and 4 (283–6336). If you don't have an e-mail connection yet, don't fret; you can check your e-mail account by going to the Radiográfica office (corner of Calle 1 and Avenida 5) and paying a $3.00-an-hour charge for unlimited use of the Internet. You can send or receive e-mail and surf the Web to your heart's content. This is also where you sign up for your Internet account.

Costa Rican Delicacies

A delightful custom in Costa Rica is the serving of *bocas,* or free appetizers, with drinks in bars—they may be fried shrimp, a chicken dish, barbecue, or some more exotic specialty. They aren't served as frequently as they used to be, especially in bars mostly patronized by Gringos, since we don't expect them. But Tico bars usually sustain this custom, so when you see someone else being served a treat, don't hesitate to ask. You may have the chance to sample a raw turtle egg—bars are just about the only place where you can legally find them.

One time I found a bar-restaurant that was still serving a variety of *bocas* with drinks, and they were exceptionally good. I told the owner that next time I was going to bring my wife to sample them. He was so delighted when I brought her in that he presented us with the delicacy of the house: a raw turtle egg apiece. Not wishing to hurt the restaurant owner's feelings, I managed to down mine in one gulp. But my wife's expression told me that I would have to somehow dispose of her raw egg as well. When the owner turned his head momentarily, I grabbed the other turtle egg, closed my eyes, performed the heroic deed, and quickly replaced the empty dish in front of my wife. The owner was so pleased we enjoyed his treats that he set us up with two more! As I recall, my appetite never returned that evening.

Dining Out

It's difficult to look at any particular restaurant menu and point out many dishes that could be described as typically Costa Rican. Curiously, in a country with so many unusual ingredients available, restaurant cuisine tends to be rather ordinary. Steaks, fried chicken, and shrimp seem to be almost obligatory on every menu; they taste fine, but after a while one gets very tired of fried chicken or steak. One of the most common complaints tourists have about Costa Rica is the large number of boring restaurants.

On one research trip I stumbled across a new restaurant that advertised "good old-fashioned American cooking." Since it was operated by an American from Los Angeles, I anticipated tasty "California cuisine." I ordered the featured dish of the evening: a specially prepared beef tenderloin. The owner assured me this was not at all like the normal Costa Rican fare. It wasn't. It turned out to be an overcooked slab of dry sirloin, topped with a slice of Velveeta cheese and doused with canned mushroom sauce. The veggies were canned string beans and carrots. So much for good old-fashioned American cooking. The last time I was in that neighborhood, I noticed the restaurant was closed, presumably due to lawsuits by outraged gourmets who object to Velveeta cheese on their steaks.

Not that there aren't some wonderful dining establishments around; it's just that you'll encounter more of the ordinary variety. Around the San José area, you can find interesting dining places, ranging from elegant French restaurants to superb pizzerias. Some excellent Chinese restaurants will surprise you with dishes that are quite different from the Oriental cuisine you are used to back home. Their style of cooking is a cross between traditional Oriental and tropical American. Also, some terribly mediocre Chinese restaurants are to be found (ask friends for recommendations).

One very common Costa Rican food—served everywhere, sometimes for every meal—is *gallo pinto,* which inexplicably translates as "spotted rooster." This is a mixture of cooked rice and black beans—sometimes mixed with cilantro and chopped onions—which are fried together until the rice turns a purple color. Mixed with eggs and topped with salsa Inglesa or salsa Lizano, it makes a filling breakfast—nutritious but boring when served at every meal.

In small restaurants away from the city, a typical menu item is a *casado*—a kind of lunch plate with beans, rice, fried *plátano* (a green cooking banana), and some sort of meat, chicken, or egg. (*Casado* means "married man"; why the meal is called this is a mystery.) *Olla de carne* is a tasty meat stew with vegetables such as *chayote,* squash, yucca, and *plátano. Arroz con pollo,* chicken with rice, is one of my favorites when properly done and not too dry. *Sopa negra* is a soup made of pureed black beans with an egg poached in it, topped with green onions and cheese or sour cream. Another favorite is *empanadas:* fried dumplings filled with meat or cheese, often sold by children who carry them around in galvanized buckets. A tortilla in Costa Rica is properly defined as an omelet made with chopped potatoes or yucca root. Mexican-style corn tortillas are popular in the countryside and are also called tortillas; these are far more common than the egg-and-yucca variety.

Great Coffee!

A big plus for Costa Rican cuisine is the coffee. Some of the best coffee in the world grows on shaded mountain slopes in Costa Rica. These exceptionally rich-tasting beans are used by coffee merchants around the world to add flavor to otherwise bland Brazilian or African varieties. In Costa Rica you can brew your coffee from 100 percent flavorful beans. We sometimes purchase coffee beans direct from the roaster and take them home while they are still hot. The use of instant coffee (a barbarous practice) hasn't caught on here. A *café con leche* with just a dash of sugar makes a wonderful starter for breakfast and is useful for washing down mouthfuls of *gallo pinto.*

Costa Ricans have an interesting way of making coffee here that gives a characteristically rich flavor to the brew. Instead of using a percolator or an automatic coffeemaker, Ticos use a wire or wooden stand holding a cloth strainer bag that hangs over a waiting cup. They place two teaspoons of coffee into the bag and pour boiling water over the grounds, letting it drain into the coffee cup below. Then for each additional cup of coffee, another teaspoon of ground coffee is added. The result is a flavorful, velvety drink that grows richer with each cup made. The grounds aren't discarded until the sack is full of grounds or until the end of the day—whichever happens first. "The aroma and essence of the coffee is much better if it isn't boiled," explained a Tico. "We call our coffee-making system a *chorreador.* It brings out the flavor without acid bitterness. This method requires more coffee grounds, but since coffee is inexpensive here, we use nothing but the best."

Cooking at Home

For those staying for longer than a vacation, an apartment or house with a kitchen is a wonderful way of enjoying Costa Rican cooking and experimenting with the unusual tropical ingredients available in the markets. Around the San José area, every neighborhood has at least one supermarket, supplemented by weekend *ferias,* or open-air markets. Every neighborhood also has its little *pulpería,* or convenience store, where you can buy items you forgot at the other markets.

Major supermarket chains are Auto Mercado, Periféricos, Pali, and Mas X Menos. The X in Mas X Menos is pronounced "por," which means "for" in Spanish, making the store's literal name "More for Less" markets. Open-air markets are held on weekends, the major ones being Saturday in Escazú, on the south side of the main square; Saturday in Pavas, about 5 blocks from the main shopping center; and Sunday in Zapote, next to the Bull Ring. Heredia's farmers' market, also on Saturday, is perhaps the best known of all, with local families selling produce raised in their backyards. Heredia's main market, open daily, is a wonderful place to browse for food, clothing, tools, furniture—whatever you can imagine.

Costa Rica's selection of fruits and vegetables is sometimes bewildering for us North Americans. In addition to delicious pineapples, strawberries, melons, and other things we are used to, you'll find *chayotes, pejibayes, palmitos, plátanos,* and other strange-looking items that will soon become standard parts of your menu. A common substitute for potatoes, the yucca root, in my opinion tastes much better than ordinary spuds. Exotic tropical fruits such as *guayabas, tamarindo, and carambolas* are exciting to experiment with and make delicious *refrescos* (blended drinks). One of my favorite *refrescos* is made by blending fresh cacao nuts (the source of chocolate) with *horchata* (a rice flour and sugar drink). My wife prefers a *batida* of fresh papaya, milk, and ice, whipped to a milkshakelike consistency.

Some fruits are so exotic that they border on fantastic—with shells, spines, and barbs—looking like something from a science fiction book cover. Especially interesting is the *marañón* fruit, the source of the common cashew nut. The nut itself grows at the end of an edible orange or yellow fruit that can be eaten raw or, more often, made into a *refresco* by blending with sugar and ice cubes. But the cashew nut itself is encased in a rubbery shell that is primed with cyanide, making it bitter and somewhat poisonous. I have to marvel over the wonderful way nature designed this fruit as a way to disperse its seeds. In the wild, monkeys, parrots, and other creatures pluck the fruit and carry it away to be consumed. When they finish eating the sweet fruit, the bitter-tasting seed is discarded, dropped on the ground to produce another tree.

Since Costa Rica is a cattle-growing country, steaks and roasts are quite tasty, with the flavor that only grass-fed beef can have, and they're inexpensive. You might be surprised to discover that pork and chicken are sometimes priced higher than filet mignon. One reason is that commercially raised pigs and chickens require large amounts of protein in their diets, which isn't available in bananas or other cheap tropical foods, so imported protein supplements bring prices up. Still, the quality of pork and chicken here is excellent. Eggs are delicious, having a brighter-colored yolk and a better flavor than we're used to up north, with our mass-produced egg farms.

With an ocean on both sides, Costa Rica, of course, enjoys a wide selection of seafood. And since shipping distances from either ocean involve just a few short hours, the sea harvest arrives fresh. Almost any kind of fish and shellfish you can imagine is available, plus some you can't imagine. You might want to try some of the shellfish and conch that thrive only around the Costa Rican shores.

Imported foods are expensive. Partly because of shipping costs and partly because of foreign exchange differentials, North American and European products can be prohibitively costly. Central American substitutes are often as good and locally grown—fresh foods are always much better than something canned or packaged.

Furnishing Your Home

It used to be that when foreign residents received their papers, they had the right to import household goods duty-free. This was a valuable consideration, since electrical appliances, televisions, video recorders, and the like are expensive in Costa Rica because of high import duties. The rules were that after the goods had been in your possession for three years, you could legally sell them, possibly turn a profit on the transaction, and then buy new ones.

To the dismay of incoming *pensionados*, this benefit was repealed in April 1992. The anguish and wailing over the loss of these privileges rocked the North American resident community to its heels. But after a series of appeals, the new laws were not applied to those who already had their *pensionado* status or those whose applications were pending.

Even though tax breaks are a thing of the past, you should be aware that duty-free imports on household goods aren't nearly as important as they once were. At one time demand for furniture outstripped the capacity to produce it. It was cheaper and more convenient to ship your used stuff from Miami than wait several months for the factory to fill your order at exorbitant prices.

Today supply has caught up with demand; you'll have no problem finding a wide variety of furniture at reasonable prices—usually less than you'd pay back home. The amount of money you'd have to pay to have that bedroom suite and living room furniture shipped from Des Moines, Detroit, Denver, or wherever would go a long way toward furnishing your new home in Costa Rica. Furniture stores have great selections, and you can visit small, family-operated factories and have pieces custom-made for about what you'd expect to pay retail. Earlier I mentioned the town of Sarchí as a place for furniture made with tropical woods. You can visit a factory there and have your pieces made to order. Chances are, you'll also find a woodworking shop near your home where you can have furniture custom-made, at prices even less than those at Sarchí.

Household appliances such as refrigerators, washing machines, and TVs can be purchased from a local dealer without waiting for months, as was the situation before. But these prices will include very high import taxes. For example, a few months ago we purchased a popular U.S.-make washer and dryer; we paid more than $600 for the washer and $525 for the dryer. We could have bought them for 40 percent less in a

U.S. appliance store. Our Tico neighbors, by the way, were astounded that we would waste money on a dryer when we could simply hang the wash on a line and let the sunshine dry it in an hour for free! But being spoiled Gringos—too impatient to wait for the sunshine and too often forgetting about the drying wash until after the next shower wet the clothes down again—we felt we couldn't live without an electric dryer.

Yes, it hurts not to be entitled to *pensionado* discounts, but Costa Ricans have been paying full price for years. What's so terribly unfair about having to pay the same for goods as your Costa Rican neighbors? You can be sure this special treatment was a source of irritation and resentment among the Costa Rican community. Perhaps they didn't blame foreigners for paying less, but they did fault their government for taxing them more.

Household Servants

The notion of housemaids and gardeners seems a bit wild for most of us when we first move to Costa Rica. (The last time we hired a cleaning lady in the United States, she charged $14 an hour and wouldn't do windows.) But in Costa Rica servants are affordable. With the minimum wage for domestic servants starting at $220 a month—this figure includes the additional costs of fringe benefits such as Social Security and a Christmas bonus—it makes sense to hire a housemaid and a gardener, at least on a part-time basis. Ticos are generally hardworking and honest, and if you can afford it, you can have someone working around the house who won't complain about doing windows.

Most North Americans report that they pay more than minimum wages; doings so makes their employees happy and loyal. However, while servants are affordable, you must be aware of the laws covering their benefits. By law, not by custom, you are responsible for things like vacations, Christmas bonuses, Social Security, and severance pay. Wages are indexed twice a year, according to inflation. You are responsible for knowing about the benefits and paying them on time. These rules are discussed thoroughly in Chapter 11. Don't hire a servant until you've read the rules!

Television and Other Media

A few years ago, in order to watch baseball or football games, you had to wait for a videocassette to be mailed from the States. Today there are six cable TV services just in the San José area, plus numerous private satellite dishes throughout the country. Costa Rica's modern television system offers six channels, some of which can be received in remarkably out-of-the-way places. On our San José cable system, we enjoyed abundant programming direct from the United States: two TV stations from Denver, one from Atlanta, and one from Chicago. Several international channels delivered programs coming from South America, France, and Germany as well. We found that watching CNN, CBS, and NBC nightly news on our cable TV made up for not having a daily newspaper delivered to our door.

Note that I described our cable TV system in the past tense; where we live now, on the Pacific Coast, our reception is two weak channels. That's the price you pay for not living near the big city. Still, video rental stores routinely stock the latest offerings from Hollywood. You'll find them in every neighborhood. It seems that the farther you are from the bigger population centers, the more video stores—understandably so, because cable TV doesn't reach far into the countryside. A recent development is the satellite-driven Direct TV connection. If you feel that watching CNN, the World Series, and late-run movies is worth about $1,500, you can have TV anywhere in the country.

In San José and most of the surrounding cities, you'll find stores selling English-language paperback books and magazines. In addition to the essential *Tico Times*, you can buy daily editions of the *Miami Herald* Latin American edition, the *New York Times*, the *Washington Post*, and the *Wall Street Journal*. These papers are a bit expensive—they arrive by airplane—but at times North Americans become starved for a big-city daily newspaper.

In San José a dozen theaters show first-run and recent English-language films, mostly from Hollywood. Tickets cost about a third of what they cost back home: from $2.00 to $2.50. The dialogue is almost exclusively English, and Spanish subtitles are printed over the lower part of the screen. This provides an opportunity to improve your Spanish skills by reading Spanish and listening to English at the same time. In many countries where almost no one understands English, the sound is turned down to a whisper, and the audience chatters away, making comments about the movie or whatever. But in Costa Rican theaters, the soundtrack runs at a normal volume so that the many Ticos who know English can listen. They enjoy sharpening their English by listening and using the subtitles to clarify the meaning. The result is that Tico audiences are as polite as you could hope for, and everyone enjoys the movies.

San José boasts nine legitimate theaters, mostly in Spanish, offering entertainment for those who are well along in their study of the language. One ongoing production is about the history of coffee in Costa Rica, tracing its arrival from Arabia, plus legends and beliefs about the wondrous substance. It is half in English and half in Spanish, with discounts for Costa Rican citizens and *residentes*. Two little-theater groups produce plays in English.

Two *folklorico* troupes regularly present traditions from various parts of the republic, one at the Herradura Hotel and another at the Melico Salazar Theater. Also, there are regular concerts by the National Symphony Orchestra. Sponsored by the government Ministry of Culture, Youth, and Sports, many visiting musicians from other countries add to the quality of the presentations.

Gratuities

Restaurants, by law, add a 10 percent service charge to the bill, then it's up to the customers if they care to leave something extra. I find that a 5 percent tip is greatly appreciated and leads to extra-special service the next time. Small restaurants out in the country often don't add tips to the bill, so it's polite to leave something. Barbershops and beauty salons expect a 15 to 20 percent tip. My last haircut cost 600 colones ($2.40) and I tipped 100 colones (40 cents).

At Christmastime it's customary to give something to the newsboy, supermarket attendants, and garbage collectors, and by law you give a yearly Christmas bonus to the maid, gardener, and any other employees. Since this Christmas bonus is not a gift or a tip but is required by law, an extra Christmas present would be considered thoughtful.

If you are a guest in someone's home where there are servants, it isn't necessary to tip them, unless they've done something special for you, such as laundry, ironing, or running errands. If a friend lends you the services of her maid, it's customary to tip and to pay for her taxi or bus fare home. Hotel chambermaids like to be tipped just as they do back home. I try to carry a few solar-powered calculators, which I hand out as special gifts for those who go out of their way for me. Gifts of this nature will be accepted as presents, while giving a cash tip might be demeaning to someone who doesn't work for tips. Items like calculators can be purchased inexpensively back home; in Costa Rica they are costly because of import duties.

Money Matters

Costa Rica's currency is the colón. As with many other foreign currencies, the colón's value fluctuates against the U.S. dollars according to supply and demand. For years rates have remained fairly stable, rising with inflation, and the currency has not been over- or undervalued. For example, in 1992 the rate was 138 to the dollar; six years later, in spring 1998, the colón's value was 250. That's a devaluation rate of about 10 percent a year—not much, when banks pay as much as 25 percent interest on colón certificate of deposit accounts. Most financial experts predict that the colón will remain stable, with devaluations paralleling inflation.

Some people feel uneasy when inflation continually deflates a nation's currency. The important point is whether the exchange rate between Costa Rican colones and U.S. or Canadian dollars is in line with reality and not overly managed by the government (a practice that has led to disaster in other Latin countries). Many people, even some economists, tend to assume that when the exchange rate is stable, inflation is under control and all is well. Ain't necessarily so. When exchange rates are steady, yet prices of goods and services rise in the host country, your dollar loses value every day! Just because a currency holds its own against the dollar isn't necessarily a sign of a healthy economy; it could be an artificial manipulation of currencies that masks serious problems. This caused the Mexican peso to collapse after a long period of currency manipulation. Therefore, do not confuse inflation rates with currency exchange rates!

Yes, a mild inflation has been going on in Costa Rica for decades, paralleling the inflation in the United States. But since the colón adjusts for this inflation as prices and wages rise, there's no appreciable change for those who own dollars. For example, prices and wages in Costa Rica today are twice as high as they were six years ago, yet we North

Americans receive twice as many colones for our dollars as we did six years ago; for those of us with dollar incomes, it's a wash. There's no foreseeable reason to expect that exchange rates will vary in any significant way in the future, other than a steady adjustment to world currencies, totally in line with reality.

Dealing in Dollars

A big business in Costa Rica is buying and selling dollars. As you walk along the streets, money changers badger you, offering to buy or sell dollars. A word of caution: street currency exchange is illegal—although the police seldom enforce the law—and some money changers are con men and shortchange artists. You might end up with a handful of Colombian-printed counterfeit bills; 5,000-colón notes are the favorite fakes. Also, because of a worldwide glut of counterfeit currency, avoid accepting $100 bills from street money changers or gambling casinos. The few extra colones per dollar you make by dealing with street people isn't worth the risk. Play it safe and cash your money in banks, *casa de cambios,* or your hotel, where it's legal and safe. By the way some hotels don't give good rates; check with the desk before changing your dollars. Also when accepting dollars, inspect them closely for rips or tears. For some reason banks refuse to accept foreign currency if it's torn even slightly. A favorite scam is for a waiter or shopkeeper to take your $50 bill, then return a torn bill (or a counterfeit) and ask you for something smaller.

Interest Rates

In early 1998 a nice rate of interest was being paid on time deposits of colones, more than 20 percent at nongovernment banks. (Dollar accounts pay about the same as CD rates in New York.) While over twenty percent sounds like a terrific return on your investment, you must consider the inevitability of the colón losing value against the dollar. You are gambling that the colón will devaluate less than expected, in which case you come out way ahead. If the rates fall at the expected rate, you'll do fine. But if for some reason the colón's value falls more quickly than the expected 10 percent, you could lose money. My guess (and it's only a guess) is that deflation of the colón will be slow and steady, as in the past. The reason I say this is that Costa Rica has plenty of foreign reserves, placing the government in a strong position to control currency fluctuations. Furthermore, in January 1996, for the first time in years, the country had a positive balance of payments—something the United States can only dream of. Again, my prediction of stability is only a guess. Also, remember that nongovernment banks sometimes don't have good track records, and it's difficult to discern which do. Personally, I don't get involved by speculating in currency. My wife helps me spend all of our money.

Banking

In many ways Costa Rica is a modern and efficient country, but for some inexplicable reason a visit to the bank is an Alice-in-Wonderland experience. It takes forever to do a simple transaction such as changing dollars or traveler's checks into colones. Although each bank handles things a little differently, it usually involves standing in two or three lines while the clerk checks your passport, examines the bills or checks, fills out forms in triplicate, and pounds everything in sight with a rubber stamp. Then you move to another line and wait until a second clerk fills out more forms in quadruplicate and does more rubber-stamping. The money is counted at least three times, then counted again as the clerk finally surrenders the colones to the customer. I fully expect someday to receive a rubber stamp in the middle of my forehead, just to make the transaction completely official.

Banks are also where you pay traffic tickets and utility bills and make Social Security payments for your maid and gardener. Since each transaction requires a flurry of forms, rubber stamps, and calculations, you can count on spending a lot of time in Costa Rican banks. Because of the time-consuming process of dealing with banks and government bureaucracy, some Ticos make their living by standing in line for you, by knowing whom to contact and when. They are called *tramitadores* (from the verb *tramitar,* meaning "to transact," "to take legal steps"). Your friends and neighbors can recommend a reliable *tramitador* to make your life easier. Many people become close friends with their *tramitadores,* dining with them and exchanging presents at Christmas.

Criticize the banking system as I do, the fact is that government banks are financially sound. Not long ago one went under. BancoAnglo, one of the big three Costa Rican banks, was forced to close its doors because of mismanagement and reckless speculation. The situation closely paralleled the savings and loan debacle in the United States. Costa Rican investors didn't panic; they simply took their passbooks to one of the other national banks and exchanged them for new passbooks from that bank. Nobody lost a nickel; contrast that with the U.S. savings and loan shenanigans. By the way, the Costa Rican bank officials responsible were immediately arrested. Now just consider how many U.S. savings and loan wheeler-dealers were even scolded, much less shown the inside of a well-deserved jail cell. Costa Rica went one step further: The government decided that those who *borrowed* money and didn't pay it back were equally guilty. It was surprising how quickly many "bankrupt" businesspeople found millions of dollars to repay their loans, rather than go to prison. Is there a lesson here?

Not all banks are government-owned. Many private banks deal with the public, usually in a much more efficient manner, at least as far as the amount of time you spend in line in front of a teller's cage. But there are two problems with private banks. One is that deposits are often backed only by the bank's reserves. In some cases, limited government funds are available in the event of default. The second problem is that some private banks are outrageously fraudulent, their reserves siphoned into private accounts in the Bahamas. Before you invest in a private bank, investigate its past performance and talk to your neighbors about its reliability. If the bank just opened last March and the main office is a post office box in Haiti, you just might be suspicious.

Until recently only nationalized government banks were permitted to offer checking accounts in both dollars and colones. Now some private banks have equal status with government institutions in this respect.

Local residents and business owners recommended a private bank to me: Banco Internacional de Costa Rica (BICSA). It has a branch office in Miami and operates under Florida's laws and regulations. I haven't used it yet, but this seems to be the most convenient way to transfer or wire funds from the United States and Canada. If it makes you more secure, you can keep most of your money in a dollar account and transfer dollars to the colón account to write checks and cover bills.

Bank accounts can be in either colones or dollars. But an unpleasant bank practice is holding dollar checks from foreign banks for up to forty-five days before crediting them to your account. (This was supposed to change as a result of the bank reform laws of 1996, but the last time I checked, they're still holding them for many days before crediting them to the account.) Another quirk is that the banks often do not have enough dollars on hand to cash a large check. You have to take a cashier's check instead. This is OK if you are making a local purchase with the money, since the party to whom you are giving the cash will probably deposit it in his or her account anyway. But when you need cash for a trip home, better plan ahead.

Bringing Your Pets

Those who cannot stand the thought of going anywhere without their pets will be happy to know that there is no legal problem in bringing them to Costa Rica. Doing so does, however, require a bit of paperwork. To get a doggy or kitty passport, you must write to Jefe del Departamento de Zoonosis, Ministerio de Salud, Apartado 10123, San José, and request a *permiso de importación* (import permit). Complete the form and send it to the ministry with the fee and documents.

You will need a health certificate for your pet, signed by a registered veterinarian, which must be certified by a Costa Rican consul. Your hometown veterinarian should be able to handle all the paperwork, which must state that the animal is parasite-free and has all current vaccinations against rabies, distemper, hepatitis, parvovirus, and leptosporosis. The rabies shots must be at least three months but fewer than three years old. Canine or feline pawprints are not necessary. Your pet then becomes a legal *residente,* with full rights of litterbox use or guard duty—however, without voting privileges.

To leave the country, your pet needs an exit permit, just as human *residentes* do. You'll need a health certificate from a Costa Rican veterinarian, complete with vaccination records. You take this document to the Ministry of Health to obtain a stamp, then to the Banco Central for a *permiso de exportación* and more stamps. Unlike a human *residente,* your pet doesn't need a certificate of good conduct to leave, so that time Fifi attacked the mailman's leg doesn't count.

Costa Ricans love their pets, but they tend not to keep them on leashes or in their yards, as North Americans do. Your free-wandering pooch or kitty could be at the not-so-tender mercy of the big watchdogs that swagger about the neighborhood, always ready to bully. Contrary to the situation in some Latin American countries, pet food is readily available at most Costa Rican supermarkets and sometimes in the local *pulpería*. Veterinarians are numerous, with at least a half-dozen practicing in the San José area. There's even one who makes house calls!

Crime and Personal Safety

I'm always surprised when friends visit us in Costa Rica and express dismay when they see wrought-iron bars on our windows. "Is crime so bad here," they ask, "that people must live behind bars?"

This question surprises me because bars on Costa Rican windows seem as logical and natural as window screens in Miami or storm windows in Cleveland. Maybe that's because my family moved to Mexico City when I was a youth, a place where homes traditionally have bars on their windows, so I suppose I grew up with the custom. The fact is, in every Latin American country, from the Río Grande to Tierra del Fuego, a home isn't considered complete without a set of decorative wrought-iron bars. To me a Latin American home looks naked without them, like a Cape Cod home without shutters or a Southern mansion without a portico and tall columns. When the first Spanish colonists came here five centuries ago, they brought iron bars with them. Roman settlers brought window bars to Spain 2,000 years ago; for all I know, the Romans picked up the custom from the Greeks, or maybe the Egyptians.

Do window bars deter professional burglars? Not really—not any more than door locks keep out burglars back home. Bars and locks simply keep out honest people. But I think they make the house look finished—plus they discourage amateur burglars and remove temptation from neighborhood kids.

Like any other place in the world, Costa Rica has crime. And without question crime rates have been increasing over the past few years. That shouldn't surprise anyone coming from the United States, where crime and personal safety have become the number one concern of the country. Take a look at some U.S. neighborhoods: The bars you see on windows and doors clearly aren't meant to be decorative; they are grim attempts to protect occupants from runaway, violent crime. The alternative to bigger and stronger bars is moving to a safer place with lower crime rates, perhaps rural Kansas or small-town Costa Rica (that's my solution).

I personally see crime as another one of those annoyances I have to put up with if I want to live here—an annoyance like potholes. To avoid destroying my car, I have to drive carefully to miss potholes. That's an annoyance. To avoid crime, I have to be careful where I park my car and where I keep my wallet. That's an annoyance. So far I haven't been affected by crime, but potholes have eaten several of my tires.

Of course, there's crime in Costa Rica; but it's of a different nature than that in the United States. It doesn't seem fair to compare the two places in the same paragraph. The difference is a growing incidence of petty crime in Costa Rica compared with a booming growth of brutal crimes in the United States. Criminals don't just rob up north; they savage and maim as well.

One big difference is the lack of rampant drug addiction among Costa Ricans. You won't find an army of desperate addicts who are forced to steal several hundred dollars each day to support a habit. The law provides a jail sentence of eight to twenty years for anyone involved in drug dealing. Drug use is considered extremely serious, and mere possession of drugs can be interpreted as evidence of drug dealing. By the way, these laws apply equally to native Costa Ricans and Gringos.

Recently the downtown section of San José was bothered by the appearance of *chapulines,* gangs of street urchins who robbed pedestrians by grabbing wallets and jewelry. (*Chapulines* literally means "grasshoppers," describing the way the kids jump on a victim and keep him or her off balance while one of them goes for the wallet.) I personally believe that incidents of this nature have been somewhat overstated. The fact that each episode made headlines in San José newspapers suggests that such incidents can't be all that common. However, the problem all but disappeared when strict laws were passed, with stiff sentences for juvenile offenders who previously avoided punishment because of loopholes in the law. Recently a San José judge handed out sentences of up to twenty-five years in prison to a band of *chapulines.*

It's best to take basic precautions when wandering about the center of San José—or any other big city in the world, for that matter. To be fair, having a wallet lifted or a gold chain stolen are crimes that plague tourists not only in Costa Rica but anywhere else in the world tourists go. Furthermore, this kind of crime can usually be avoided by taking reasonable precautions. Residents and long-term visitors infrequently haunt bad areas of downtown San José after dark, and they know how to avoid pickpockets.

The overall rate of burglaries in Costa Rica is much lower than that in the United States. But a high percentage of break-ins are performed on foreign-owned homes. Burglars know that the average Gringo has a nice VCR, a TV, a microwave, and maybe a stereo. Here again, a little precaution is in order. Besides a decorative set of bars, it's worthwhile to contribute to the neighborhood *guardia,* the watchman who patrols your neighborhood on foot or by motorcycle. Every block has a couple of them. Because of these *guardias,* most middle-class neighborhoods are often as safe as similar places in the United States, where a police car cruises by once a day—maybe.

If you're going to be gone for some time, a housesitter might be in order. Costa Rican burglars rarely enter a house when they think somebody might be home. Making friends with your neighbors is a great insurance policy, since they'll watch out for your vacant home, just as you take care of theirs. And as in any country, the farther you live from the big city, the lower the crime levels.

Golf Courses

When I first started writing about Costa Rica, golf courses were almost nonexistent. This disappointed many tourists who feel that a vacation isn't complete without a few rounds of golf. For golfers looking for a place to spend a long time or retire in Costa Rica, the near absence of golf was a severe drawback.

Why the scarcity of golf courses? It's partly a matter of econonics. During the rainy months, when golf course maintenance is limited to cutting grass, tourists are few. In the dry season, when lots of tourists are here, expensive and scarce water must be expended. Another factor is that golf is not a Tico tradition. The main sport here is soccer, a team sport, with strenuous running, kicking, and body contact. The excitement is contagious, with everybody cheering wildly for his or her team. Ticos have difficulty understanding golf as a sport. What they see is a few lackadaisical people fooling around with clubs. Someone hits a ball, then rides a sluggish cart to where the ball lands, and then whacks it again. Nobody cheers. Nobody gets excited. There aren't any spectators. It doesn't make sense to Ticos.

Since only an estimated 400 Ticos play golf, and without enough tourists and year-round Gringos to play, investors were hesitant to build new courses. For years the Costa Rica Country Club nine-hole course and the Cariari eighteen-hole layout were the only golf courses in the country, and both were private. So if you were addicted to golf, you were restricted to living in the Central Valley, and you had to join a club. Because of the increase in long-term foreign residents and the recent revival of tourism, the situation is changing. As of summer 1998 thirteen golf courses are in operation. Some are for members and guests only, but eight are open for public play. Nine more golf courses are under construction.

Developers are enthusiastic about golf's future here. As tourism increases and more and more full-time Gringo residents are moving to Costa Rica, more courses will be opening. Following is a list of golf courses open or due to open soon in Costa Rica (from the *Tico Times*).

Costa Rica Country Club West. In the San José suburb of Escazú; opened 1944; nine-hole; members only and guests.

Cariari Golf Club. General Cañas Highway, near San José; eighteen-hole, par-seventy-one championship course; hotel guests, club members.

Los Reyes Country Club. San Rafael de Alajuela, near San José; nine-hole; members, guests of certain hotels.

Tango Mar. On the tip of Nicoya Peninsula; nine-hole, tough executive course, par thirty-one; hotel guests only.

Rancho Las Colinas. Near Playa Grande, Guanacaste; nine-hole, par-seventy-two championship course; members and public. Another nine holes are planned.

La Roca Beach Resort & Country Club. North of Caldera on the Pacific coast; nine holes scheduled for 1998, another nine by 1999, with a third nine possible; par-seventy-two championship course; members and public.

Melid Conchal Golf Club and Resort. Playa Conchal, Guanacaste; nine-hole, with another nine holes scheduled; par-seventy-two championship course; hotel guests and public.

Parque Valle del Sol West. San José suburb of Santa Ana; nine-hole; additional nine holes could be added; public at present.

Los Sueños Marriott. Playa Herradura; scheduled for December 1999; eighteen-hole, par-seventy-two championship course; hotel guests and public.

Tulin Resort. South of Jacó Beach; eighteen-hole, par seventy-two; scheduled for 1998; members and public.

Cacique del Mar. Playa Hermosa, Guanacaste; eighteen-hole par seventy-two; scheduled for 1998; members and guests only.

Monte del Barco. Resort north of Liberia, Guanacaste; scheduled for December 1998; eighteen-hole; members and public.

Resort Rancho Mary La Cruz. A half-hour north of Liberia; nine-hole with another nine holes scheduled for October 1998. It will be an eighteen-hole, par seventy-two; members and possibly the public.

Future courses. Several are planned or under consideration near Flamingo, Tamarindo, and Playa Tambor, as well as near the community of Atenas, a half-hour west of San José.

What Do You Do in Costa Rica?

Whenever a Costa Rican resident goes home to the United States or Canada to visit friends and relatives, one of the most frequently asked questions is, "What in the world do you *do* all day in Costa Rica?" The question is accompanied by the same look of pity I might give a friend who is hopelessly addicted to soap operas or *Family Feud* reruns.

For some reason people picture our lives in Costa Rica as total boredom. They see us sitting in a jungle and killing time by counting army ants, or snoozing the day away in a hammock tied between two coconut palms. There's nothing wrong with these pastimes—only I never was good at numbers, and I seldom have time for luxuries such as hammocks.

When asked this question, my inclination is to return a look of pity and inquire, "What do *you* do all day long in that boring place where *you* live?" However, I usually contain the sarcasm and simply reply, "It isn't what I *do*—it's what I *don't* do. I don't mow lawns, fix plumbing, or wash the car. My wife doesn't do laundry, make beds, or wash windows. We pay $1.50 an hour to have somebody take care of those chores so we can do things we *want* to do rather than chores we *have* to do."

The following is an example of a typical day in my life in Costa Rica. This is what I *do* all day:

5:15 A.M. A band of howler monkeys happen to have bunked down for the night in the trees behind our house. With incredibly loud roaring calls—sounding like wounded jaguars—they warn neighboring bands where they are. Answering growls and roars come from all directions; there are at least a half-dozen troupes in our vicinity. My wife doe not notice; she's used to garbagemen making noise back home; she can sleep through anything. During my working career early rising was part of the daily routine. So naturally, now that I'm retired, the first thing I do when I wake up every morning in Costa Rica is to roll over and take a little nap.

6:00 a.m. Time to get up and enjoy another leisurely day in paradise. Since our usual bedtime is 9:30 P.M., we've had plenty of rest. Coffee on the veranda is next on the agenda. The rich aroma of Costa Rican coffee finally awakens Sherry. While waiting for the coffee to finish brewing, I go outside to water the papaya plants and ferns; the gardener won't be coming this week, because of his mother-in-law's birthday.

6:15 A.M. We settle back in the wooden rockers we bought in Sarchí and enjoy our steaming coffee. Parrots scold each other as they chatter and flit about the forest, only a few yards from our veranda. Chacalacas, motmots, and other mysterious birds add their voices to the morning serenade. When sunbeams begin striking the forest floor, the monkeys finally shut the hell up and start leaping from tree to tree along their "monkey trails" as they move toward today's feeding area. It could be a ripening fruit tree, flowering vines, or whatever else is on their seasonal menu. On the ground below our veranda, pizotes and armadillos scurry about as they scrounge breakfasts of insects and fallen fruit on the forest floor. Another sunrise in paradise.

6:30 A.M. Over our second cup of coffee, we start planning our day. "Today for sure," we resolve, "we'll go to the beach to jog and swim a little." Since the beach is less than 400 yards from our house, that doesn't seem like such a radical resolution. But somehow the unexpected always happens. We haven't been swimming in weeks. But come what may, *today* we play in the surf!

6:45 A.M. Miguel, the teenager who picks up extra money by doing chores around the house, knocks at the door. I put on my sandals and go to the bodega to get paint and brushes so Miguel can get started painting the wall and iron gate of our garage. They don't really need painting, but he needs work.

7:00 a.m. By now the local bakery is open, so I jump in the car to score some hot croissants for breakfast. Before I can get home with them, a friend flags me down and informs me of a property owners' meeting at 9:00 A.M. This is bad news, because I'd volunteered to teach a computer class at noon, and meetings often go past that time. So much for the beach this morning. OK, then, this afternoon.

7:10 A.M. When I return with the croissants, my wife reminds me that I need to put gasoline in the car because she plans on going shopping in town this afternoon. That's when I remember that the mechanic is expecting me to bring the car in at 7:30 for an oil change and tuneup—important in the dry season, with dusty roads. In Costa Rica you keep your appointments with *el mechanico* and *el dentista.*

7:25 A.M. After a hurried breakfast I drive the car to the gas station–garage for fuel and maintenance. While I'm waiting, my contractor stops by to discuss the new bedroom and bath we're adding to our house. "You must go with me to Santa Cruz tomorrow," he informs me, "to pick out the floor tile." Hmm. . . that means I'll have to cancel tomorrow's appointment with the insurance agent and find someone to take over tomorrow's computer class.

8:15 a.m. The mechanic discovers he doesn't have an oil filter for my car—too late, because he damaged the old one removing it. "On my mother's grave," he swears, "I'll have a new filter before noon." Sure. But this is Costa Rica, and I happen to know that his mother lives in Heredia. Noon tomorrow is more likely.

8:45 A.M. I hitch a ride to the residents' association office with the driver of a dump truck. He extracts a promise from me that I'll help his twin sons with their English lessons this afternoon; there's an exam tomorrow, and they're worried that they aren't prepared. The only time I can do this would be at 1:30, after the computer class. I arrange to meet them at the library then. Looks like I skip lunch again.

9:00 a.m. I arrive at the association meeting, but we have to wait for a quorum before we can transact any business. In the meantime the association president and his wife extend an invitation for cocktails at sunset—at 5:30. (The sun goes down early in the tropics.) I accept the invitation, with the provision that we can be excused by 7:00. We've agreed to meet friends for dinner at a new Italian restaurant on the beach.

11:00 A.M. The meeting over early, I catch a ride to the garage with one of the committee members. Miracle of miracles, my car is ready! On my way back to the house, I encounter a friend who explains that his car won't start and asks whether I could possibly drive him to his house for a toolbox. Of course.

11:30 A.M. I arrive home, hoping to have time for a quick shower before going to the library, where the high school kids will be waiting for their daily one-hour computer session. But Sherry informs me that the hot-water system isn't working. That means I'll have to find out where the electrician is working this afternoon and ask him to help us. Reluctantly, I take a cold shower.

11:50 a.m. Just enough time for Sherry to drop me off at the library. On the way she tells me that our maid invited us to attend her daughter's confirmation on Sunday and that the Wentworths want us to come to their ranch to see their newborn colt on Sunday afternoon. That means no beach time Sunday either.

NOON. I arrive at the library on time, but to my dismay one of the computers is having an intermittent hard-disk problem. That means I'll have to stay after the tutoring session to isolate the trouble; we can't afford to lose one of the library's four computers.

Then I remember—I had promised to stop in and see an invalid friend this afternoon. Somehow I have to find time today, because tomorrow is accounted for, as well as the day after. Maybe I can stop by after I fix the computer and still make it to our friends' house for sunset cocktails—provided that my wife finishes with her shopping and picks me up at 4:00 P.M. as she promised.

I firmly resolve that Monday, come what may, we're going to the beach to jog and swim. Then I remember: Monday's the day the homeowners chose for their semimonthly beach cleanup get-together. Oh well, at least we'll be on the beach.

But to get back to the question, "What in the world do you *do* all day long in Costa Rica?" The answer is, "We wake up in the morning with absolutely nothing to do, and by noon we know we'll never catch up!"

Miscellaneous Information

Electricity The same as in the United States or Canada—110 volts alternating current. Short power failures are common. Keep candles and matches in a place where you can find them in the dark.

Time Costa Rica is on Central Standard Time, but because the length of the days is virtually unchanged over the seasons, Daylight Saving Time is not observed.

Holidays Sometimes it seems as if every time I go to the bank to conduct business, it's closed for a holiday. Costa Rica celebrates more than a dozen national holidays and uncounted numbers of local fiestas that call for closing the bank. Watch the *Tico Times* for announcements of upcoming holidays, and plan your official business around those days. The country's biggest celebration starts a couple of days before August 2, when thousands of people walk along the highways in a pilgrimage to Cartago to honor the national saint, the Virgin of Los Angeles. Drive cautiously at this time.

January 1: New Year's Day

March 19: St. Joseph's Day (patron saint of San José)

Easter Week: Thursday through Sunday

April 11: Juan Santamaria's Day (national hero)

May 1: Labor Day

June 29: St. Peter and St. Paul's Day

July 25: Anniversary of Annexation of Province of Guanacaste

August 2: Virgin of Los Angeles Day (patron saint of Costa Rica)

August 15: Mother's Day

September 15: Independence Day

October 12: Columbus Day

December 8: Feast of the Immaculate Conception

December 24 and 25: Christmas Eve and Christmas

Religion Although the country is predominately Catholic, it isn't fanatically so. All religions are accepted with tolerance and goodwill. You can find English services in just about any denomination of church or synagogue you can think of.

A Healthy Country

Costa Rica is a healthy place to live. The United Nations recently noted that Costa Rica is in first place in Latin America for development of preventive and curative medicine, ranking with the United States and Canada among the twenty best in the world. Infant mortality is lower in Costa Rica than in the United States, and the average life expectancy is longer. This is not happenstance; the Costa Rican government spends a great deal of money on health care.

For example, in many Third World countries you play a game of Russian roulette when choosing a restaurant. A dining room can look wonderful, with white tablecloths, gleaming silverware, and tuxedo-attired waiters, but the kitchen can be a virtual cesspool. Not so in Costa Rica. If a restaurant looks good, then its kitchen will probably be just as nice. I've found very few places where I would hesitate to eat, and I've never been served spoiled food. (I can't say that about some restaurants in the United States.) This is due in some measure to the high standards of the underground water supply but also to the Ticos' natural inclination toward neatness and order. The level of cleanliness of Costa Rican restaurants is remarkable.

Another factor in restaurant safety is the relative scarcity of houseflies in Costa Rica. Since this is the tropics, you might expect to see more insects than you would in the temperate zones of North America, and you do, but in balance. For some reason you'll see remarkably few houseflies, true villains in spreading disease. In San José and other towns on the Central Plateau, you can eat outside at a sidewalk cafe without sharing your lunch with flies. This seems strange to visitors from North America's Midwest, where the fly population blooms in the summer to a plague. Yes, an occasional fly might drift past, curious as to what you are having for lunch and hoping to join you, but nothing like you expect back home in the summer.

The same thing goes for mosquitoes: In the dry season they are often as scarce as houseflies. In many areas of Costa Rica, people don't use window screens. (I wouldn't advise this, because you never know what might fly into the bedroom at night.) When in an area where dengue fever is known, mosquito repellent is essential. Mosquitoes can carry this flulike illness, which has also appeared in the southeastern United States. So far it's affected only a few parts of Costa Rica: around Puntarenas and Cañas. A concentrated campaign to wipe out the particular mosquito that carries the virus is under way.

You Can Drink the Water!

As part of its commitment to serving the public, the Costa Rican government has spent large sums of money on water and sewage treatment. Unlike the case in most Mexican and Central American cities, safe drinking water is found in San José and other major towns around the country. Most smaller towns have excellent-quality water, as do most hotels, where drinking water comes from safe wells. The government strictly monitors these water systems, even those private ones used by a handful of people. Every two months, at a minimum, tests are made for purity.

There are, however, a few places with questionable water supplies, where ordinary precautions should be observed. In some areas amoebas and *Giardia* are not unknown, but local people are aware of this and will warn you. Escazú, a ritzy suburb of San José, is an example of a place where drinking water has been known to be unsatisfactory in the past. The problem is intermittent, so if you are renting a place here, check with neighbors and follow their example.

Medical Care

The United States' health care system, with its exclusion of nearly forty million citizens from the ranks of the medically insured, is a major reason some folks think favorably about living in a country where health care is not only available but affordable. In a typical U.S. hospital, for example, patients with Medicare coverage usually pay more—just for the deductible share of an operation—than the total surgical and hospital bill would cost in Costa Rica!

In the United States should you visit an emergency room, you would have to provide proof of a hospitalization plan or a personal credit card. If you have neither, you could be told to get lost. If you have Medicare, you will find many doctors who won't accept it. In Costa Rica when one goes to an emergency room in any government hospital, there is no charge for resident, visitor, or even someone in the country illegally! This affordable medical system is another of the benefits Costa Rica enjoys because there is no military or defense industry to absorb resources. Statistics show that the general level of care is equal or superior to that in the United States—and it's available to all citizens, not just those who can afford premiums.

Why is quality health care inexpensive in Costa Rica? A prominent physician (in private practice in San José) explained it this way: "Here, our government considers medical care a public service and obligation, just as it considers education and highways a public responsibility. The government builds hospitals and trains medical specialists to serve the people, not as a business. But in the United States, medical care is a profit-making industry, a big business where profits are maximized to the highest point people can pay. Here, a doctor working for a government clinic earns between $800 and $2,000 a month. In the USA, where doctors work for profit, $20,000 a month is more common."

The doctor went on to say, "Where there is no competition, medical specialists can charge what they like. But here in Costa Rica, we have competition between our free, public hospitals and private clinics staffed with private doctors such as mine. We private doctors must keep our fees in line or we lose our patients to free clinics."

Health Tourism

In 1996 the Costa Rica Tourism Institute announced a government-sponsored Health Tourism Project, the only project of its kind in the world. The idea is to maximize the use of government hospital operating rooms and equipment (which are idle a good portion of the time) by "renting" the facilities to qualified private physicians. By combining modern surgery with pleasant tourist surroundings for recuperation, the joint government-medical project is expected to boost tourism. Part of the plan includes the use of bed-and-breakfast rooms for pre- and postoperative care.

Dr. Longino Soto Pacheco, the Health Tourism Project's director, said, "Here we can do the same surgery on the very same type of operating tables, with medical equipment of the same quality you will find in the States, and with surgeons trained in the same medical schools" (from *Business Costa Rica,* December 1995).

In the United States a typical heart bypass operation currently costs $50,000—just for the surgeon—plus big bucks for the hospital room, anesthesiologist, medication, and other medical fringe benefits. Some heart surgeons in the United States will schedule five heart bypass operations the same day; this assembly-line technique raises the surgeon's income by $250,000 for one day's work! However, in Costa Rica the total cost of a heart bypass operation is currently $15,000—that's "out the door," for everything. In other words, the complete process—including pre- and post-operative expenses—could be about what you pay in deductibles on a typical major medical policy in the United States. Currently Medicare won't cover out-of-the-country care, but the Costa Rica Tourist Institute will try to show the U.S. government how taking advantage of health tourism will save large sums of money. Expected services will include a full range of surgical procedures, including a kidney transplant center operated by a world-renowned surgeon specializing in renal transplants.

Medical Bills

In San José a routine visit to a private physician's office costs between $17 and $35. As of summer 1998 a day in a first-class private hospital costs about $90! (Hospital food is excellent, by the way, not the skimpy, tasteless food we're used to in U.S. hospitals, but delicious and usually more than you can eat.) That $90 rate is at the country's most expensive hospital—for a private room, a private bath, and a color television, plus an extra bed and meals for an *acompañate,* or companion. (It's customary for a family member or friend to spend the night in your room after an operation or when you are in serious condition, at no extra charge.)

If you are willing to put up with sharing a bath with the room next door and can do without your own private phone, the cost drops to almost half. And for a shared room and shared bath, you'll pay less than $40 a day. A day in a first-class hospital in Costa Rica costs about the same as a moderately priced hotel room! Compare these prices with those in your community. In the United States if you can get out of a hospital for less than $1,500 a day, just for the room, consider yourself lucky.

Choosing a Doctor

Foreign residents can "buy into" the Social Security system (*Caja,* as it's called in Costa Rica) by paying a fee from $40 to $50 a month and then going to government hospitals for treatment. However, since medical care is free, it isn't surprising to find the public system well used and crowded. When people don't feel quite up to snuff, they traipse off to the hospital to see a doctor. Of course, for emergency treatment there is no problem—you are seen immediately—but for an ordinary office visit with a government doctor, you could find yourself standing in line or sitting in the waiting room for a long while. For elective surgery you can expect a wait of several months for your turn.

However, there is a better way: Choose a family doctor who is in both public and private practice. See him or her as your private doctor by making an appointment whenever you have a minor problem, and paying for an office visit. But if something expensive ever comes up, such as a major operation, your doctor will check you into the government hospital for free treatment—by the same doctor.

Even if a patient chooses a private doctor and uses a private hospital, costs are ridiculously low compared with those in the United States. For example, in San José the typical bill for a gall bladder operation is $2,500, and for an appendectomy, $1,200 to $1,800.

Again, for those with Medicare, be aware that it is not valid outside the United States. However, those under seventy years of age can buy a health insurance policy from the National Insurance Institute (INS). Until 1998 the cost of a policy for someone between ages sixty and seventy was about $415 per year. (Premiums are based partly on age, partly on health experience.) However, in 1998 the premiums were boosted 30 percent, bringing the total cost to $533. These increases are under review and may be adjusted downward. (If a person belongs to a residents' association, such as the American Legion or the Association of Residents of Costa Rica (ARCR), the government grants a 15 percent reduction in premiums.) Still, compared with the private insurance in the United States, the costs are inexpensive: $46 a month. This policy pays 80 percent of hospitalization (private room), postoperative care, medicines, lab tests, X rays, CAT scans, cardiograms, therapy, home care, and support systems. For surgical fees the policy pays 100 percent, up to a maximum set level. Doctor visits are also covered to the limit of the schedule. The limits of the policy are said to be generous, taking into account the low medical costs in Costa Rica.

All retirees we interviewed swear by the quality of Costa Rican medical care. I can tell you my personal experience: I went to a doctor with a bad case of the flu, severe back and neck pain, and a fear that I had pneumonia. The doctor decided that I was going to be OK, but he suggested that I go to the hospital for a checkup and a rest. "It costs less than a hotel," he explained.

I requested a shared room, but since the hospital wasn't full, they did not put another patient in with me; essentially, I received a private room for a two-bed ward rate. After three days of tests, medication, and tender loving care (plus great meals), I was presented with a bill that made me feel even better. The entire cost of three days in the hospital, including electrocardiogram, blood tests, and X rays, was less than if I had stayed in a moderately priced hotel and dined in ordinary restaurants for those three days!

Dual System

Many Costa Rican doctors, after graduating from medical school, go to universities in the United States for further study and to do residencies. This is particularly true for specialists; since Costa Rica is such a small country, there aren't enough patients with the same problem to give a doctor the opportunity to see the wide variety of patients needed to get experience in his or her specialty.

I asked a physician from the United States who had retired in Costa Rica some years ago, "Why would a Costa Rican doctor, who does a residency in the United States or Canada, return here to work for Costa Rican medical earnings?"

"You have to understand," he replied, "that most doctors only work half-time for the government. The rest of the time, they work for themselves. Take the case of a cardiologist who charges $50 an office visit. If this doctor sees five patients a day, that's $250 a day, or about $50,000 a year, plus his salary from the government. When you consider that income taxes and the cost of living are far less here, and that high malpractice premiums aren't necessary, a huge percentage of the doctor's earnings are available for savings or investment. Even though Costa Rican doctors earn a fraction of what U.S. doctors do, they live here just as well or better, and they can live in Escazú instead of Kalamazoo!"

Hospitals in San José

Three large Social Security system hospitals provide San José with round-the-clock emergency care—with regular hours for laboratories, X rays, pharmacies, and doctor's appointments. These are the Calderón

Guardia, San Juan de Dios, and Mexico. Some private hospitals are the Clinica Santa Rita, the Clinica Biblica, and the Clinica Catolica, all excellent hospitals—the Clinica Biblica being the newest and most modern—that offer the same services as the government hospitals but with no waiting for elective medical care. Note that the term *clinica* usually indicates private hospitals or clinics, available to anyone.

Next to the Clinica Biblica is the Clinica Americana, an office complex with a group of English-speaking doctors, most of whom did residency in prestigious U.S. university hospitals. The KOP Medical Clinic in Escazú specializes in treating foreigners, with a staff that speaks English, French, Spanish, and Japanese. They offer a wide range of services, including obstetrics, gynecology, pediatrics, and dermatology.

Some emergency rooms specialize; for example, Hospital Mexico specializes in heart problems, and San Juan de Díos has a burn center. All towns of any size will have a hospital, and those that are too tiny often still have a doctor or paramedic and emergency equipment.

Rest Homes

Care for infirm elderly patients is excellent in Costa Rica, with the cost paid for by the government. However, I believe that this is something available only to long-term residents who become infirm after becoming *pensionados* or *rentistas*. To receive residency permission, one needs to pass a health examination, and I cannot imagine a doctor giving an Alzheimer's patient, for example, a clean bill of health. However, if you develop Alzheimer's or some other condition that requires long-term care after you have been living in Costa Rica as a resident, that's a different story.

A government facility probably won't be suitable for a foreigner, because of language and communication problems. But several private full-care facilities are able to address the needs of non-Spanish-speakers. (At least one of these offers specialized care for Alzheimer's patients: Golden Valley Hacienda in Alajuela; also in Alajuela is the Villa Comfort Geriatric Hotel, which specializes in folks who are not bedridden but who need care in everyday living.) The cost is about $1,500 a month for round-the-clock care.

A facility in Los Yoses, the Hogar Retiro San Pedro, was given high praise recently by an American lady for the care there. Another facility is the Hogar para Ancianos Alfredo y Delia González in Heredia. This one is in the process of starting something new in Costa Rica: a residence-development of individual cottages for senior citizens who do not require full care. Housekeeping services and meals will be provided, as will recreational facilities and physical therapy services. In addition to medical care, the facility will have recreational, hobby, arts, and travel programs for its people. Residents must be over sixty-five and able to purchase a cottage. A catalog can be obtained by writing to Apdo 138 in Heredia.

Office Visits and Hospital Rooms

The following rates by Costa Rican doctors for office visits were published by the newspaper *La Nación*. Understand that the maximum rates are average maximums and depend on the type of clients, the location of the doctor's office, and the professional standing of the physician. Those practicing in the more expensive parts of the San José area could charge more than the average maximum; those in more isolated areas, less.

Speciality	Minimum Fee	Maximum Fee
Gynecology	$18	$35
Pediatrics	$17	$30
General medicine	$25	$30
Oculist	$25	$30
Cardiology	$25	$35

Below are comparisons between two private hospitals in the San José area.

Room	Clinica Biblica Rate	Clinica Catolica Rate
Two-bed ward	$66	$48
Three-bed ward	—	$40
Intensive care	$150	—
Small room	$72	$65
Private room	$90	$78

Dentists

The University of Costa Rica trains medical specialists of all kinds, including highly skilled dentists, periodontists, and orthodontic surgeons. Like medical care, dental care in Costa Rica is affordable. I go to an English-speaking dentist in Pavas who has a very modern clinic. After he received his degree in Costa Rica, my dentist did postgraduate work in the United States.

When asked about Costa Rican dental prices compared with those in the United States, the dentist replied, "Depending upon where you live in the United States, dental care there can be three to six times as expensive. For example, in Costa Rica the standard price for a porcelain cap is $135. In Los Angeles the same work costs from $600 to $700. A bridge typically costs $375 here, but a similar job in Los Angeles would cost at least $1,800. I've had patients who fly here, pay for their hotel, food, and airfare—and still save money."

What about quality? "Dental work in Costa Rica is equal to that done in the USA," he replied. "There is absolutely no difference in the competency of the dentists. However, the quality of dental laboratory work is usually better here in Costa Rica. Don't misunderstand, the USA also has excellent dental labs, but because they can get the work done cheaper in the Philippines, many dentists routinely send bridgework and dental caps overseas, to low-cost laboratories. The quality just isn't up to the standards of Costa Rican or American labs. If I were to have caps or bridgework done in the USA, I'd certainly insist that my dentist use an American dental laboratory."

The following average rates by Costa Rican dentists were published by the newspaper *La Nación*, from data from the Colegio de Cirujanos Dentistas de Costa Rica. The fees can be higher or lower than shown here, depending on the area and the dentist's clientele. I know of one dentist in Rohrmoser who charges $60 for cleaning teeth, another dentist in Pavas (10 blocks away) who charges $25, and the other day a dentist in Nicoya charged me only $12.50 for an excellent job of teeth cleaning. The Costa Rican national average is $18.50; my dentist in California charges $80.

Service	Average Fee
Cleaning	$18.50
X ray (routine)	$25.00
Full-mouth X ray	$27.50
Filling, one surface	$12.50
Fillings, three surfaces	$21.00
Crown and metal bridge	$60.00
Dentures, upper	$100.00
Dentures, upper and lower	$200.00

Plastic Surgery

Costa Rica has gained worldwide recognition for another of its medical services: reconstructive surgery, commonly known as plastic surgery. San José is becoming known as "Beverly Hills South" because of the number of people coming here for body renewal. Several excellent surgeons specialize in face-lifts, liposuction, breast reconstruction, and other corrections of nature's mistakes. Not only are Costa Rican plastic surgeons ranked among the best in the world, but their fees are based on Costa Rican medical standards: in a word, inexpensive.

Why would Costa Rica be so popular with those wanting to rid themselves of wrinkles? Besides affordable costs and quality surgery, it turns out that San José is a perfect place to slip away to have an operation because of its climate—never hot, never cold—which makes recuperation faster, safer, and more comfortable. Since the healing process takes three or four weeks, many patients find this a great time to learn Spanish in one of the many "total immersion" schools around the city. These schools provide for homestays with a Costa Rican family and have small classes or even individual instruction if you prefer.

Another attractive thing about Costa Rica as a base for cosmetic surgery is that many folks feel embarrassed about having their friends and family know they are going to have it done. Therefore, a growing number of them vacation in Costa Rica, where they are unlikely to run into acquaintances; they have the operation; and they return home a month later, when all traces of the surgeon's handiwork have disappeared.

What does all this cost? Happily, the cost of a face-lift, a breast job, or a tummy tuck with liposuction—including surgery, postoperative care, and hospital stay—is less than one might pay just for three days in a hospital in the United States! For example, a complete face-lift costs from $2,000 to $4,000, plus $900 for operating room and recovery days in the hospital. The same operation in New York or Los Angeles would be $22,000, plus a lot more for the hospital.

San José's leading plastic surgeon is Dr. Arnoldo Fournier, who did his residency in reconstructive surgery at New York's Columbia University and who has the oldest established plastic surgery practice in Costa Rica. Dr. Fournier charges $800 to $1,200 for an eyelid operation when done separately. Nose surgery or liposuction to abdomen and thighs costs about $1,500 to $3,000, compared with U.S. rates of about $10,000 for the same procedures.

How safe is it? Costa Rican hospitals are excellent, with all modern equipment. Personnel are highly trained. Dr. Fournier points out, "Most of my surgery is done under local anesthetic and sedation. The patient is given some pills a couple of hours prior to the operation, and intravenous medication is given by an anesthesiologist during surgery. This is much safer than using a general anesthetic. Some patients just stay one night in the hospital and then check into a bed-and-breakfast for a few days. Others prefer to stay awhile, since hospital rooms don't cost any more than a first-class hotel."

For more information you can write to Dr. Fournier and ask for his free booklet, *A Brief Introduction to Plastic Surgery*. The address is P.O. Box 117–1002, Paseo de los Estudiantes, San José, Costa Rica, Central America. This publication explains thoroughly what to expect, illustrates the procedures with detailed drawings, and gives pre- and postoperative advice. For those connected with the Internet, there's a World Wide Web page on plastic surgery at: http://www.cool.co.cr/usr/fournier/fournier.html

THE REAL ESTATE GAME

Because North Americans in Costa Rica don't feel the need to group together—living in compounds or sealed-off neighborhoods as they do in other foreign countries—housing selection is far more open. Costa Ricans and North Americans are so similar in temperament and personality that most Gringos feel comfortable living just about anywhere in the country. Since juvenile delinquency isn't out of control in residential areas and because neighborhood kids are generally well behaved, we North Americans don't feel threatened as we might in some lower-economic areas back home.

Granted, North Americans do tend to congregate in the more expensive areas—nice homes, condominiums, and plush housing developments. But not everyone can afford to live in these neighborhoods, and not everyone wants to live in an English-speaking enclave. Therefore, you'll find foreigners scattered all over the Meseta Central and, in fact, all around the country.

One expatriate who has lived here for twelve years with his family of five said, "We live in a Costa Rican barrio with Ticos who are typical of most Costa Ricans I know. They love their family, neighborhood, and country, and [we] all work together at watching out for each other. . . . Our home has never been broken into, and we don't live in a fortress. We have no walls, pit bulls, Dobermans, or security systems. Five minutes and a crowbar could gain entry" (letter to the editor of the *Tico Times* by Steven Corgan, December 15, 1995).

Another thing that makes living in Tico neighborhoods easy is that even though Spanish is the dominant language, most Ticos have been exposed to English in Costa Rica's excellent school system. (However, that doesn't make them fluent in English, any more than your two years of high school Spanish made you fluent.)

Renting

Starting around 1994, rents and housing prices leveled out and have stayed steady since. This is true at least for the Meseta Central. Some hot beach properties will always rent for whatever the market will stand, and rents in these areas fluctuate with the season. A tip: For getting the best dollar value when renting in a beach area, make your deal in September or October—the slowest months of the year—when homeowners are eager to have tenants through the rainy season. At that time you have bargaining power.

When you first arrive in Costa Rica, you are likely to want to rent for a while, to get an idea of where you want to live. Neighborhoods vary greatly in quality of shopping, access to transportation, compatibility of neighbors, and, of course, price. There are some areas where you definitely wouldn't want to live—you can usually detect "bad vibes" quickly—and there are other areas that may look great at first, but later you could be sorry you didn't know about another, more interesting neighborhood. Take your time when looking for a place to live, and ask many questions of fellow expatriates.

To get an idea of what you might have to pay to rent a house or an apartment, check the *Tico Times* classifieds for a wide range of rents. The last time I looked—in Summer 1998—houses and apartments were offered at rents ranging from $250 to $2,500 a month (and even higher). While the $2,500 place should be spacious and luxurious, chances are, the $250-a-month place could be perfectly livable and just as nice as places back home that rent for twice that amount. Don't rent on price alone, however; check out the neighborhood closely.

For many Costa Rican families, the idea of paying even $250 a month is prohibitive. So if you are looking for the rock bottom in rents, check the classifieds in the Spanish-language newspaper *La Nación*. The ads in that paper are read by local people who do not have the ability to pay higher rents.

Most people, when trying out Costa Rica for livability, don't enter into long-term rentals or sign leases until they are certain they want to settle in for a long time. An ideal way to savor living in the country, particularly on the Meseta Central, is to rent an apartment by the month or the week. Short-term rentals are particularly useful when determining which neighborhood you'd like to settle in.

San José has several *apartotels*, small furnished apartments complete with cable TV, telephone, and cooking utensils—in short, everything you need for a trial of Costa Rican living. Several apartment complexes regularly advertise rates of $50 a day or $900 a month for a three-bedroom apartment, others from $225 to $495 a month for a one-bedroom place that includes telephone, TV, and washing machines. You can pay a lot more, but these apartments seem OK by my standards. (Of course, I'm easily satisfied. I do, however, insist on wall-to-wall floors and, preferably, a waterproof ceiling.)

Another excellent way of discovering whether you like a neighborhood or a city is to rent a room in a Costa Rican home. Because of pressure on hotels for tourist rooms a few years back, many private families converted spare bedrooms into rentals for the busy seasons. They're delighted to host North Americans on their visits, to take them into their homes and treat them as part of the family. A bonus to living with a family is the opportunity to perfect your Spanish by total immersion in the language. Most language schools encourage students to stay in private homes and routinely make rental arrangements for the students. Typically, a family will charge from $80 to $150 a week for a room, which includes two meals a day (breakfast and supper) and your laundry.

Don't confuse the private home setup with traditional bed-and-breakfasts. Many bed-and-breakfasts around the country are similar to small hotels, but with a tasty breakfast thrown in. Bed-and-breakfasts range from cheap, near downtown San José, to expensive, in the suburbs, depending on the luxury of the accommodations. The *Tico Times* lists many renting for about the same as an ordinary hotel.

Buying Real Estate

Many if not most countries in the world severely restrict the rights of foreigners to buy property. Some absolutely prohibit it. Not Costa Rica; this is one country where you needn't be a citizen or go through all kinds of legal gymnastics in order to own property. If you're financially capable of buying it, it's yours.

The standard recommendation to visitors is to wait at least six months before buying property. However, many catch real estate fever within the first few days of their initial visit and end up buying something anyway. For a while the buying spree in Costa Rica diminished somewhat, but people from all over the world are still plunking down money to buy something—anything—before it's all gone. Starting in 1997 the market picked up and is gaining speed once more. My guess is that the boom will continue, with predictable cycles of frequent selling followed by slack periods, just before another frenzy of buying and selling.

For twenty years armchair experts have been saying that Costa Rica real estate is overpriced, that the market has peaked and is sure to tumble. Overpriced, compared to where? Clearly, you can buy a home in Nicaragua, El Salvador, or Panama for a fraction of the price in Costa Rica. If you want to live in Nicaragua, be my guest. These same experts have been predicting the collapse of California real estate for twenty years. Yet prices keep going up, despite the fact that you can buy cheap property in places like Oklahoma, Nebraska, or Kentucky. The reason Costa Rica and California real estate keeps appreciating is a basic principle called "supply and demand." When a surplus of buyers feel they'd rather live in San José than Managua, prices will be higher in San José. Should they prefer Santa Barbara to Souix City, home prices will rise to meet the demand. When demand falls off, as it did in Costa Rica from 1994 to 1997, of course prices will drop. They didn't drop very far, however, and in 1998 home prices began rising once more.

Legalities of Buying Real Estate

Although buying property in Costa Rica should be rather straightforward, it can be tricky if not handled carefully. The following are some points to keep in mind. For complete details see Chapter 18.

The first rule is to find a competent, English-speaking attorney to handle the deal for you. This can be a challenge in itself. Inquire around the North American community for recommendations. You can also inquire at your embassy for a list of reputable attorneys. Some claim that attorneys from one of the "old families" are best, because they know a lot of people in the bureaucracy who can make things easier.

You need a lawyer to be sure the person who is selling you the property actually owns it. This is a common scam: pretending to be the owner of property belonging to an absentee owner, and selling it several times to gullible buyers. Your lawyer will also make sure that liens, mortgages, and second deeds aren't attached to the property like warts on a toad.

The second rule: Never count on a verbal contract for anything. A handshake means nothing. You may think you have a deal, but when you return with the cash, someone else owns the place and is moving in furniture. Get everything in writing, after you are completely satisfied that the property is registered and actually belongs to the seller and that the seller is who he or she claims to be. This seems elementary, but you'd be surprised how often buyers don't bother to check!

An attorney told of a client who insisted on buying a piece of view property against the lawyer's advice. The attorney reluctantly investigated and found that not only was the seller asking twice the value, but he knew the land belonged to someone else, a man who had bought the property twenty years earlier and forgot about it. To complicate matters, the real owner had died and his heirs couldn't be located. That land will be vacant for some time.

Since Costa Rica is so small, the government is able to keep land records in one place, at a central title registry called the Registro de la Propiedad. All liens and attachments must be registered here, and the books are open to the public. Even though the process of checking out a deed takes a short time, your attorney needs to know how to go about it. If you find nothing registered against the piece of real estate, you can safely transfer it to your name; any outstanding debts or obligations not registered are none of your concern. But don't feel smug until you make sure that your lawyer actually registers your new property and the documents are stashed away in your safe-deposit box.

The third rule: Do not trust the seller or agent just because he or she is a fellow North American! There's something about Costa Rica that seems to bring out latent tendencies toward larceny in our compatriots. An astounding number of confidence men come out of the closet the moment they arrive in Costa Rica. Mostly they are rank amateurs, but since they deal with people like you and me—also rank amateurs in business deals—they can cause much damage before they are finally stopped. This leads to the fourth rule: Make sure the lawyer you hire represents only you, and not both parties! Legally, an attorney can represent both sides; if his first client is a crook—look out.

In Costa Rica installment sales are not the norm; you need to plop cash on the barrelhead for most property transactions. When you consider that interest rates often top 40 percent, you'll understand why. Real estate agents should charge a commission of 5 percent of the sales price; be skeptical of those who insist that 10 percent is the customary commission. Closing costs can amount to another 5 to 7 percent—customarily split between buyer and seller. The lawyer's fee is about 1.25 percent. Conveniently, prices are usually quoted in U.S. dollars.

Brokers and sales personnel aren't regulated in Costa Rica as they are in the United States or Canada. As a result, fast-track wheelerdealers often get into real estate sales. Some have been known to boost the sales price of property by 50 to 100 percent over the asking price, keeping for themselves the difference between the owner's asking price and the actual sales price. Ask local property owners for broker recommendations, and try to contact the seller personally before closing the deal. When selling property, be wary of a brokerage agreement that doesn't pay you the full sales price less commission!

The fifth rule: Above all, do not be so overwhelmed by the beauty and tranquillity of Costa Rica that you pay the first price asked. Ticos can display irrational streaks of optimism when valuing their properties. Foreigners, bloodthirsty for profit, can be even worse. Determining the actual value of properties is difficult, because there are no "comparables" to gauge value as we are accustomed to back home, where selling prices are a matter of record. In Costa Rica everyone knows how much is asked for a property, but the actual price is always kept a guarded secret, because property taxes and transfer fees are based on the selling price. Incidentally, my attorney tells me that although it's customary to fib a little to tax collectors about the sales price of a property, if you get too creative about your fibs, they can arbitrarily assign a value to the property, no matter how much you paid!

Naturally, the farther from the city or ocean, the less expensive the property will be. But that private, isolated, mountain-slope location with a gorgeous view of the valley could be an open invitation to thieves whenever you go shopping.

The sixth rule: If you're buying unimproved land, be sure you can bring electricity and year-round water to the property. (Some parts of Costa Rica suffer water shortages every dry season.) Make sure the soil is suitable for a septic system. If sewage can't be absorbed, it will sit around, back up, and make your new home smell like an open cesspool.

When buying property, if the title is in the name of a Costa Rican corporation, or *sociadad anónima*, that's good. If not, one of the first things you'll want to do is form a corporation. This may sound strange, but there are several advantages. The section on off shore corporations in Chapter 18 explains how corporations are set up and how they are used in buying property. Although offshore corporations are sometimes used for avoiding taxes, hiding assets, and other marginal activities, there is nothing at all questionable or illegal about using corporations for real estate ownership. The big advantage of property registered in the name of a corporation is the ease of transferring ownership. Instead of going through the expensive procedure of transferring property to your name, you simply purchase the corporation's stock, take over the books, and you are now the owner.

Beachfront Property

Real estate is booming along both coasts. Prices in some areas are going wild, although other places still have bargains available. The situation is somewhat murky, because some properties that are being bought and sold have tough building and ownership restrictions that you might not be told about until you're ready to start construction. Foreigners are supposedly limited as to ownership of oceanfront property, but they manage to sidestep this law by putting their land into Costa Rican corporations.

Property owners are restricted as to how close to the beach they can build. The most important point to bear in mind is that you cannot actually own beachfront property; it must be leased from the local municipality. Make sure you're comfortable with this concept before deciding on that wonderful stretch of coconut trees and sand.

Chapter 18 discusses beachfront property in great detail, but generally, the law goes like this: The first 200 meters ashore, starting halfway between low-tide and high-tide lines, is the "maritime zone," and it belongs to the municipality. It cannot be sold, but it can be leased. (This lease is called a "concession.") The first 50 meters from the beach is the "public zone," which belongs absolutely to the public, off-limits to construction of any kind.

Construction between the 50- and 200-meter points must have the permission of the municipality. Building permits are sometimes issued only for tourist-related projects. It's also my understanding that permission to build commercially can be withheld from noncitizens until they have five years' residency. Therefore, that $35,000 lot on the beach is not an outright purchase; you actually pay that money for the right to renew a lease every five years. It's yours provided that you do everything right, make the lease payments, pay taxes on time, and obey all the rules.

Caution: A seller may claim that an existing building that falls within the first 50-meter mark is legal, because it's been "grandfathered." That's possible, but more likely someone in the past ignored the rules, and the bureaucracy hasn't gotten around to enforcing the laws. The government could force you to dismantle the buildings and restore the property to its original state, when and if it chooses to do so. Check grandfather clauses with a skeptical eye and a good attorney.

Squatters

Anyone who has followed the battles between North Americans and squatters in the *Tico Times* is aware of hair-raising stories concerning squatters and legitimate property owners. The popular name for a squatter is a *precaista.* If you're thinking of buying a piece of rural property, you need to be aware of the squatter problem. The problem is with agricultural land, not residential property.

We've all heard stories of North Americans who purchased lovely tracts of forested land with the intention of building a home someday and then, when they returned a few years later, were surprised to find the land cleared and someone farming it.

If the property you are interested in has an extra house and a Tico family living in it, beware. Don't let the seller glibly pass this off as the "caretaker's residence." It could be a squatter's home! "This family takes wonderful care of the place!" the seller might exclaim. "They just never leave the property unattended." The seller should add, "They'll never leave, period!" Make sure you see documents proving that this is indeed a caretaker employee, not a squatter. In order to be an employed caretaker, the employee must receive the legal minimum wage rate, including Social Security, and all other legal benefits. The papers proving all this must be up to date. Insist on your lawyer examining the proof. If someone is paid to simply look over the property on a regular basis, make sure there's a written receipt that he is being paid for this service and is not a squatter himself.

To most of us the idea of someone simply moving in on your property is outrageous; it's trespassing; it's theft! Can this really happen in a law-abiding country like Costa Rica? Aren't property owners protected by the law? Isn't all of this illegal?

Well, it turns out that to an extent, it is legal. There are laws to the effect that unowned or abandoned property is open for homesteading, just as it was in the early days of the United States and still is in some western states. These Costa Rican laws were intended to prevent a few wealthy people from hogging land they don't use and don't need. This is precisely what happened in all the other Central American countries; 2 or 3 percent of the people own 90 percent of the land. One reason Costa Rica is so much better off than its neighbors is that citizens have access to land. The laws are well intentioned and fair. The problem lies in how these laws are interpreted and who is doing the interpreting. Too often the bias is in favor of the squatter.

Just when is a piece of land abandoned? One law, which seems clear, states that after property goes unattended for ten years, whoever has been using the land in a "continuous, open, and peaceful manner" for those ten years may apply for a title. And the person will be successful unless the original owner has a good lawyer and a valid excuse. Another principle of law is that the squatter must show that he had reason to believe the land was abandoned; this means that someone who was being paid to watch your land can be removed if he attempts to take it over for himself. (Remember, you need receipts.)

Typically, the scenario goes like this: A choice piece of unattended property becomes a tempting target for a *precaista*. He'll construct a cabin and plant a crop in the hope that he won't be discovered for a year. If the occupancy is less than a year it's considered trespassing and is handled by the Ministry of Interior and the courts. If the trespass is less than ninety days, you call the local police, and they are obligated to evict the squatters and "present you" with a paper that confirms that you are the true owner of the property. (If the police fail to act, your lawyer can do something about that.) But let it go a full year and the situation becomes serious. The owner usually has the option of paying the squatter for his expenses and "improvements" or else going to court. ("Improvements" could be cutting down all your beautiful trees and selling them to make a pasture of your forest.) When the bill is too high—you can be sure it will be padded—sometimes it's cheaper to walk away. Understand, these problems seldom occur anywhere but on agricultural land. Land zoned or used as residential property doesn't fall into the category of this law.

The solution to this problem is a matter of prevention. While you are out of the country, have a friend or a management agent drop by the property at least once every three months. At this point, a simple complaint to the police is usually enough to boot someone off your land. Be sure to keep records of expenses and improvements to the property as proof that you haven't abandoned your land. Any place where there are a lot of foreign property owners, you'll find someone who watches property as a paid service. However, be absolutely sure you know who is caretaking your property, and keep records that he is being paid. My attorney advises, "Hire someone to check on the property, and then hire someone else to check on the person checking on your property." The last thing you want to do is hire a squatter to watch over your property!

Occasionally a problem arises when a foreign resident decides to return to the United States for an extended stay and has to lay off the maid, gardener, or other employees. If the property owner isn't familiar with the laws and neglects to pay workers' benefits such as severance pay, accrued vacation, and year-end bonuses, the employees could feel justified in taking over the land as compensation. Chapter 11 covers this in detail.

However repugnant the idea of squatting may be to you, it is important to operate within the law. After all, *precaistas* have rights, like it or not. One lady, who had just purchased some property, told me she had been informed that "the only way to deal with squatters is to burn down their houses," and that's what she intended to do if she ever found any on her property. I was horrified to think of someone on a tourist visa, a guest in the country, taking the law into her own hands! This is the way the problems start, and problems of this nature have been known to escalate into gunfire! Sometimes squatters are well organized and have their own ways of striking back; the best advice is to leave this problem to the law. The law may work slowly, sometimes not at all, but this is better than killing or being killed for a piece of farmland. I have friends who have had no problem kicking the rascals off their land, and the police burned the squatters' shacks themselves.

If you are an absentee owner of undeveloped land and have reason to believe that your property is a target of squatters or property theft scams, you should do the following: Make sure you are the legally registered owner, and if you live out of the country, ask your attorney to conduct a title search from time to time to make sure you are still on the title. Let the neighbors know who you are and that you own the property. Fence the property if possible, and post signs. Have a friend walk the property boundary lines every two months and file a complaint against any squatters encountered. If you hire a caretaker or agent to watch the property, make sure you have signed receipts showing that you've paid the caretaker for this purpose. Otherwise your trusted caretaker could end up becoming a squatter. Understand, these precautions are only for undeveloped property that is left untended by absentee owners for long periods. Other properties are relatively safe.

Building Your Own Home

When my wife and I first visited Costa Rica back in 1972, like all first-time visitors, we began looking for some excuse to stay, some way to earn a living, and we looked at property with dreamy eyes. We fell in love with a marvelous tract of ten hectares of coffee trees perched on a mountain slope overlooking San José. It had a modest owner's home of frame construction and a slightly larger house for the caretaker and his family. The price was only $18,000.

By the time we returned to Costa Rica, two years later, the property had been sold and was back on the market for $26,000. Of course, we just knew that the real estate market had topped at a crazy level, so we reluctantly gave up our dream of owning ten hectares of coffee. However, every return trip brought us a new conviction that we were foolish for not buying something last time, because the market had to be at an absolute top. "It can't possibly go higher!"

This process continued for more than twenty years, until we finally stopped kicking ourselves for not buying last time, and we started seriously looking for property. We found a good deal on a condo near San José, a place with a wonderful view and convenient to everything we needed. But after a while the condo seemed to be frivolous, because we found ourselves spending more time away from there, renting places near the Pacific beaches. So a new search began with an exciting possibility: building our own home!

We faced two choices. The first option: a lovely view of the beach—up on the side of the mountain. But this type of lot was a ten-minute drive to the beach; walking was out of the question. The second option was something within easy walking distance to the beach, where we could hear but not see the surf. The bonus was a low price, one-third the cost of a view lot.

We located a gentleman who had bought a lot near the ocean, in a development that featured a golf course as part of the design. Twenty years later the golf course had not materialized, and the forest crept up to and encompassed his lot. When the buyer, an avid golfer, realized that a golf course was not in the picture, he lost interest. Fortunately, he was willing to sell at what we considered to be a bargain price.

On the advice of our lawyer, we decided upon a local contractor rather than one from some other part of the country. The reason: Local people have their own crews and know whom to hire. They also know the local officials and have little trouble cutting through red tape. After interviewing several retirees who had experience with local builders, we asked for bids.

The plans were drawn on napkins while sitting at restaurant tables, and ideas were tossed about as to what would be the best design. To our surprise all three building estimates came to the exact same amount, about $30 a square foot for a quality home—sitting 28 feet in the air on one end—of reinforced cement, stuccoed concrete block, and tile. The bonus was that by perching our home on concrete pillars, we would have an eye-level view of monkeys, parrots, and butterflies from our veranda.

When estimating how long it would take to build the house, our contractor wisely said, "I can finish it in three months, *no hay problema.*" But since this is Costa Rica, he promised it would be built in five months. "That way you will be happy if I finish in four months," he said.

A work crew set about cutting just enough trees to lay out the house. I watched over them to make sure they didn't cut too many. They thought this amusing, and I made friends with several of them. They started calling me "don John" (a term of friendship and respect accorded to those older and more wrinkled than you). They still do—long after the house has been completed. As I drive to or from the village, someone is always waving at me and saying, "*Hola, don John!*" I've gotten into the habit of waving at everyone, for fear I might hurt someone's feelings at not being recognized.

Watching over the crew is a good idea, by the way. Not because they will loaf, but because when you go away for a few months, contractors have a tendency to take their men and go work elsewhere. You can't blame them, because there is a labor shortage from time to time. They figure they can always get back to your house before you return. It does not always work that way.

As construction got under way, I discovered that we needed some bureaucratic busywork. One required item was a *plano catastral*—a legal description of the property—which was kept at my lawyer's office along with the corporation books for the property. I drove to San José for the required documents. When I announced to the lawyer's secretary that I needed a *plano castrado*, she eyed me with surprise and then explained that I probably wanted a *plano catastral*. It turns out that a *plano castrado* is a "castration plan." I quickly agreed that was not precisely the plan I had in mind! Other requisites were a set of architect's plans and a building permit. *No hay problema*, I was told. What with a little bureaucratic delay, they were delivered to my hands six months after we moved into our house. *No hay problema.*

During the early construction phase, I stayed at a nearby bed-and-breakfast, and I arose at dawn to hang around the building site and observe the wildlife that is so bountiful at daybreak. Monkeys, coatimundis, parrots, and other animals put on an early-morning show.

Hanging around my building site at dawn brought surprises other than wildlife. I discovered something about the Ticos who worked on my project: Not only did they arrive on time for work, but most were early—quite unlike the case in other Latin countries I can think of. Starting time was 6:00 A.M., and at exactly 6:00 work commenced in earnest. They worked hard, with regularly scheduled breaks, until 3:30 P.M. (a nine-hour day). The famous *mañana* mentality wasn't apparent on this job. On the other hand, they were well paid by Central American standards and enjoyed a comparatively high standard of living. I'm not saying all Tico workers are like this; I'm only relating my experience.

A major problem I feared was that the hubbub of workers, pounding hammers and general noise, would frighten away the forest wildlife. That would essentially destroy the value of our property, since the forest denizens were to be the showcase of our new home. We were pleasantly surprised when that problem didn't materialize. In fact, during construction an unruly gang of howler monkeys congregated in the trees around the building site, and spent hours shouting insults and making caustic remarks in monkey language about my work crew's sex habits.

Don't misunderstand, our building experience was not all peaches and cream—all expected problems raised their ugly heads, and a few creative problems joined in the fun. We quickly learned a Spanish lesson: the difference between *Hay un problemcito* ("There's a little problem") and *No hay problema* ("There's no problem"). Essentially, it's as follows: *Hay un problemcito* translates "We gotta a big problem here, pal, and it's gonna cost big-time dinero." On the other hand, *No hay problema* usually translates "There's a problem, but it ain't my problem!"

However, after four months—a month earlier than promised—we had our dream house in Costa Rica. Would we do it again? I would. My wife wouldn't.

Business Opportunities

Many countries severely restrict foreign business investment. Eager to develop their own industries, these governments give special tax breaks and favors to local businesspeople and throw roadblocks in the way of foreign investors. The rationale behind this practice is that foreign investors only want to take advantage of low wages and slack government controls to generate high profits, which are then spent in the foreigners' home countries. The only benefit to the host country is a number of minimum wage jobs that don't pay workers enough to purchase the products they create. When working people can't earn enough to be consumers, all businesses in the country suffer. Often an appalling increase in poverty ensues with workers toiling ten to twelve hours a day just to keep food on the table. Merchandise that isn't exported is dumped on the market as cut-rate competition to local businesses and manufacturers, forcing them to lay off employees and often to go out of business.

Costa Rica takes a different attitude toward foreign investment. The government welcomes outside money as a way to spur development, yet it strictly enforces labor laws and keeps wages at a fair level. As a result, the average Tico worker has enough disposable income so that stores, shops, and businesses flourish.

Any investment that promotes tourism, creates jobs, and doesn't harm the environment is considered especially welcome here. Another plus: Most foreign investors in Costa Rica live in Costa Rica. For them the whole point of going into business is to be able to enjoy living in Costa Rica. They spend or reinvest profits in the country, further bolstering the economy.

To attract desirable investments, Costa Rica offers generous incentives and tax breaks. Depending on the type of business, there can be a twelve-year exemption from income taxes as well as waivers on import duties. If ecology is concerned—particularly projects involving reforestation—tax exemptions can be forever!

Consequently, a growing number of businesspeople and investors are discovering that Costa Rica, in addition to having a wonderful climate for vacations, also offers a pleasant business climate. Among the things Costa Rica has going for it are political stability, a strategic location, a relatively inexpensive and dependable labor force, and an up-to-date infrastructure. Governmental incentives, in addition to tax breaks, include lines of financing for specific industries, elimination of customs duties on importation of primary materials and equipment, and a Free Trade Zone program. In recent years millions of dollars—approximately 65 percent of which are of U.S. origin—have been invested in Free Trade Zones.

This Free Trade Zone program was developed for foreign-owned firms for the operation of export enterprises and related industries. Generous tax exemptions are granted on all types of equipment, machinery, merchandise, and goods needed for operation. Depending upon where the enterprise is located, up to ten years' tax exemptions are granted on property, real estate transfers, net capital, and assets. Up to 100 percent exemptions on profits or other taxable income are granted for the first eight years of operation and are granted at a lower rate for the next four years. Firms operating in Free Trade Zones can also sell up to 40 percent of their production in Costa Rica, with approval of the Ministry of Economy, Industry, and Commerce. (Regular customs duty must be paid on these sales.)

Anyone who owns a business is permitted to import many items necessary to operate the business, without the usual import duties. This can be important. For example, while the owner of a motel or other tourist facility is restricted in the importation of an automobile, tax breaks can be granted when importing a passenger van, because he needs it to transport clients. The owner of a farm can buy a pickup or four-wheel-drive vehicle at reduced duties because it's necessary for operation of the farm. However, there's been a crackdown on buyers of nonessential pickups, so this tax break has become difficult to obtain unless you really qualify for it.

Investments of $50,000 or more in specially approved projects qualify the investor for residency and, eventually, a Costa Rican passport. A popular $50,000 investment is in reforestation projects; some businesspeople in Hong Kong are buying these as an insurance policy, so that should the takeover by the Chinese Communists become onerous, they can escape to Costa Rica. With $150,000 the investment can be in any enterprise.

Reforestation projects aren't just a matter of deciding to start planting. You need to present detailed plans prepared by an approved forestry technical expert (a member of the Forestry Professionals of the General Forestry Office). The property, once planted, can be resold, as long as the purchaser agrees to continue with the reforestation project. Furthermore, serious questions as to profitability need to be addressed. There's more about reforestation later in this chapter.

Going into Business

Before we delve into the subject of going into business in Costa Rica, you should ask yourself some important questions. Do you really want to move to a beautiful country and spend your time working at a business? Ask yourself whether you'd be better off birdwatching, swimming, or tanning on the beach instead of doing bookkeeping, tending bar, or changing linens in your bed-and-breakfast. Do you feel up to the challenge of dealing with a quixotic, entangled bureaucracy, in a language you don't entirely understand? And finally, if it's so easy to start the business you have in mind—and make large sums of money from your idea—why hasn't somebody else already filled that niche?

Too often, dreamers feel confident that all that's necessary to become a successful businessperson in Costa Rica is to show up and dazzle the country with entrepreneurship. Well, yes, it happens sometimes, but mostly to those who know what they are doing, employing skills and special knowledge gained from business experience in their home country.

But if you're one of those who needs to be doing something and volunteer work doesn't fill the bill, then you might consider joining the numerous foreign business investors already in Costa Rica.

Many North Americans who go into business in Costa Rica don't bother qualifying under the $50,000 or $150,000 investment laws, since tax advantages accrue to any qualifying business and because a Costa Rican passport isn't an enticement to those already holding U.S. or Canadian passports. Residency papers can be easily obtained under the *residente rentista* provisions of the laws (explained in Chapter 12). Also, your choice of investment doesn't need to be approved by the government.

Since most businesses are registered in the name of a corporation, even a foreigner holding tourist papers can effectively control and manage the enterprise. While it is against the law for a noncitizen to work at an ordinary job without permission, it's perfectly OK to oversee your own business. Discretion is required here, however, since part of the scheme is to create jobs, and if a business owner is doing work that could be performed by a citizen, complaints could arise. I know of one case in which a foreign couple built a small business and managed it entirely by themselves (working very long hours, incidentally) to save the $1.50-an-hour wages they'd have to pay a Tico. Local government officials hinted that perhaps they should hire some help, and the officials were slow in granting permits, as a way of reinforcing the hint, until the couple finally hired much-needed employees.

Some North Americans have done exceptionally well in Costa Rican business ventures. They bring enthusiasm, expertise, and imagination, often re-creating successful enterprises they operated in their home country. One businessman from Illinois, who started a successful beach resort about ten years ago, said, "It's interesting to see who makes money here and who goes belly-up. The successful ones are those who come here because of the attractive Costa Rican lifestyle and who go into business as a means of staying in Costa Rica. They usually make money despite themselves. The ones who face one disaster after another are those whose main interest is making a pile of money."

Foreigners often feel they can be successful in tourist-oriented businesses because they understand the wants and needs of other foreigners who visit Costa Rica. Restaurants and bars are popular ventures. However, as in any business endeavor, you should know what you are doing, particularly in the restaurant or bar business; the failure rate in Costa Rica is unusually high. Motels, hotels, or bed-and-breakfasts fare better, although demand for new rooms has slowed considerably. In some areas entrepreneurs have overbuilt. A thorough market analysis is essential before buying or building that little hotel you've always wanted.

Real estate sales and development have created fabulous success stories as well as woeful tales of spectacular flops. Too many wheeler-dealer types start developments that look great on paper but never get past the fantasy stage. Be cautious about floating your investments on blue-sky dreams.

You needn't start your own business; numerous in-place enterprises are always available through ads in local newspapers. Of course, just as is the case back home, you need to investigate why the business is for sale. Maybe the reason is too much work, not enough profit, or illness, or perhaps the owner feels it's time to cash in the equity and stash the profit. Don't consider buying a business unless you're competent to handle it and understand exactly why the enterprise is up for sale. What makes you think you can make money at this if someone else failed?

Among the many businesses advertised in the *Tico Times* are bed-and-breakfasts, car rental agencies, pharmacies, travel agencies, and lots of bar-restaurants and discos. Apartment buildings, hotels, and beach resorts are always on the market, as are teak and palm-oil plantations (often not a good idea, as I'll discuss shortly).

Checking It Out

Newcomers to Costa Rica are tempted by all sorts of "free" seminars to help them get settled and to make decisions on how and where to invest. Unless you were born yesterday, you know that the free lunch went out with the nickel beer. That's not to say that you can't learn something from these seminars, so long as you keep in mind that the presentation will be tilted toward selling a particular product. Never let anyone pressure you into parting with your money on the basis of a sales pitch. Always check with independent experts before considering investing, and then check out the experts. To be fair, I must admit that the few free seminars I've attended were quite informative, and I found surprisingly little sales pressure.

Still, it's just as easy to lose money in Costa Rica as it is back home. For a stranger in a foreign land, it's even easier. You must know what you are doing. Business consultant Ray Nelson says, "My best advice is to come here for six months and look around. Study the existing businesses and find out why some are successful and why others fail. Above all, don't jump into a business just for the sake of being in business—particularly a business that you don't know much about."

Because of Costa Rica's liberal attitude toward foreign business ventures and sometimes lax regulation, a surprising number of foreigners feel as though they have complete freedom to operate as they wish and that ordinary laws and ethics don't apply. This is probably why Costa Rica draws more than its share of swindlers, crooks, and con artists.

The Costa Rican government does what it can to keep on top of offenders, but it's impossible to do much more than prosecute crooks after the damage has been done. And this rarely happens, because the swindler simply skips the country before the trial date. For this reason look very carefully at any business deal presented to you. All too often ostensibly honest businesspeople surprise everyone by turning out to be swindlers. Make sure you have a good, English-speaking lawyer check with all the proper government agencies and verify the integrity of your deal before risking your hard-earned money.

Popular scams include phony mutual funds, nonexistent banks and so-called tax-shelter investments; gold mines; hotels and resorts that never leave the drawing board; real estate that is sold to several people, property that didn't belong to the seller in the first place; and teak, macadamia, and jojoba plantations—all the get-rich-quick schemes you can imagine.

After pointing out all the pitfalls of going into business, I have to admit that many people are having fun doing so. You can feel a dynamic sense of progress and excitement in Costa Rica. This is the country of the entrepreneur, of wide-open opportunity, cheap land, dependable labor, and honest government. Modern-day Costa Rica is reminiscent of the old frontier days of the United States and Canada, full of success stories about North Americans who've opted to "start all over again." Just be aware that there are failure stories as well.

Agriculture as Investment

Because of incredibly rich soil and year-round growing seasons, Costa Rica is an agricultural paradise. The country is checkerboarded with crops of all descriptions. Just about anything grows here, with bumper crops the rule rather than the exception. Rich volcanic soil and a rainy season that coincides with the peak growing season makes farming a dream in Costa Rica. Therefore, agriculture would seem to be one of Costa Rica's best bets for investment. It is, actually, but it can also be Costa Rica's biggest investment disaster for novice farmers and for those who don't understand the ground rules. Just because crops grow well doesn't guarantee you are going to make money.

One longtime agriculturist who has struggled to make a living in Costa Rica says, "Farming is a great way to go broke even if you are an experienced agriculturist. There are too many unknowns and too many marketing problems." He added wryly, "If I had invested the same amount in real estate as I spent trying to get an orange grove started, I would be a rich man by now."

Newcomers are bombarded with brochures, advertisements, and lecturers, all promising huge profits from oranges, macadamia nuts, black pepper, and other such crops. Seminars on teak, mahogany, and other exotic woods tempt investors with promises of a 30 percent return on the dollar. Most of these promotions feature absentee management; you put up the dough and the company handles the rest. Other investors plan on living on the property and actually doing the growing, harvesting, and marketing all by themselves.

Of course, growing and harvesting are the nitty-gritty of agribusiness, but a third factor, marketing, is truly the key. Without a marketing strategy all your efforts in growing oranges or bananas are in vain and your crops a waste, except for whatever you and your family can eat. One farmer pointed out, "If you don't have a contract, you are banging your head against the wall. What are you going to do with a field full of pineapples without buyers? Local marketing is the only way to move them, but there is only so much local demand. Bananas are the country's top crop, but a little guy can't compete with the huge multinational corporations. Coffee growing is a small-scale operation, that's true, but world prices fluctuate so much that you often can't make money."

One ex-farmer narrated some problems he encountered trying to farm profitably in Costa Rica: "We had some great orchards, with good production, but we couldn't get marketing contacts. Local markets can absorb only so much citrus fruit, and high export costs kept our products out of range for foreign markets. The only money appeared to be in marketing juice. So a few of us citrus farmers decided to invest in a juice extraction plant. But before it could be completed, a government plant went into operation, causing our project to go bankrupt."

Next he tried growing starfruit. "We did great at first," he said, "because we were the first to put it on the market. But the problem was, a starfruit vine bears a thousand fruits, and each fruit has enough seeds to grow a thousand plants. Before long, starfruit flooded the market and we couldn't give it away. Then we looked toward Europe as a market for starfruit juice. That worked out great for a time, but competition reared its head again. European buyers began demanding concentrate rather than juice, and we couldn't afford to build a concentrate plant."

A longtime Costa Rica resident who dabbles in agriculture for fun advised, "It's a mistake to blindly take the word of promoters and developers who claim huge returns from agricultural projects. If you don't know Spanish and don't understand Costa Rican labor laws or the legal system, you are going to have a tough time under the best of circumstances. If you don't understand the problems of production and marketing, then you have no business trying to be a tropical agriculturist." He added that an investor in agriculture shouldn't buy a farm unless prepared for continuous, personal, hands-on management. "Absentee ownership seldom works," he emphasized.

But what about all those advertisements for plantations of high-profit crops? Listed here are some problems and questions related to me by farmers:

- Black pepper at one time was indeed a profitable crop, but East Indian overproduction has dropped the price. Buyers are insisting on low prices because they use black pepper as a loss leader in their marketing strategies.

- Jojoba bean production was once popular, but like many other crops, jojoba wasn't native to this area and a glitch in the climate killed off most of the trees in one season.

- Macadamia trees take a long time to produce and then are susceptible to pests; the wrong spray can kill the trees.

- Hawaiian papaya is becoming popular for shipment to Japan. But this market is very selective, with buyers handpicking and accepting only about 30 percent of the crop. Another problem with papaya and other crops is that Japan and other countries usually insist on certification of medfly-free crops. The hard part is getting medfly-free certification. It's difficult enough in places like California and Florida and is extremely difficult in Costa Rica.

Teak plantations are getting the biggest push in Costa Rica at the moment. According to promoters, this is a surefire venture that will pay huge dividends. One company advertises that a $6,500 investment "will earn almost $300,000 over a ten-year cutting period." I asked an American agriculturist about this. This was his opinion: "First of all, teak isn't native here, and nobody knows what the production will do or what kind of wood it will produce. It takes about fifteen to twenty-five years for the trees to be big enough for harvesting, and we won't know for sure until then. That is a long time to wait for profits." The *Tico Times* once ran an interesting series of investigative feature articles on teak as an investment. The controversy is ongoing, so before you invest, do some investigation on your own. You're likely to find investors who feel they've made a mistake.

Tourism and Investment

Tourism has become Costa Rica's top industry, bringing in even more cash dollars than the export of coffee or even the number one crop, bananas. Tourism's importance as an economic resource for the country cannot be overstated; neither can its opportunities for foreign investors be overlooked. Most hotels and tourist facilities constructed in the past five years have been financed through outside investment. In the past eight years, more than 6,000 hotel rooms have been added to the country's inventory. Every week sees new bed-and-breakfasts opening their doors to tourists. Yet despite all this action, we still couldn't find vacancies along the Guanacaste Coast during Christmas week! Instead of hotel room prices dropping because of increased competition, rates edged upward—not drastically, just enough to prove that there is still space for more tourist businesses, albeit with larger vacancy rates than before. Again, do a careful market analysis before adding new rooms to the inventory.

Ecotourism Investments

As pointed out earlier, Costa Rica's environment combines several tourist attractions. Visitors are drawn here to enjoy a unique climate, lovely facilities, gorgeous beaches, and Costa Rica's ecological wonderland. Therefore, with a new awakening of environmental awareness on our planet, it's no surprise that Costa Rica attracts large numbers of affluent visitors who insist on seeing these wonders firsthand, sights not available anywhere else on the tourist circuit except in a zoo or a greenhouse arboretum. They go out of their way to come here, to enjoy the sensation of walking through a rain forest hoping to catch sight of a quetzal bird, inhale the odor of tropical blossoms, and hear the bizarre calls of howler monkeys.

Accommodations are a secondary consideration for many of these visitors. If they wanted discos, shopping, and spiffy beachfront hotels, they wouldn't travel all the way to Costa Rica. Most come here for something special. They pay well for the privilege of viewing tapirs, ocelots, beautifully colored butterflies, and magnificent flowering trees, all in their natural settings. This idea of combining vacations with ecological marvels in a tropical paradise is called "ecotourism."

Traditional tourist resorts, in order to attract visitors, must invest heavily in great views, tennis courts and golf courses, luxury rooms, and first-class restaurants. Then after they've sunk a fortune into a project, there's always a danger of someone building an even more expensive resort next door to lure away clientele, making the place obsolete. The facility must be top quality and well maintained to stay even with today's competitive market. Without something special tourists have little reason to patronize a particular resort.

Ecotourism, however, is a game played in a different league. An intriguing feature is that it doesn't necessarily require an enormous investment in land and accommodations. The point is that ecotourists search out facilities located away from fancy hotels, discos, and boutiques. The best nature preserves are located on almost inaccessible mountaintops or hidden away on isolated beach coves far from shopping centers, beauty parlors, miniature golf, and other "necessities" of civilization. It isn't necessary to provide nightlife, gourmet restaurants, and deluxe accommodations. In fact, most visitors would be disappointed if they found them.

Land for ecotourism developments can be incredibly inexpensive, because it has little commercial or agricultural value, is difficult to reach by automobile, and is of interest only to ecologists and special types of tourists. If visitors have to fight their way over rocky, muddy roads to arrive at their nature accommodations, so much the better. This adds to the feeling of isolation from civilization. If getting there requires an hour's boat trip, having to wade the last 50 yards to get to shore, ecotourists don't complain. It's part of the adventure. Let me hasten to add that it's also less expensive for the investor.

Investment in a successful eco-project can be quite modest, and tourists will still be eager to visit. They're satisfied with small and sparsely furnished rooms, a community bathroom, and meals that consist of rice, beans, and fish. At an ecotourism development they're happy to find space available. Some places put guests in tents, where they sleep on cots, use outdoor showers, and wear rubber boots to breakfast. And ecotourists love every minute of it! In ecotourism you have two choices: Either you put up with what is available or you don't enjoy the ecological treasures Costa Rica has to share.

Ecotourism dining rooms operate on the same premise. Instead of a fancy menu with a list of gourmet selections, the kitchen serves up one meal for everyone. The food is tasty and well prepared, that's true, but from the management's position very efficient and cost-effective. Ecotourists don't complain if *gallo pinto* is served three times a day, if fried yucca and *plátanos* replace baked potatoes, or if smoked pork chops are served instead of steak. After working up an appetite slogging through dripping forests and climbing mountain trails in search of elusive butterflies and toucans, they'd probably enjoy my cooking!

In addition to getting into business with the lowest possible investment, ecotourism entrepreneurs derive satisfaction from working toward the preservation of the environment. If they didn't feel that way, they probably would have gone into some other endeavor. Visitors feel that they too are contributing to a better world by supporting environmental understanding and education. That investors break even and occasionally make money while doing what they enjoy is a pleasant side benefit.

The Costa Rican government welcomes and encourages this type of nondestructive development. Every hectare of cloud forest or primeval beachfront used as a living museum is a hectare saved from chain saws and cattle grazing. Some ecotourism projects have even gotten off the ground through grants from U.S. government agencies or from conservationist groups.

Investing in Costa Rican Stocks

Investing in Costa Rican stocks is not something I'd recommend, even if I were a competent player in the stock market. I've had my problems with U.S. stocks and bonds and would never encourage someone to jump into something I or they knew nothing about.

The Costa Rican stock exchange (known as the Bolsa) has some unique problems. One is that the most successful companies are privately owned, by families, and aren't found on the stock market. Unlike the United States and Canada, Costa Rica doesn't have a watchdog government agency looking over the shoulders of corporation officers to ensure business is conducted in an orderly and competent manner to protect stockholders. My understanding is that reporting to stockholders can be erratic and sometimes fraudulent.

This is not to say that the Bolsa in general is not on the up and up. Many knowledgeable investors have money in the Costa Rican stock market, and they seem to be satisfied. The key word is *knowledgeable*. If you know what you are doing, be my guest.

Working in Costa Rica

A question often asked is "How can I get a job in Costa Rica?" The answer is, "It can be done, but it's not easy." The Costa Rican government discourages foreigners from competing with citizens for work. In order to work legally, you'll need a special permit, which involves proving that you are uniquely qualified for a job that can't be done by a Tico. Foreign companies are entitled to a percentage of noncitizen employees, but in practice they seldom fill this quota. The reason is simple: They can hire all the qualified Tico employees they need, and foreigners don't want to work for Tico wages.

An exception to this nonemployment of foreigners is in teaching. A qualified English as a Second Language teacher can usually find work and get a permit. But the wages are so low that most don't feel it's worthwhile. English-language schools in the San José area often have positions open for qualified high school or elementary school teachers, but you must have credentials or some speciality that makes you valuable. Again, the pay won't be exciting. (High school teachers earn a little more than $15 a day.)

This isn't to say that there aren't a large number of foreigners working illegally in the country. Some work in real estate sales, property management, and tourism. A few with special skills work in construction—usually on a temporary or emergency basis. Sometimes foreigners working as contractors are not hassled by the local government—because they hire workers and provide jobs. Unless the foreigners are obviously taking work from Ticos, their activities are often ignored. But the bottom line is that working without a permit is illegal, and you can be deported for doing so. After you've had your residency for five years, you can apply for a *carta libre,* a permit to work freely, and can then accept any type of work without restriction.

Examples of Business Ventures

In the course of researching business opportunities in Costa Rica, I've met many foreigners who've made the decision to become entrepreneurs. Their experiences vary, as do their levels of enthusiasm for being in business. Here are a few examples.

Nightclub/restaurant. It looked like a good deal; every weekend as many as 300 people crowded into the Cebolla Verde (the Green Onion) to dance to a rock-and-roll band. They paid 1,000 colones apiece cover charge. The nightclúb/restaurant sat on the road between Escazú and Santa Ana, two of the more affluent areas of the Meseta Central, areas where many North American expatriates reside. With crowds like this, how could you miss?

But after Robert Masek (from California) bought the Cebolla Verde, he and his partner, Graham Henshaw (from England), discovered they weren't making money, despite the throngs of patrons and the crowded dance floor. It turned out that the youthful crowd came to dance, not to drink or eat. The cover charge went to the band, and the customers bought one soft drink or beer to last the night.

The partners soon realized that the success of the restaurant depended on food—not entertainment—and on attracting customers who had money to spend. So they fired the rock-and-roll bands and concentrated on meals. Business dropped off, then started building up, but slowly. They needed something special to bring people in. They decided to try spit-roasting a pig every week as well as serving American-style prime rib. This worked, bringing people from all corners of the area to sample this hard-to-find fare. Not only did the partners attract more Gringos, but a large contingent of affluent Ticos are now regular customers.

Graham's advice to anyone wanting to go into business in Costa Rica is, "First: Spend at least six months here, looking around and doing market studies. Second: Either do something you really know well or else do something you've always wanted to do but don't have to make a living at doing."

Trout farm. The Costa Rican government has been encouraging the establishment of fish farms as supplementary income for farm families. A government agency imports eggs and fingerlings from Alaska and Idaho and makes them available at cost. A group of Canadians, Americans, Europeans, and Ticos living near San Isidro de General decided to take advantage of this unique business opportunity.

They leased some land high on the mountainside and raised about $100,000 to build the necessary tanks and equipment. The property is strategically located at the edge of the Chirripó Reserve, with cold water cascading down the mountain peaks (Costa Rica's highest) to feed the tanks needed for breeding and hatching fish. "There aren't any farms or homes above us to pollute the water with insecticides or sewage," Chuck Narry, one of the partners, pointed out. "And since trout like cold water, they thrive."

The partners' lease is an interesting arrangement. The Tico landowners leased the land with the proviso that they share equally in the enterprise. The Ticos agree to supply the labor, while the foreigners supply experience and capital. The group purchased several thousand hatchlings from the government and started their first crop. The first batch of broiling-size trout sold out immediately in local grocery stores. The dream looked as if it were coming true. At the time I interviewed the entrepreneurs, an order of 175,000 hatchlings was due, and they felt sure they would be getting orders from all over the country, from restaurants, from upscale supermarkets, and, eventually, for export.

"However, a big problem is, most pieces of equipment we need don't exist here," Chuck Narry said. "We either have to make it ourselves or order it from the United States and pay an enormous duty. We even have to make our own fish feed." One headache they don't have is problems with employees. Since the workers own the land and are part-owners of the business, labor relations are ideal.

Bakery. When I met Ron Kozlowski a few years ago, he was in the process of constructing a bakery and learning how to handle Costa Rican workers. The construction stage wasn't easy. "I had good employees," he said, "and they worked very hard, but sometimes they drove me wild. One day I had to go out of town, and when I returned, the workers had built a wall where there wasn't supposed to be a wall. I had to sledgehammer it down and start over." Today Ron has one of the best-constructed buildings and a thriving business in the village of Dominical.

An ex–Navy Seal, Ron is a deep-sea diver specializing in underwater welding, and he spends half the year working, the other half in Costa Rica. Rather than go into debt, he built the bakery from savings and his paychecks, thus avoiding the horrendous interest rates common in Costa Rica.

"I decided to specialize in Tico-style baguettes, European-style croissants, and desserts. Getting quality merchandise for the deli and ingredients for baking and cooking is my biggest problem," said Ron. "For example, the secret to good pizza is the gluten flour for the dough. Then it has to be cooked in a brick oven. Otherwise, the crust comes out like crackers instead of real New York–style pizza." His clientele is about half Ticos and half Gringos, and he is proud of this: "It shows that everybody appreciates my attempts to bring them something different."

Ron's advice for newcomers: "Do your homework, and anticipate at least a third over cost." His biggest problem: "Electricity bills. Because I'm on a commercial rate, I pay $1,200 a month for the bakery-deli. Yet I have two private homes, with two refrigerators, two stereos, and so forth—and the bill is $25 a month!"

Massage therapy. After Joe Goodman graduated with a degree in political science, he came to Costa Rica in 1975 for a vacation. He decided he wanted to stay and made application for residency. After eight years of managing hotels and agricultural projects, he decided he wanted to do something different. He went back to the States to study physical therapy and returned to take jobs as a therapist and masseur for a health club in a luxury hotel in San José and work with a chiropractic orthopedist.

After a few years Joe became tired of the city and wanted to get away to a small town in the tropical part of the country. So he made a deal with a small motel on the Pacific Coast where he could have a room and place to do massage in exchange for managing the motel when the owners weren't around.

About becoming a resident, Joe said, "It's not easy to establish residency, and it never has been cheap. It requires lots of patience. Plan on spending triple the amount of time and money you originally planned on." As for advice for those going into business, he added, "Don't sell the business back home. Rent it, lease it, or let someone else run it while you come down here and look around—get to know the country. Often folks settle in someplace without knowing what's happening elsewhere and are sorry they hadn't seen everything before making a decision."

Rental cabins. When Richard and Ann Dale retired from a successful retail furniture business, they looked forward to moving from the harsh winters of Washington, D.C. They methodically started exploring Caribbean islands one by one in search of a retirement home. Nothing seemed right.

At that time their oldest son, a postgraduate student in biology at Harvard, had been traveling in Costa Rica. He began telling his parents interesting tales of that country: monkeys, parrots, nice people, and so forth. It sounded so attractive that Richard and Ann decided they had to visit, just in case this might be their retirement Eden.

"Everything seemed so natural after the Caribbean Islands," Ann explained. "There everything seemed artificial; even water was often imported." They found a delightful lot on the Bar River—just a few meters from the main road and the beach—and decided to build a 2-story home with both a river and an ocean view. However, after a busy life of business, they became restless and decided to add a few cabins on the property and rent them out. This was the start of their small motel, now with five rustic cabins that rent for about $30 a night. They added a floating dock and some rental kayaks and inner tubes for their customers' float trips on the Río Bar .

"An interesting part of the construction phase was that the workers weren't familiar with power tools," said Richard. "Machetes and handsaws were their basic implements." After careful instruction and training, as well as some close calls, the workers learned to handle drills, power saws, and electric sanders. It wasn't easy. "Once a worker had a power saw cradled in his lap when he plugged it into the power," said Richard. "Fortunately, it was upside-down, so he wasn't injured. Another time a power sander sitting on a work bench zipped away at high velocity when the cord was plugged in. But today they are excellent craftsmen."

Bed-and-breakfast. Around the turn of the century Barrio Amón was the most elegant residential area in San José. High-society families lived in opulent mansions, arguably the Costa Rican equivalent of San Francisco Victorians. But as the wealthy moved to Escazú or Barrio Escalante, Barrio Amón fell into disrepair. Then a few years ago, the barrio was "rediscovered" by entrepreneurs who acquired the mansions at bargain prices and began restoring them as hotels and bed-and-breakfasts.

Carl Stanley, who had extensive experience restoring Victorians in the Monterey, California, area, decided to try his hand at creating a bed-and-breakfast. His purchase was the 1910 residence that once housed a wealthy coffee-growing family. The twenty-room mansion had 14-foot ceilings and a desperate need for refurbishing. "It was in terrible shape," Carl said. "I spent two and a half years in restoration, another year setting it up as a luxury inn." Furniture pieces in each room are exact replicas of those depicted in old photographs taken in the house seventy years ago. He named the bed-and-breakfast Casa Verde de Amón. "Last year I received an award for the best restoration in Costa Rica," he added proudly.

When asked for advice for folks who are considering coming to Costa Rica to enter business, Carl Stanley said, "If you can be successful in the States, you have a chance at being successful here. The catch is, you'll have to work twice as hard and for less money. You go through a learning curve. You come with great expectations but you go downhill for a couple of years until you become *chispa*—that is—'streetwise.' "

"You simply cannot come to a Third World country and expect to make money without learning the language, working intensely within the culture, the bureaucracy, with the workers," he added. "The problem is, too many foreigners here tend to live in isolation, in their own English-speaking world. Yes, a man may marry a Tica, but she protects him from everything Costa Rican, and together they remain in their isolated world."

Supermarket. Billed as the "Biggest Little Supermarket in Guanacaste," the Pura Vida Market in Garza was started by Richard and Ginger Powers, from Manhattan Beach, California. When asked, "What made you decide to go into the grocery business in Costa Rica?" Richard replied, "Originally we were thinking of a bed-and-breakfast, but it seemed everyone had the same idea. We hit on the idea of a supermarket when Ginger started complaining about the availability of good food. The markets were dark inside, vegetables old, and things were difficult to find. She said, 'Somebody should put a supermarket in here.' And I said, 'Why don't we do it?' " They had never been in the grocery business before, but the more they thought about it, the more obvious it became that a supermarket could be a success. They were correct, for the store made money the first year it was open, something they didn't really expect.

"The best thing about the business is that it makes enough money to provide a living so we can afford to live here. The worst thing is that it doesn't provide enough income to do everything we'd like to," Richard said. Since their children are enrolled in a private school in San José, they need to rent a home there in addition to the lovely home they built in Garza.

After writing about the Super Pura Vida for the previous edition of *Choose Costa Rica*, Richard and Ginger bowed out of the scene and leased the store to Marsi and Tim Marsh, also from California. Originally Marsi came here to teach school to English-speaking children. She had assumed that with all the North Americans living in the area, there would be a need for a teacher. To her dismay she discovered that most residents' children were already out of college and had children of their own, but back home.

Bar and grill. Bill and Pam Lancaster—who used to have a bar and grill in Key West, Florida—came to visit friends who owned a bar in Nosara. Before they realized what was happening, their friends talked them into taking over the business temporarily. Their friends were tired of working and wanted to return to the States, so Bill and Pam found themselves back in the business. The friends never returned.

"We had to learn to work with new foods, new liquors, and a totally different way of doing things," Pam said. "At first language was a problem, but fortunately, many of our customers are English-speakers. They come because of the Florida-style food we serve. Interestingly, that's also why many Ticos come to our place [Bill's Bamboo Bar]. They're curious about American food and often order one dinner to divide between two or three of them, just to try the different cuisine. I make sure they get a huge serving and extra plates so they can make up their own little portions."

When asked about the downside of running a bar and grill in Costa Rica, Bill replied, "Well, the margin of profit is so low, you can be sure you'll never get rich. With beer selling at a dollar a bottle, it turns out the Gringo's cheapest form of entertainment is drinking at Bill's Bamboo Bar!" Then he added, "It does provide a living, though—and we didn't expect to get rich in Costa Rica." Pam added, "One good thing is that your investment is minimal, at least when compared with the U.S. licenses, insurances, liabilities, and business problems."

What advice would they give to someone wanting to go into the bar business in Costa Rica? Pam said, "The best thing would be to find someone who is willing to walk you through the legal steps, explain the lease laws, how to purchase supplies, and on and on. Maybe offer to work in a business for a month in exchange for the experience." They seem to be doing something right, because they recently opened another restaurant in Nosara, called "Marlin Bill's."

Fishing charter service. Tom Cochran loves to fish, but while working as a contractor in the United States, he couldn't find the time to wet a hook. "It only seemed natural to get into the fishing business when I moved to Costa Rica," he said. "I'd be out fishing anyway, so why not make money while I'm having fun?" He bought a small boat, just large enough to carry a few passengers, and he went into the charter business.

"The best part about being a professional fisherman is that I enjoy every moment, and my clients always turn out to be friends," he observes. "The worst part is that there aren't enough clients. But I go fishing anyway." When asked if he makes a profit, Tom says, "I really haven't figured that out yet. But I'm having lots of fun." To supplement his income, Cochran does some contracting, building homes for newcomers.

Hotel and bars. Pat Dunn, owner of San José's Dunn Inn Hotel, came to Costa Rica some fifteen years ago at the request of his father, who wanted to know if this would be a good place for retirement. Pat liked it so well that he decided to move here himself. His father decided to stay at home.

Pat's first venture was a bar in San José. After owning several bars, he found a dilapidated old mansion in Barrio Amón, which at that time was a slightly seedy, old section of town. Pat envisioned a comeback for this once elegant neighborhood, and he began rehabilitating the building as a tasteful hotel. He was correct, for today Barrio Amón is a popular place for bed-and-breakfasts, upscale hotels, and good restaurants.

"Costa Rica is a virgin territory in some ways," Pat says. "If you're willing to work hard and if you find the right niche, you can make it. Too many come here with the idea that they can dazzle Costa Rica with their brilliance. They soon learn the hard way that it doesn't work like that." Not knowing Spanish proved to be Pat Dunn's biggest frustration. Fortunately, he married a Tica businesswoman who helped him across the rough spots.

One piece of advice he offers to those thinking about going into business in Costa Rica: "Do it straight and right, and don't pay off anyone." He explained that at first he tried to cut corners by paying bribes to get things done quickly. But that turned out to be a mistake. Someone was always ready with an outstretched hand. "It takes a little longer to play by the rules, but in the long run you'll be ahead," he notes.

Where to Go for Business Help

Listed here are a number of sources for help and advice for those interested in going into business or investing in Costa Rica. These are folks who've been around Costa Rica for a while and who are up on the latest scams.

First, look for the Costa Rican–American Chamber of Commerce's publication *The Guide to Investing and Doing Business in Costa Rica.* They also publish a monthly magazine, *Business Costa Rica.* The Chamber's phone number is (506) 220–2200; fax, (506) 220–2300; e-mail, amchamcr@sol.racsa.co.cr.

The Canadian Chamber of Commerce plans to hold meetings every other month to advise countrymen; dates should be announced in the *Tico Times.*

For investments check with the National Securities Commission (Victor Chacón or Oscar Mora, 506–233–2840; fax, 506–233–0969) or the Costa Rican Stock Exchange (506–222–8011; fax, 506–255–0131). Just because a stock is registered doesn't mean it is approved or a good investment, but it does mean that certain minimum standards are met. Other sources of information are the Costa Rican Coalition for Development Initiatives (506–220–0036; fax, 506–220–4754) and the Center for Promotion of Exports and Investments (Oscar Ureña, 506–221–7166; fax, 506–223–5722).

Doing Business via the Internet

An exciting development in communications, the Internet, has brought Costa Rica closer to the rest of the world. This explosive technology is an important tool for all levels of government, business, and academia, bringing lower communication costs and access to worldwide markets. The Costa Rican government recognizes the value of the Internet by bringing it to the country at a $25-a-month hookup charge. By the beginning of 1998, the number of commercial Internet users was estimated at 5,000 and hundreds more were connecting to the country's academic node. From anywhere in the world, you can connect with the Costa Rican–American Chamber of Commerce, read the *Tico Times* or *La*

Nación, or contact one of the more than one hundred businesses—Costa Rican and American—that currently have home pages on the Web.

If you have a computer and have access to the Internet, you might be interested in contacting my World Wide Web site. I will try to keep up to date on new laws, changes in real estate trends, and events in the country that may be of interest to investors. The URL on my home page is: http://discoverypress.com/

For information on buying property, setting up a corporation, or opening bank accounts, see: http://discoverypress.com/crinet.html

The Costa Rican–American Chamber of Commerce has its World Wide Web page at: http://magi.com/crica/amcham.html

Hiring Help

During World War II the Costa Rican government passed a series of progressive labor laws that remain on the books and are strictly enforced. These laws seek to avoid conflicts between workers and employers by setting out concrete employment rules and a system of wages and benefits. In effect, these laws take the place of union contracts between worker and employer, guaranteeing individual workers benefits they probably couldn't negotiate on their own. If you look at the rules from the viewpoint of the worker, they are only fair and certainly not unreasonable from the standpoint of a considerate employer.

Therefore, hiring a maid, a gardener, or an employee in your business involves more than a simple understanding about wages and conditions as is the custom back home. Because we North Americans aren't used to such formal relations with employees, and because we are likely to be hiring workers, even if just domestic help around the house and garden, the rules need to be spelled out in some detail. Following the laws to the letter prevents serious and unexpected problems.

Briefly, here are some ground rules: The employer is responsible for making Social Security payments for an employee as well as deducting contributions from the employee's wages. All workers are entitled to paid vacations. After a thirty-day trial period of employment, an employee is entitled to severance pay as well as notice before being laid off. A Christmas bonus is neither a gift nor a nice gesture but instead an obligation mandated by law. The employer is required to give three months of maternity leave at half-pay. All these rules are detailed below and should be studied carefully before hiring any help. One other piece of advice is to purchase accident insurance for your employees, even if they are only part-time. The cost is minimal, and they'll appreciate the extra coverage. You'll also protect yourself, should something horrendous happen to your workers.

Good Labor Relations

Recently I spoke with a lady who was visiting Costa Rica with the intention of starting some kind of business. "When hiring workers," she said, "I understand that the secret is to just hire them for eighty-nine days and then lay them off. That way you aren't responsible for benefits such as severance pay, and vacations. Once they work ninety days, you are obligated; so you simply hire new workers every eighty-nine days!"

This upset me, and I told her so. Although her information was incorrect, that wasn't the point. The Costa Rican people work very hard for a fraction of the wages employees receive in the United States or Canada, and the law guarantees them certain benefits. It seems repugnant to me to try to chisel them out of their rightful wages. Attitudes like this can do nothing but tarnish the reputations of other North Americans. Those who have lived here for a long time generally realize the wisdom of paying their help more than the law requires. "I try to make it so my maid can't afford to quit," said one lady. "She is wonderful, and I couldn't stand to lose her."

Word quickly gets around the neighborhood if you are a good person to work for (or a chintzy one). If you earn a poor reputation as an employer, your job applicants will be those who can't hold a job elsewhere. Then you'll wonder why your employees are lazy, don't show up half the time, or have a tendency to steal!

After I gave the newcomer a piece of my mind about her attitude, she explained that she had heard that if you lay workers off after they've worked more than ninety days, you must pay eight years' salary as severance pay. She heard wrong again. The facts are these: For each year worked an employee is entitled to severance pay of one month's salary—up to a maximum of eight months' pay. That is eight *months'* salary, not eight *years!*

From a worker's point of view, this is only fair. Let's suppose that after eight years of faithful service, it becomes necessary to let your housekeeper go. For eight years the severance pay amounts to less than $1,500. Does that sound outrageous for eight years of loyalty and hard work? If it does, then maybe you deserve workers who are lazy, don't show up half the time, or have a tendency to steal.

Roger Connor, of Plinio's hotel and restaurant in Manuel Antonio, told of his experience hiring Costa Rican workers. "It's important to gain their trust," he said. "They don't know anything about you or how you are going to treat them. At first I had trouble attracting the best workers. But I treated people fairly and tried to keep them busy during slack seasons so I wouldn't have to lay them off. Before long I earned a good reputation. Now I have a waiting list of people who want to join my staff."

Conditions of Employment

1. Length of employment. The first thirty days of employment are a trial period, and either employer or worker can terminate without notice. However, vacation pay and *aguinaldo* (Christmas bonus, described later) must be paid in addition to wages if the employee has worked more than twenty days in that month's time period. Thereafter, for each month worked one day's vacation pay is due, up to two weeks of vacation for a full year's work. Many employees, either by custom or through union contracts, receive three weeks' vacation. My understanding is that an employee may work through his or her vacation, provided that the employee receives an additional day's pay for each day worked. (I'm not a labor lawyer, however, so you will want to confirm this point if it arises for you.)

2. Wages. Minimum wages depend on the job and skills required. As of January 1998 the lowest minimum wage was $6.87 a day or about $35.00 a week. This would be for a farmworker or unskilled laborer. Construction workers earned $7.89 a day, or $39.45 a week—although in practice most are paid more than this. Bartenders, cooks, and others employed in the restaurant industry have a minimum daily wage of $7.63. While these wages may seem low, bear in mind that they are more than twice those in other Central American countries.

An interesting facet of the wage structure is that a maid, gardener, or chauffeur who lives in your home is considered to be receiving an additional 50 percent of his or her salary as "payment-in-kind." In other words, if you pay a live-in maid the present minimum wage of $121 a month, the actual salary is considered to be $181.50, or 50 percent more when figuring benefits. This is important, because the gross salary (salary plus payment-in-kind) is used to figure the *aguinaldo*, Social Security payments, and severance pay. A catch here is that an hourly employee who regularly receives a lunch at your home is also considered to be receiving a 50 percent payment-in-kind, so your Christmas bonus, severance pay, and vacation pay have to be based on this. If you feel that you are already paying the hourly employee enough, you can save money by *not* providing lunches at home!

3. Working hours. The maximum for domestics is twelve hours a day, although almost nobody expects more than eight. The standard is usually an eight-hour day and a five-day week. For regular employees other than domestics, work on Saturday and Sunday is at double-time rates. For those working in businesses or industries that traditionally operate seven days a week, the rules are a bit different.

4. Social Security. An important obligation for employers, one taken quite seriously by the government, is Social Security. This critical institution pays for health care, sick leave, and disability pensions. You, as an employer, must pay 20 percent of a worker's gross salary and must deduct 9 percent of the worker's wages and pay both portions of the tax to the Caja Costarricanse del Seguro Social. Make sure your workers understand that you are withholding the taxes from their pay. Otherwise their share of taxes could come out of your pocket. Some people pay both sides of the Social Security payments as a bonus for a good employee.

Within eight days of hiring an employee, you must notify the local Social Security office. Doing so is vital, because should a worker become ill or injured on the job, you could be liable for medical bills and 50 percent of the employee's salary for the duration of the sickness for life, should the disability be permanent). When your employee is covered by Social Security, your liability is limited to the first four days salary; Social Security takes over from there. To prevent abuse of this law, you, as the employer, are entitled to demand a health certificate from the worker (*carnét de salud*) when the employee is hired and every six months thereafter. This is provided at no cost to the employee by the Seguro Social Hospitals.

Pregnancy is a different situation. Your employee's blessed event will obligate you to some additional employee benefits. Employees are entitled to a month's rest before the baby is born and three additional months afterward—half the salary to be paid by the employer and the other half by the government. By the way, firing a worker for being pregnant is frowned upon, and you will need to validate your reasons for firing other than pregnancy.

5. Christmas Bonus (aguinaldo). Sometime between December 1 and 20, employees are due an *aguinaldo*. For those who have worked a full year prior to December 1, the bonus is a month's pay. For those who have worked more than the thirty-day trial period but less than a full year, the payment is prorated over the time they have worked. Thus, a person who has worked three months gets three-twelfths of one month's pay. Remember that employees who live in or who regularly receive at least one meal a day also get a Christmas bonus based on the payment-in-kind, or an additional 50 percent.

6. Notice and severance pay. Workers employed more than ninety days and less than a year are entitled to two weeks' notice before being laid off. After a year one-month's notice is required. If you don't or can't give notice, you must pay the employee full wages for the notification period.

Unless an employee quits, you are obligated to pay severance pay dependent upon length of employment: up to three months, none; from four to six months, two weeks' pay; between seven months and one year, one month's pay. Then you must pay an additional month's pay for each year or fraction over six months worked. In no case can this payment be more than the equivalent of eight months' salary.

Again, remember that this is based on gross pay (including 50 percent payment-in-kind, if applicable). It doesn't matter if the worker immediately finds a new job; you still have to pay.

A worker can be fired at any time during the first thirty days for any reason, with no obligation other than the *aguinaldo* and wages due. Furthermore, a worker who fails to give notice (*preaviso*) before quitting forfeits the *aguinaldo*.

Employee Obligations

According to government regulations, workers can be held responsible for damages they have caused, whether intentionally or due to imprudence, or "inexcusable neglect." A domestic worker can be discharged without receiving severance if "notorious lack of respect or civil treatment is shown," which should be backed up by witnesses. You had better have good proof, though, because in doubtful cases the Ministry of Labor tends to side with the worker.

When an employee is laid off, it is usually a good practice to make things crystal-clear by having him or her sign a statement (in Spanish) to the effect that all benefits have been paid. Include the severance pay, vacation pay, Christmas bonus, and any salary due up to the time of separation. Have the employee sign the document in front of a witness. Should the employee be quitting voluntarily, be sure to note that in the document.

Minimum Wages

Because Costa Rica's economy is booming, little unemployment and much competition exist for good employees. Consequently, real wages are often higher than the minimum wages listed by the government. For a realistic figure you'll need to consult your neighbors to see what they pay domestic help, or talk to other businesspeople to find out what they consider appropriate salaries for employees. At present, construction workers are in exceptionally short supply, and they earn much more than minimum—in some parts of the country, double minimum wages. Many workers earn commissions and bonuses on top of minimum wages, so in reality these figures are simply basic starting points for wage rates. Those North Americans who successfully operate their own businesses unanimously agree that paying good salaries means happy employees who are loyal and hardworking. For an up-to-date list of minimum wages, either visit the local Surcusal Seguro Social (Social Security office) or ask your employee to get a copy of the list for you. The following wages were in effect in 1998 and will be adjusted upward twice each year (to account for inflation). Basically, salaries as measured in colones have risen considerably, but in dollars very little.

Minimum Wages for Various Professions*

	Daily	Monthly
Unskilled workers	7.45	193.64
Taxi driver	10.07	262.80
Schoolteacher	—	508.32
Industrial engineer	—	508.32
Truck driver	8.26	198.84
Salesperson	7.61	229.44
Commercial pilot	—	475.07
Clerk-typist	10.01	260.48
Librarian	10.01	260.48
Dental assistant	—	231.23
Doctor, lawyer, dentist, accountant	—	508.32
Domestic servant	—	193.64
Journalist	—	626.05
Gardener	7.45	193.64

* In dollars, from the Ministro de Trabajo y Seguridad Social, as of January 1998, for the province of Guanacaste.

BECOMING A RESIDENT

When I first visited Costa Rica, immigration rules were rather strict. A Canadian citizen was permitted a ninety-day visa; an American citizen, only a thirty-day one. Before you could get a visa or tourist card, you needed to show a return ticket and enough money to last the stay. A thirty-day extension could be applied for, but it was easier to take a bus to Nicaragua or Panama, stay overnight, and apply for another thirty-day visa. I heard stories of visitors who overstayed their limit being placed on the next plane or bus out of the country, with NO RETURN stamped on the passport.

Then it got to be easy. Anybody with a passport received a full ninety-day visa, just for the asking, just for stepping off the airplane! The way it works today is that after your three-month stay, you need to leave the country for seventy-two hours—perhaps a visit to a beach in Nicaragua or nearby San Andreas Island in the Caribbean—and then you have another three-month sojourn. There's been talk of cracking down on those who've repeatedly taken advantage of the laws allowing them to leave the country every ninety days, stay out for seventy-two hours, and then return—those so-called perpetual tourists. However, as of summer 1998 this law hasn't been enforced rigorously, except against undesirables. You can still do repeated seventy-two-hour turnarounds. If you are going to stay year-round in Costa Rica, you might as well consider applying for residency. Once your application is in, you don't have to worry about leaving while your residency is being processed.

Even though the rules have tightened somewhat, they are still exceedingly liberal compared with those in most other countries. In the United States, for example, if you stay one day over your visa, you will never be permitted to return! It's embarrassing to contrast the openness of Costa Rica's immigration with the closed-door policy the United States shows Costa Ricans when they want to visit Disneyland or Las Vegas. To receive a temporary visa, a Costa Rican must visit the embassy, hat in hand, and prove beyond the shadow of a doubt that he or she has every intention of returning to Costa Rica and has no possible motive for staying in the United States. It must be a humiliating experience to be denied a visa because your job doesn't pay a salary high enough to convince an embassy employee that you're sufficiently trustworthy to visit Hollywood and return.

For example, I have a Costa Rican friend who won two air tickets for Miami in a raffle and went to the U.S. Embassy for a visa for her and her daughter. Now, when you apply for a tourist visa, among other things you must show a bank book as proof of your affluence and intention of returning. My friend's husband is a successful contractor and always keeps large sums of money in his account to cover his payroll, materials, supplies, and everyday expenses. So my friend was confident that this healthy bankbook would impress the embassy clerk who was handing out visas. But when he noticed that the account held more than $10,000, he tossed the bankbook back at her, saying, "Drug money!" He motioned for her to step aside so he could process the next person in line.

Actually, for North Americans Costa Rican immigration rules are even more liberal than I've just outlined. At present if you stay longer than permitted, the penalty is a weak fine of 320 colones a month (about $1.28, at today's rates) for the overstay, plus a $35.00 exit permit. You don't even have to go to the Costa Rican Tourist Institute to apply for the permits; a travel agent can take care of the tax and fine. It used to be that you had an extra thirty days after paying your fines to leave the country. But today you only have five days—certainly not unreasonable. I've met folks in Costa Rica who came several years ago on a tourist card and are still here without renewing their cards. One couple bought land, built a motel and restaurant, and operated a successful business, never so much as asking government permission. However, if you plan on living here more or less permanently, you should check into becoming a legal resident at some point.

From time to time the government declares an amnesty; those who've been in the country illegally for a certain amount of time—say, two years or longer—can apply for permanent residence. And those who are operating successful businesses are also sometimes permitted to apply for residence papers. Those who qualify under amnesty rules are particularly lucky, because they don't have to certify that they won't work and therefore they aren't restricted from holding jobs.

Understand, I'm not recommending that anyone overstay his or her visa or try to ignore Costa Rican laws. I'm simply reporting how the laws are being enforced at this time and how they are being applied toward foreigners who have the wherewithal to support themselves, who may invest much-needed capital in the country, and who won't be taking jobs from citizens. Those who are indigent or who get into trouble may not find the laws applied quite so gently. Stricter enforcement could occur in the future, as is the case for Nicaraguans and Panamanians who have slipped across the border as economic refugees.

Residency in Costa Rica

When the thirty-day rules were in effect, just about the only way Americans could enjoy more than a short visit was to apply for a permanent visa. To encourage foreigners to apply for residency, the government used to offer some enticing benefits to retirees. Retirees received huge exemptions from import duties on household goods, appliances, and automobiles. With import taxes on automobiles in the 100 percent range, you could bring in a new car, drive it for five years, and sell it for as much as you paid for it!

For years these valuable duty-free imports were major reasons for wanting legal residency. As you might imagine, these tax-free imports became a point of contention between Costa Ricans and foreign residents, with the local people complaining that it was unfair for them to pay more taxes than foreigners. Because of complaints from citizens and pressure from the World Bank and the International Monetary Fund, the Costa Rican government canceled these benefits for newcomers in 1992. Those who entered the country before the laws were changed were granted "grandfather" status.

Today, with longer stays possible, the necessity of obtaining legal status is not as pressing as it once was. For someone like myself, who can be satisfied with living half the year in Costa Rica and the other half in my home country, there's no clear advantage to becoming a legal resident. One can own property or a business and can travel about the country with nothing more than a tourist visa. On the other hand, there are restrictions and obligations on *pensionados* and *rentistas*—not ponderous ones, but they involve a certain amount of red tape. For example, you must prove that a certain amount of monthly income has been deposited in a Costa Rican bank. On a regular basis, you must provide police certification of good conduct, and you must live in Costa Rica for at least four (nonconsecutive) months of the year in order to hold on to your *residente* status.

For those who will be staying pretty much full-time in Costa Rica or who plan on entering business and working as a manager in the business, the resident option is probably the best way to go. Once you have the papers and as long as you fulfill the residency obligations, you are completely legal and can enjoy all the rights of a Costa Rican, except voting. Becoming a legal resident of Costa Rica doesn't affect your U.S. or Canadian citizenship in any way, shape, or form.

Categories of Residents

Immigration and applications for residency are handled by the Coast Rican Tourist Institute. Basically, it recognizes four classes of legal immigrant residents: Residente Pensionado, Pensionado Rentista, Techos de Paz, and Rentista Inversionista. After two years of residency under one of these categories, you may apply for permanent residency, and then you have fewer restrictions—for example, you can work without permission from the government.

Residente Pensionado. This category pertains to retired people with pensions of $600 per month or more. Social Security is usually sufficient to qualify for this status. A total of $7,200 a year must be deposited to a colón account in a Costa Rican bank and proof of this shown to the government every year. No law says that you can't take the money out of the bank right away and change it to a dollar account or that you have to spend all of it; you have only to prove that you've brought that amount of dollars into the country. Some people deposit the full amount at the beginning of the year to get the requirement out of the way.

For a married couple the person without retirement income is considered a dependent, and no extra income is required (that is, only one pension per family.) Children under the age of eighteen (or under twenty-five, if in school) are also considered dependents. Social Security is sufficient proof of income. This is the option most retired people go for.

Pensionado Rentista. This category is for those who are not old enough to retire or who do not have a pension, yet who want residency in Costa Rica. Applicants must prove $1,000 a month income ($12,000 a year), deposited in colones to a Costa Rican bank under the same rules as regular *pensionados.* The income must come from an investment such as a certificate of deposit or annuity that will guarantee an income of at least $1,000 per month, and the income must be guaranteed for at least five years. The financial institution must agree to notify the Costa Rican government if the money is withdrawn. Younger people and those who want to go into business often choose this option.

For many people, qualifying for this status is difficult due to the large amount of money needed to be invested to return $12,000 a year income. (It would take almost $250,000 invested at 5 percent.) One way to immediately acquire residency status is to deposit $60,000 in an interest-bearing dollar account in a Costa Rican bank. The bank then pays you $1,000 a month, or $12,000 a year (plus interest), from this account for a period of five years. Deposits in state-owned banks are government guaranteed without limit, and most bank interest in Costa Rica is tax-free.

Techos de Paz. Some folks would rather use $60,000 to buy a house, start a business, or make some other investment in Costa Rica. For this reason there's another recent development: the *Techos de Paz* (Shelters of Peace) Investor Residency Program. This program requires a minimum investment of $50,000, of which $10,000 is channeled to purchase housing bonds issued by the Banco Hipotecario de la Vivienda (the country's local home mortgaging institution) and used to finance low-cost housing. The rest of the money can be invested in whatever endeavor you like, not just a government-approved investment. The good part of this scheme is that you obtain immediate residency, can work at whatever job you care to take, and aren't restricted to stay in the country for any period beyond one day per year. The downside is that the $10,000 you invest in the Banco Hipotecario is nonrepayable. In effect, you are buying immediate, nonrestricted residency for $10,000. The Association of Residents of Costa Rica (ARCR) can help with both of these alternative methods of obtaining residency.

Rentista Inversionista. People who are serious about going into business prefer this category. It requires a $50,000 investment with an approved tourism or export business, $100,000 in a reforestation project, or $200,000 in any other type of business. If the investment is in an existing company, you need to submit the firm's latest balance sheet and a statement indicating its profit-and-loss situation.

You understand, of course, that you needn't become a resident to own or operate a business in Costa Rica; you can do so on a tourist visa. Many foreigners invest far less and don't bother with residency. However, they are ostensibly restricted to management duties and not permitted to work at ordinary tasks in the business. This is not always enforced, especially if the person working isn't displacing a Costa Rican worker.

When it comes to investment in a business or a reforestation project, please exercise extreme caution. As mentioned elsewhere in this book, Costa Rica is teeming with sharks just waiting for fish like you and me. Reforestation investments are highly promoted as lucrative investments. You should be cautious of overly optimistic claims; teak promoters have poor track records in fulfilling their promises. Consult a *good* lawyer.

What Do You Get with Residency?

As a resident of any of these four statuses, you have the following benefits and requirements:

1. You have all the rights of citizenship except voting.
2. You can own and manage businesses, but you aren't permitted to earn a salary from a Costa Rican employer or company. You can pay yourself dividends, however. Once your residency is permanent, you can work.
3. You must reside in Costa Rica the equivalent of at least four months a year, not necessarily contiguous months. Once you have permanent residency, you are expected to visit Costa Rica once a year, for at least one day.
4. You must renew proof of stable and permanent income annually until you have full residency.

The Red Tape

The question of whether to become a legal resident or to visit using a tourist card varies with the individual. Some feel that four or five months is all they want to stay, so why bother with the red tape of papers? Others plan on making Costa Rica their primary home and therefore see benefits in becoming residents. It all depends upon your circumstances. One benefit is that residents receive a 50 percent discount on in-country airline flights as well as certain other breaks, such as reduced entrance fees to parks.

To make an application, you can either do it yourself or hire someone to go through the red tape for you. The process requires a deposit of about $100 and about $30 for fees, stamps, and forms. It could take from a few months to a year before approval comes through, depending on how thorough your preparation and who is assisting you. Meanwhile your residency status is legal and won't be challenged.

Ask around the North American community for recommendations of a good lawyer or an experienced *tramitador* (a person who knows which lines to stand in and knows whom to see to get your papers processed promptly). Some people I've talked to have had good experiences with *tramitadores* they located through classified ads in the *Tico Times*. But be careful; hiring someone who doesn't know what he or she is doing not only takes a lot more time but could be a waste of money if the person does not or cannot follow through. More information on immigration and residency can be found linked to my Internet Web page at http://discoverypress.com/costa.html

Pensionado Association

Yes, some individuals have done the paperwork on their own, but you'll hear sad tales of woe from those who have tried it without knowing what they were doing. Few people enjoy standing in line, facing the indifferent attitudes of some clerks or the hard-to-understand questions and information in Spanish. One way to avoid this is through the Association of Residents of Costa Rica. Among other things, this organization specializes in obtaining residencies, and it charges reasonable fees, considering the amount of time you save. A provisional membership is $100, entitling you to apply for residency through the group and to attend social events and meetings. Regular membership is $60 a year.

Further benefits are as follows: The association can make sure your annual papers are up to date, translate and notarize your documents, renew the required Costa Rican ID card, help you get a driver's license and other special permits, and assist you in buying an automobile. The organization will also do English-to-Spanish translations and authenticate a photocopy of your resident's *carnét* so that you can leave your original at home.

Members are eligible to receive doctor and hospital care in the National Health Services System, under terms of a special contract. This relieves you of the obligation of standing in line each month to make your payments. The organization pays it on a three-month basis and sends you proof of payment for the current month, which entitles you to medical service. The association also publishes a newsletter six times a year. For more information write ARCR, Apdo. 232–1007, Centro Colón, San José, or call (506) 233–8068 (fax: 506–222–7862). The ARCR has a comprehensive Web site at http://www.amerispan.com/arcr/

Paperwork

In any event, the process of getting your resident papers is best started by you, right in your home country. It's much easier to get these at home than by mail from Costa Rica. The four main items you need are listed below, and in all cases processing must be done through your local Costa Rican Consulate. They charge about $40 per document.

1. Income certification. This is the first and most important step; it's often complicated and difficult. Rules and proof of income differ between *residente pensionados* and *pensionado rentistas.* Social Security or other government pension money is the easiest to prove. Ask for a statement from the pension source confirming that you have at least $600 a month pension, and have that notarized at a Costa Rican Consulate in your country. If the pension is nongovernment, you'll need notarized letters that the pension is for life and two letters from bank officials testifying to the soundness of the company's pension plan.

The guarantee of income for *rentistas* is $1,000 in interest and dividends from banks or investment houses. The decision on whether your income qualifies is made on a case-by-case basis. You'll need statements establishing that this income is guaranteed for at least five years, and you'll need to renew these guarantees every succeeding five years. The Costa Rican Consulate can help you with this. Again, it's important to have the notary certification and authentication of the documents done by a consulate in your home country.

2. Birth certificate. This is needed for you and each of your dependents.

3. Marriage certificate. Proof of previous divorce is not necessary.

4. Police certificate of good conduct. Obtain this at your last place of residence, and make it the last document you receive. Have the police certify a set of fingerprints as well; ask the Costa Rican Consulate for the necessary forms. Make the good conduct verification your last step, because it's only valid for six months from time of certification. If you get this document first and then spend a lot of time with the other papers, it could expire before your application gets under way. I know of people who've had to return to the United States to get another conduct certification because theirs was more than six months old. You'll also need certificates of good conduct for dependents over eighteen.

Note too that if you are traveling with children, some special rules apply. Apparently, these rules apply more for Costa Rican citizens than for tourists, and even though they don't seem to be strictly enforced, it's important that you be aware of them. When a child traveling without both parents stays beyond thirty days, the child falls under the jurisdiction of the Patronato Nacional de la Infancia, a children's welfare organization. In order for a child to leave the country without both parents, it might be necessary to have a permit notarized by the Patronato offices on Nineteenth Street and Sixth Avenue in San José. I've never heard of any tourist being hassled for this, but if just one parent is traveling with a child for long periods, it might be a good idea to have a notarized statement of permission from the other parent.

And remember, just having your documents notarized is not enough. The documents must be taken to the Costa Rican Consulate in your country to verify the notary's validity and certification. The notary isn't merely verifying your signature, but also that the documents are valid and that they belong to you. Not following each step correctly is responsible for the many delays and obstacles you often hear people complain about.

Other details can be taken care of in Costa Rica at the time you make a formal request for residency. You'll need twenty photographs for adults (seven profile and thirteen front shots) and sixteen photos for minors (seven profile and only nine front shots). Several certified copies of your passport are required, and you'll fill out a questionnaire of personal information. You may be required to take a physical exam. As a retiree, you'll have to sign a statement that you won't work for pay while in Costa Rica (without authorization) and that you'll spend at least four months a year in Costa Rica. (As stated earlier, the months needn't be consecutive.)

From here on, it's filling out forms, standing in line, waiting for stamps and signatures, standing in more lines to put a deposit in the bank, going hither and yon, to stand in still more lines—most of which can be done by your surrogate, the *tramitador.*

COSTA RICAN SCHOOLS

Because of Costa Rica's high literacy rate and excellent educational system, a greater percentage of people speak English here than in any other Latin American country. As you try practicing your Spanish with folks you meet, you'll notice that some will insist on speaking English; they love the opportunity to practice with a native English-speaker. This is good news for most North Americans; they can get by while they're trying to learn Spanish. Fluency is greatly enhanced when you can throw in an English word when the Spanish word eludes you.

Unfortunately, many North Americans live in Costa Rica for years without learning any more words than are needed to deal with the gardener or the gas station attendant. But those who take the trouble to learn Spanish will find they are appreciated by Ticos. Knowing the language opens many doors that would otherwise be closed to you. Being able to communicate with anybody, instead of only those who speak English, permits interaction with a whole new set of potential friends and acquaintances.

An excellent way to study Spanish and to learn about Costa Rica at the same time is to enroll in one of San José's many Spanish-language schools. Language acquisition is big business here, with at least twenty schools in and around San José offering intensive Spanish classes. Throughout the country you'll find individuals who are happy to give private, one-on-one Spanish lessons. Some schools keep the class size to three or four students, thus ensuring that each person has maximum attention from the teacher.

Most schools offer programs that include living with a Costa Rican family. By interacting with a local household, you learn how to cook Costa Rican food, where and how to shop, and how to deal with servants—those ordinary, everyday routines of life that can be so different from circumstances back home.

Combining school with homestays with Costa Rican families speeds the learning process; you are in a round-the-clock Spanish environment. Weekend excursions with teachers and fellow students to various tourist locations combine learning and vacation into a very pleasant package.

In previous editions of *Choose Costa Rica,* I listed individual language schools, their facilities, and their tuition. But there are so many good schools today, so many opening from time to time, and all so heavily advertised that I felt it impossible to list them all. The *Tico Times,* other newspapers, and tourist publications are full of advertisements for language schools. Tuition is reasonable because of the competition. Ask around for recommendations and interview the schools personally to make your selection. Any school will gladly place you in a Spanish-speaking home with two meals a day and laundry. Homestay meals are often not served on Saturday and Sunday; arrangements may have to be made individually on this. Many schools include free airport transfers. Some will pick you up at your door every morning, take you to school, and return you in the afternoon.

Recently a friend came to me, obviously distraught. "Tell me about schools in Costa Rica," he demanded. "I'm seriously looking for an alternative to the school system here in the United States. I need to find some place where my kids have a chance to grow up safe and sane." It turned out that a young boy in his children's school had been robbing other children at knifepoint and hadn't been discovered until after he had attacked a dozen or so victims. Another boy had been caught passing out samples of drugs to his classmates. "I'm ready to go anywhere to give my kids a chance," my friend insisted.

While I wouldn't want to send anybody off to a foreign country just for the sake of the children, it's my understanding that Costa Rica does have a lot to offer in the way of private education. It's also my observation that drug use and juvenile delinquency are infinitely less of a problem than in the United States. Juvenile gangs and graffiti are rare to nonexistent in Costa Rica. Graffiti is mostly limited to announcements like "Alfredo loves Alejandra." One particular piece of graffiti near downtown San José has me puzzled—it says, "*Santa Claus y Batman son socios*" ("Santa Claus and Batman are partners"). Explain that, if you please.

In the San José area, you can choose from nineteen English or bilingual private schools. Some schools present classes half in Spanish, half in English; others are basically English-language schools. Some offer classes from prekindergarten through high school; others, just the first three to seven grades. The all-English schools are very popular with upper-class Costa Rican families, because they are seen as prep schools for U.S. universities. Just to give an idea of costs, here are a few examples of schools in the San José area. The stated tuitions are subject to change and are only approximate. Most schools charge an enrollment fee or a one-time family membership fee in addition to the tuition.

- The Country Day School is a prestigious institution in Escazú, with classes from prekindergarten through the twelfth grade. It is Costa Rican accredited and has 650 students, with classes all in English. The enrollment fee is $300 a year plus $3,510 tuition for grades one through twelve. Kindergarten and preparatory school is $1,810 for a half-day.
- The Costa Rica Academy is another popular school and charges similar tuition. It is accredited by Costa Rica and in the United States by the Southern Association of Colleges and Schools. It's located in Ciudád Carari, west of San José, on the way to the airport.
- The largest academy is Lincoln School, in Moravia, on the northeastern side of San José, with 1,600 students. Tuition for high school is $128 a month; for grades seven through nine, $93 a month; and for lower grades, slightly less.
- Escuela Britanica teaches half in English and half in Spanish, kindergarten through eleventh grade. It's located in Santa Catalina on San José's west side and has 800 students. Grades nine through eleven require $147 a month tuition, lower grades, less.
- A new entrant in the bilingual education scene is Conbi College, which offers preschool, primary school, and high school classes.

Universities and Foreign Students

Students from abroad are welcome at Costa Rica's many universities. There are four public universities and nine private institutions. The largest of the schools is the University of Costa Rica (UCR), with about 35,000 students; it's main campus is located in San Pedro, on San José's northeastern edge. Most Costa Rican students have scholarships and pay little or nothing. Tuition for resident students is about $70 a semester; foreign students are charged more, with rates available on request.

The Universidad Nacional has about 13,000 students and has several campuses scattered about the country, as does UCR.

Private universities offer programs ranging from MBAs to degrees in theology, tropical agriculture, and conservation. Most welcome foreign students, charging tuitions of about $100 per class and $5,600 for an MBA degree.

Importing vs. Buying a Car

Public transportation in Costa Rica is more than adequate, and many folks here do perfectly well without an automobile, yet having your own wheels is a luxury some refuse to forgo. Since car rentals cost between $800 and $1,200 a month, after a while the savings involved in owning your own car become quite evident. The equivalent of a year's rent would purchase a nifty used, four-wheel-drive vehicle.

An additional benefit of driving your own automobile is not having to worry about collision insurance deductibles. You see, rental cars come with $750 deductible insurance, or $1,500 if the car is stolen or totaled. Every scratch they can find or invent goes on your bill. I firmly believe that some rental companies must make more money charging customers for tiny scratches than they do on car rentals. If you own your own vehicle, you can take the scratches as learning experiences, and fender-benders are covered by your personal insurance on the car.

There are places in Costa Rica where it just isn't practical to visit without a vehicle. True, buses make it just about anywhere you can imagine—some places I'd hesitate to take a four-wheel-drive—but after you get there, then what do you do? If you have to walk 5 kilometers to the nearest store or restaurant, you are stuck. Without a car your choice of hotel accommodations is governed by where the bus stops. With your own transportation you can shop around for the best place to stay and then use your wheels to select the best restaurants or hunt out the nicest beaches (which are usually a long way from a bus stop).

Buy or Import?

Chapter 16 gives details on driving your vehicle down from the United States. That's an option for the hardy, one not to be undertaken lightly, but it can be fun too. If you don't choose to drive, you are left with the alternatives of buying a vehicle in Costa Rica or shipping one down from the North. There are advantages to both options. Which option is better depends on several conditions in effect at the time you need a vehicle.

One condition is import duties, which change from time to time according to the government's resolve to limit the number of additional cars coming in to clog the already overcrowded highways and byways. Another obvious factor is the current market for used cars in Costa Rica. After a wave of imports in 1994, the asking price for autos took a nose-dive. People who used to make a good living importing cars from Florida suddenly began looking for other businesses to sustain them.

There are two schools of thought about buying vehicles in Costa Rica. One side claims that cars here are maintained in excellent shape because they are so expensive; folks protect their investments with loving care. The other side claims that Costa Rican roads are so full of bumps, and Costa Rican drivers so wild, that cars age quickly beyond their years.

No matter which school of thought you favor, take my advice: Never buy a refurbished taxicab! Taxis in Costa Rica go through absolute hell, driving all day and all night, cruising over rough streets—stop and go, stop and go—the worst kind of wear. How can you tell if a car is a rebuilt taxi? Don't ask me; you need to find an expert mechanic you trust and have him inspect the vehicle. I have a friend in San José who restores taxicabs for a living. He has a great body-and-paint man and a skilled upholsterer on his staff. I've seen vehicles limp in looking hopeless and strut out looking brand-new. I've studied these cars in minute detail, but I swear, each looks showroom fresh!

Hidden Costs

At the end of this chapter, you'll find thumbnail sketches of used vehicles offered for sale in spring 1998 in the *Tico Times* classified section. This should give you a notion of relative values of cars compared with what they're worth in your hometown. Adjust these prices to reflect the extra taxes you'd have to pay on an imported car.

Custom duties on imported cars are sky-high. Theoretically, taxes start at 100 percent of the new-car price, plus sales tax, and drop down each year for about five years. Thus, a six-year-old car should be taxed at about 30 percent of its list price new. This isn't as simple as it sounds, however, because lately they've decided to add in other factors. The U.S. "blue-book value" of the vehicle is considered as well as the actual condition of the automobile. Also, the amount of duties keeps changing as the Congress and Ministry of Customs vacillate on how to apply customs duties. Decisions have changed several times just in the past year. Pickup trucks used to receive favorable treatment from tax collectors, but no more. My best advice is to ask friends for recommendations for a customs agency or a *tramitador* who knows how to get things done. They can tell you exactly what you'll need to pay in taxes.

Shipping Your Vehicle

Cars can be shipped from either Atlantic or Pacific ports to Costa Rica. But the cheapest and fastest way is from Florida or New Orleans. Most people say they paid $400 to $800, depending on the shipping line and availability of space. From California costs are higher: I paid $1,300 from San Francisco. From Florida the destination port is Limón; from California it's Puerto Caldera (near Puntarenas). The shipping line will prepare the documents stateside and take care of details once you deliver the car. Don't fail to ask for full-coverage insurance; it's not terribly expensive. If you don't mind paying more, you can ship your car by airplane from Miami. My understanding is that it costs about $1,300. The car will be waiting for you when you arrive!

In any event, you will need a Costa Rican customs agent to handle the paperwork once the car arrives—ask around for recommendations. If you want to pick up the vehicle at the port rather than wait for it to arrive in San José, you'll need someone to accompany you to the dockside customs warehouse to attend to the paperwork there. This need not be an expert, just a Tico who speaks good Spanish and who can ask which lines you must stand in. Some folks have used a bilingual cab driver.

My Personal Experience

I chose the option of shipping my automobile to Costa Rica rather than buying one there. I realized that it was going to cost a small fortune, but I figured it was worth the trouble; the car was in exceptional shape and had exceptionally low mileage—a 1967 Volkswagen Bug that had spent sixteen years of its life in a garage.

We began the process by calling shipping companies in nearby San Francisco, shopping for the lowest cost. Estimates ranged from a high of more than $2,000 to the bid we accepted of $1,300. The difference was that for $2,000 you got a container for your vehicle alone and for $1,300 other merchandise was included in the container.

The shipping line (Maruka) handled most of the paperwork for us and gave us a date to deliver the car to the docks. We said goodbye to our little car, apprehensive of its voyage, despite the full insurance that was covered in the fee. We were told that the car would arrive twenty days later at Puerto Caldera, near Puntarenas. So we flew to Costa Rica to be ready to greet our Bug when it arrived.

After our anxiously calling Puerto Caldera every day, the ship finally arrived ten days late. We found out that ten days one way or another is average for cargo ships on the West Coast. A Tico friend and I hurried to the port and began our first inquiry of a long day's asking questions, standing in line to fill out papers, getting signatures, and standing in line for more papers and signatures. We also had to drive into Puntarenas to purchase three months' worth of liability auto insurance. This cost only $10, one of the lesser amounts for the day.

The most expensive cost was $85, to open the container. Another Gringo was trying to get his car at the same time, and when he complained about the $85, he was told, "You don't have to pay it. If you'd rather, you can wait until the container arrives in San José and wait until the customs officials get around to opening it. That could take a month or more." He paid the $85.

I highly recommend taking a pleasant-mannered Tico with you if you go through this process. My friend handled things very smoothly. He joked with the clerks, he patted them on the back, and we bought soft drinks for a couple of helpful workers. Not once did anyone suggest a bribe, nor did we offer one. The result was that, by the end of the day, we had a bevy of friends in all corners of the huge customs office. (In fact, when the ordeal was over, one of the clerks came out and towed my car to get it started when I discovered the battery was dead.)

Finally, with fifteen minutes to go before the customs office was ready to close for the day, I was told, "All you need now are four copies of each of these documents, and you can pick up your car."

I eagerly rushed over to the copy machine and stood in line. Ten minutes to go, and my turn was next! But to my extreme dismay, the clerk shrugged and said, "Sorry, the machine is out of toner. You'll have to come back tomorrow."

This is where our friendships paid off. One of the clerks we had been joking with rushed over and took the documents from my hands. "Wait here," he commanded. "I'll copy these in my boss's office." He came running back with the copies with four minutes to spare.

When I finally got my VW started, I drove to the exit gate and handed the guard a stack of documents that weighed almost as much as the car. He looked through them carefully, handed me the originals, tossed the rest into what looked like a wastebasket, and motioned me on. Now I believe I know what they do with all those duplicate and triplicate forms.

At this point the car was in the country legally, but only for ninety days. In order to make the car a naturalized "Tico," it had to go through the main customs warehouse in San José. Supposedly, this is a simple matter requiring two days in the warehouse while papers are filled out, the car inspected, and license plates issued. Unfortunately, the government was in the middle of a campaign to cut the number of warehouse workers, so employees were protesting by working "by the book," as slowly as possible. In Costa Rica this can be *very* slow.

"When can I get my car?" I asked hopefully.

"Ordinarily, it would be two days, señor, but with this slowdown, it will take two weeks. God willing."

I called my customs agent to complain. He calmed me down by saying, "I'll talk to the chief. We can get your car in a week. God willing." I returned to the customs warehouse in two days to see if I couldn't hurry things along, and I arrived just in time to hear the chief explain to another Gringo that his car would be out of hock within a month. "God willing."

I was going to ask how long God had been involved with Costa Rica customs, when the chief saw me and smiled broadly. "A miracle! The papers came through on your car just an hour ago." To be fair about all this, I must point out that the strike was an untimely event, and apparently God only works part-time for customs. Most people tell me they've had to wait no more than the expected two days for their car.

I drove away in ecstasy, thinking that my problems were over, that my car was a genuine Tico now, entitled to all the freedoms of the road of any other Tico automobile. Not so. Next I had to go through a safety inspection in order to get papers that could then be presented to another office for clearance to get a piece of paper that was pasted on the windshield until my license plates were ready.

At this point I gave up and turned the papers over to a *tramitidora* who went to work. She knew exactly where to go, what line to stand in, and whose bread to butter. Three days later my VW Bug was a naturalized citizen of Costa Rica! After waiting a year and a half for my license plates, I found someone who earns a good living by making plates in his garage, so for an additional $25 I now have license plates. Eventually, they'll have the plates for me; I only hope the Volkswagen is still running by then.

"Pura vida!"

Used-Car Prices

The following is a typical offering of used cars listed in spring 1998 in the *Tico Times* classified pages. As is the case anywhere, you can tell little about the condition or value of individual cars, but you can derive some idea generally of prices and can then compare them with those in your community. Remember that having a Tico license plate is very important. If the vehicle isn't a naturalized Tico, you'll have to add lots of money on top of the purchase price, maybe 100 percent. You can generally tell from the asking price if Costa Rican plates are on the car, because if they are not, the price will be unusually low.

'92 CHEVY PICKUP, 4x4, extended cab, 5-speed. $15,000 plus taxes.

'89 MITZUBISHI MONTERO, 4-dr., 6-cyl, automatic, air-cond., loaded, taxes paid, very good condition. $13,500 firm.

'89 TOYOTA, 6-cyl., 4-dr., radio, air-cond., fuel injection, all extras. $14,000 plus taxes

'89 VOLKSWAGEN GOLF, diesel, 4-dr., 5-speed, air-cond., 50,500 miles, $8,400.

'87 TOYOTA PICKUP, double cabin (4-door) 4-wheel-drive, $10,000.

'94 FORD AEROSTAR, like new, $8,400, plus taxes

'91 FORD EXPLORER, Eddie Bauer, $18,300.

'89 FORD, TRS WAGON, New tires, $6,500.

'90 FORD AEROSTAR Van, 7 passenger seating, excellent condition, $4,800 plus taxes.

'92 CHEVY S-10, x-cab, 6-cyl., auto., air-cond., 64,000 miles, new tires. $12,000, taxes paid.

'91 PATHFINDER, 4X4, Loaded, Costa Rica plates. $21,500.

'87 SUZUKI SAMURAI, Tico plates, good condition. $5,000.

'88 MITZUBISHI RAIDER, auto, ex. cond., $9,200.

'91 SUBARU LEGACY, 92k miles, new tires. $12,000.

'90 MAZDA PICKUP, 33k miles, auto, Tico plates, $8,500.

'85 MERCEDES 230E, 60k miles, perfect cond. $10,000, taxes paid.

'94 DODGE CARAVAN, perfect, extras. $22,000.

'89 JEEP CHEROKEE, air-cond., exc. cond., taxes paid, $12,000.

'94 TOYOTA LANDCRUISER, auto, full extras. $28,000 plus tax.

'74 VOLKSWAGEN BEETLE, exc. cond., $3,950.

'88 NISSAN STANZA, 4-door, full size. $3,500.

'93 HONDA CIVIC, $6,800 plus taxes.

'88 HYUNDAI, air cond., sun top, automatic. $3,950.

'89 JEEP CHEROKEE, 6-cyl, automatic, $9,275 plus tax.

'87 VW RABBIT, 4-door, air-cond., $4,800 including taxes.

'90 DODGE RAM VAN, 62k miles, taxes not paid. $5,000.

'91 SUZUKI SIDEKICK, 4 dr., auto., 31K miles. $14,000.

'83 MERCEDES, taxes paid. $8,000.

GETTING TO COSTA RICA

The most practical way to get to Costa Rica is by airplane. Most people travel this way, even though fares are scandously overpriced. For the exceptionally hardy, automobiles and even intercity buses are alternatives. It's theoretically possible to travel as far as Guatemala City by train, but the logistics of doing this are best left to wild adventurers who are willing to put up with incredibly uncomfortable and unreliable facilities. Ship travel is all but impossible, too. Cruise ships touch at Costa Rican ports, but you cannot book a one-way passage.

Central America by Air

The quickest and easiest way to get to Costa Rica is by air, but this, of course, restricts the amount of belongings you can take—things you may need for a long-term stay. Those of us who live here full- or part-time always enter with as much luggage as we can get away with, packed with personal things we need from home and items difficult to find in Costa Rica. We send "wish lists" to our friends to carry in their luggage when they visit. They bring everything from paperbacks and videotapes to bedding and automobile parts.

A number of airlines schedule regular service to Costa Rica: American Airlines, United, and Continental, among others, and inexpensive Canadian charter flights fly from Vancouver and Montreal. Mexico's Mexicana Airlines flies to Costa Rica, as do several other Central American airlines, such as TACA, Aviateca, COPA, and SAM, which fly from Miami, New Orleans, Houston, San Francisco, and Los Angeles.

Costa Rica's own airline, LACSA, sometimes beats the price of U.S. airlines, but generally the carriers keep their prices similar. Some lower-priced fares involve stopping several places along the way. On our last trip from Los Angeles, we stopped in Acapulco, San Salvador, Managua, and, finally, San José.

Getting the best fare may involve shopping around a bit. My experience with travel agents is that not all of them can find the least expensive way to travel. You can often save money by calling the airlines yourself and shopping for their best rates and either making your own reservations or requesting that your travel agency make them for you (costs the same either way). I saved $160 on my last Costa Rica tickets this way. Check directory assistance for airlines' toll-free telephone listings. You'll spend time on the phone, listening to boring music while waiting for a clerk, but you could save dollars. Be sure to ask about special promotions, which can save you a bundle. Sometimes the clerk won't know until a month in advance just how much, if any, of a price discount will be available.

Costa Rica's Airport

Costa Rica's main international air terminal is the Juán Santamaría Airport, near San José. It's clean and modern, and customs inspection is relaxed. Airport taxis to downtown San José are plentiful and prices competitive. Ask a local person about the current fare to downtown; for a year or so, the price has been around $10 to $12, and drivers will accept dollars for the trip. By the way, airport taxis aren't permitted to go to more than one hotel or address per trip, so if you share a cab with someone, you'll have to go to the same destination. If you don't have much luggage, you can take a bus to downtown San José or nearby Alajuela for about 50 cents. There's a bus stop in front of the terminal, and buses run every few minutes.

Money changers hang around the taxi stand, so this might be a convenient time to change a $20 bill into colones if you can't wait until you get to your hotel. Be cautious, though; street money changers can be quick-change artists. Know exactly how much money you give them, and count your change carefully. Having a calculator in your hand makes them think you know what you are doing. I wouldn't change anything larger than a $20 bill, if at all. Money changers don't want traveler's checks, by the way.

A brand-new international airport near the Pacific Coast city of Liberia is finally open for business. It's been completed and ready to open for some time now, with the first official inauguration held twenty years ago and several other grand openings since, each time with service predicted to begin shortly. At each inauguration ceremony officials from the tourism ministry, travel agencies, and businesspeople all celebrate the impending opening of this new facility. The last inauguration was in

November 1995, with President Figures flying into the airport from Washington, D.C. This time they are finally open for business. LACSA flies several times a week from Miami, and charter flights from Toronto are landing now. With the Liberia airport in service, Guanacaste's Pacific Coast towns and resorts will boom. The economy here is already healthy, but this will boost it even higher. A friend flew in from Miami the other day, with about two and a half hours' flight time and two and a quarter hours' drive time from Liberia to a Pacific beach resort—a total travel time of less than the drive from San José to his destination!

Central America by Bus

For those with lots of time, patience, and a sense of adventure, it's entirely possible to travel from the Mexican border to Costa Rica by bus. As a matter of fact, my wife and I did exactly that during our first visit to Costa Rica, twenty-five years ago. We didn't do it to save money (although it's a cheap way to travel); we just enjoy bus travel in foreign countries and happened to have unlimited time for our vacation. With somebody else driving you get to see the countryside and enjoy visiting the cities in a much different way from flying over at 33,000 feet. Like driving to Costa Rica, however, a bus trip is something you need to think over carefully. It takes a stalwart traveler with a highly developed sense of adventure and lots of free time to enjoy this trip. A friend related the following itinerary for his trip in 1997.

My friends caught the Ticabus at its San José terminal and headed to Guatemala City; tickets cost $43.63. The bus stopped at the Nicaragua–Costa Rica border for customs inspection. The total border cost for both Costa Rica and Nicaragua was $8.75.

The first night they spent at the Ticabus terminal in Managua. They stayed in the small hotel at the bus station, humorously called the "Ticabus Hilton." Rooms cost $6.00 per person and were modest but clean. The bus left early the next morning and stopped at the Honduras border for passport stamping and $4.00 for exit and entry fees. (An alternate route stops over in Tegucigalpa, Honduras, instead of San Salvador.)

Going through Honduras was fairly fast. The bus's next stop was at the El Salvador border, and exit stamps again cost $4.00. Entering El Salvador requires a visa that you can get from an embassy by mail, at no charge. If you don't have a visa, you'll have to pay $10 for a tourist card.

The bus stopped for the night in the city of San Salvador. At the nearby San Carlos Hotel, the room rate was $10. The bus left at 6:00 A.M. At the Guatemala border another stop was made for exit from El Salvador and entry into Guatemala. The costs were $2.00. The bus arrived in Guatemala City at about noon.

In Guatemala they caught a bus that went to Tapachula, Mexico for a fare of $21. The line was Galgos Bus line, also comfortable and providing very good service. From Tapachula to Mexico City, they traveled on the Cristobal Colon line—the best bus on their entire trip. The ticket cost was $40.00. The bus had hostesses and plenty of room to stretch out and enjoy the sixteen-hour trip to Mexico City. From Mexico City the twenty-four-hour trip to Juárez (on the border across from El Paso) cost $80.

Even though Mexican first-class buses are OK, often having a bathroom, stereo music, and sometimes even an attendant serving coffee and soft drinks, this was the longest, most difficult leg of the trip. Because of the long distance between the United States and the Guatemala border, the numerous bus changes and long hours made for an uncomfortable trip. (An alternative might be to fly from Tapachula or to break up the trip, with stopovers for sightseeing in Mexico.)

The total cost per person for bus fare and fees came to $221.38. This is not a trip for the fussy or overly fastidious, because hotel accommodations are basic to rustic, and you'll feel constrained to stay near your hotel and/or the bus station. I don't advise exploring the cities of San Salvador or Managua during the overnight stops, except in the company of other bus passengers—preferably Central Americans who know what they are doing.

The fun part of this bus trip is making friends with other travelers. Those passengers who live here are eager for you to enjoy their country, and they'll point out landmarks and highlights as you cruise along. While having lunch at the rest stops, passengers make plans for having dinner together at the next overnight stop. By the time my wife and I reached San José, we had made many friends and received several invitations to visit Costa Rican families.

Driving to Costa Rica

One of the first questions folks ask when thinking about spending a long time in Costa Rica, is "Can I drive my car there?" The answer is, "Yes, but it ain't easy."

My first Pan-American Highway experience happened many years ago—before the turmoil in Central America—when my wife and I drove our 1967 Volkswagen Bug from San Jose, California, to San José, Costa Rica. We thoroughly enjoyed ourselves. It was an interesting experience, one we wouldn't have missed for anything.

For a while civil war in Guatemala, El Salvador, and Nicaragua brought tourist automobile travel through these countries to a virtual standstill. But even then some intrepid tourists insisted on driving, merely changing the route somewhat. They traveled the Pacific coastal route through Guatemala, avoided El Salvador by detouring through Honduras, and then carefully skirted trouble spots in Nicaragua. I tried to get through in 1983 but returned to Mexico after tiring of gun barrels being pointed at my forehead at every military stop. Today with the return of peace to the region, automobile travel is once again routine.

Our last adventure took place in December 1996–January 1997. The actual driving time from the Arizona border at Nogales was about eight or nine days. But not being in a hurry, we spread the trip over a full month. We stopped to visit friends in Lake Chapala, Oaxaca, and Guatemala City. We also detoured to spend some time at the marvelous Mayan ruins in Copán, Honduras.

It was an unusually pleasant drive. From the time we left Nogales until we reached our home in Costa Rica, we encountered not one military stop, saw no military presence, and were halted only a few times for routine checks of the car—presumably, to make sure it wasn't stolen. At none of the borders did they inspect our luggage or do anything other than glance in the back of our station wagon. Please realize that this good experience could have been due to an unusually lucky series of circumstances and may not be typical. Also, we were careful not to do anything stupid, like driving after dark. So don't think I'm suggesting that everybody will have a breeze. It's a long, hard trip, with some bad roads as well as good ones. Sometimes the accommodations are awful; sometimes they're delightful. If you can speak some Spanish, it would be helpful, but we encountered other travelers who spoke very little yet were making out OK.

With the exception of the amazing and efficient toll roads in Mexico, the Central American portion of the Pan-American Highway today consists of low-speed pavement—sometimes pockmarked, occasionally smooth with dual lanes—with infrequent stretches of gravel. Nicaragua has the worst pavement of all, with more potholes than blacktop left on the highway.

Mexico, however, offers new four-lane divided pavement, with 75-mile-an-hour speed limits. The tolls are expensive, so much so that often we were the only vehicle in sight. But the price was worth it. We set our cruise control and zipped along as fast as we cared to. The downside is that you see little of Mexico, other than fields and backcountry.

Every day was a new adventure, a new challenge, full of photo opportunities and stimulating encounters with other travelers and local people. The most annoying part of the journey was the delay and inconvenience while crossing borders. Sour-faced officials examine your papers with suspicious eyes, then hand out a sheaf of forms to be filled out in triplicate. Then they rubber-stamp everything in sight. (Oh, how they love rubber stamps!) You go from one official to another for what seems an eternity. Finally, you are allowed to leave the country, only to drive 50 feet into the next country and start the process all over again at the next customs office.

I recall that during the Somoza regime, the Nicaraguan border was absolutely the worst. The personnel were arrogant, corrupt, and sadistic as they bullied travelers. One particularly nasty customs inspector searched through my book bag, looking for subversive literature. Since he read little English, he demanded to know what each book was about. His face turned livid when he found a sociology textbook among my belongings, with the word *sociology* prominently displayed on the cover.

"Socialism!" he shouted in a grim voice. "This book is about socialism!" I tried to calm him down by explaining that sociology is something like psychology. But when he opened the book to the first chapter, which was titled "Revolutions in Social Theory," things hit that proverbial fan. The book stayed behind at the border, though I was permitted to enter the country, albeit with some suspicion. Another man had a khaki-colored field jacket expropriated because it was "military equipment."

Ironically, when the Sandinistas first took over in Nicaragua, travelers reported that the only easy border crossings were in and out of that country. Apparently, Sandinista customs inspectors were somewhat laid-back, casually waving Costa Rica–bound tourists through, saying, "Have a good trip!" (Maybe General Somoza took the rubber stamps with him when he left. He took everything else.) But Nicaraguan border guards soon learned the ways of bureaucracy; traffic today flows with the same consistency of cold molasses as the other crossings.

Today the worst border to cross is into Guatemala. There I made the mistake of waiting with the car, as the *tramitador* suggested, and giving him the money to pay the fees. Wrong! I soon figured out that I needed to go with him and pay the fees myself. After that no problem. No *mordidas* (bribes) of any consequence at any border crossing—even when I offered a bribe in order to get through quickly. The easiest border stop was Costa Rica, where it took less than a half-hour and where border officials actually smiled and joked with us. (I hope this story doesn't get anybody fired!)

Even if you speak good Spanish, I highly recommend that you hire a *tramitador* to help you through customs, especially at the busy crossings. (Costa Rica is an exception.) There are always kids hanging around who, for a fee, will run your passport and car papers around to the places where they will be rubber-stamped, have stamps affixed, and signatures scrawled upon them. It's difficult to tell which are legitimate charges and which are *chorizos* or *mordidas*. Which of the kids to hire? I always pick one who is a little older and looks aggressive. He will not be shy about elbowing others aside to get to the front of the line so that the officials can look at your papers first. If you speak good Spanish, you might do OK without a *tramitador,* but you might also spend a lot of time in line. If you don't speak Spanish, don't try it alone. One recent traveler reported that the border officials wouldn't deal with him until he hired a *tramitador.* The cost is usually $10, but you can bargain. Get the price fixed before you start.

We didn't drive through El Salvador, though not because we wanted to avoid it; our visit to Copán, Honduras, happened to route us around El Salvador. The border crossing from Guatemala to Honduras at that point is exceptionally easy and painless.

The secret to stress-free traveling in Central America is to "hang loose" at the customs stops; don't get upset—try to laugh at the process. Handing out a few $5.00 bills from time to time helps smooth over the problems.

This is perhaps the most difficult part for Americans: paying money for people to do the jobs they're already paid to do. To us this is wrong, it's blackmail, it's theft, and it's humiliating. If you insist on looking at it this way, the border-crossings are going to be bad experiences. You need to look at the process from the viewpoint of the border-crossing employees. To them accepting money in order to help you is a perfectly natural and legal process. The government pays customs and immigration workers minimal wages with the full knowledge that they'll make it up in tips from the travelers. So the tougher they make it, the more travelers will be willing to pay. Like it or not, that's the way it works, and nothing you do will change the system. The customs workers see absolutely nothing wrong with the process and can become highly frustrated when confronting a stubborn, belligerent tourist who tries to single-handedly change the system by refusing to pay for quicker service.

Driving the Pan-American Highway isn't easy, mind you, but then it never was a journey to be taken lightly. We're talking mile after mile of marginal highways, poor hotel accommodations, frustration, and red tape at every border crossing. Yet I've interviewed a dozen travelers who made the trip between 1993 and 1998; all shrugged off these inconveniences. They felt the important thing was that they got their vehicles and belongings through intact, and they had fun doing it. Most described their trip as an adventure they wouldn't have missed for anything. Most also said they wouldn't care to repeat it!

On the Road

From the U.S. border at Brownsville to Costa Rica, the drive is 2,300 miles. From Mexicali the distance is 3,700 miles. Your car should be in good condition, with new steel-belted tires, a spare, an emergency toolkit, road flares, and flashlights with extra batteries.

Unleaded fuel is usually available nowadays, especially in larger towns. Always get out of the car and supervise the gas station attendant while he services the car. Attendants have been known to accidentally put diesel fuel or leaded gas into a car requiring no-lead fuel. And make sure they turn the pump back to zero before they start, so you don't end up paying for gas you don't get. (I've never had this happen in Costa Rica.) You might carry a hand calculator so as to make sure you are paying the correct amount and getting the right change, too. Even if you don't know how to figure this out, the attendant will think you do, and he won't cheat. Another trick that station attendants in Mexico will try to pull on you (cabdrivers do the same): When you hand them a 100-peso bill, they quickly switch it for a 50-peso note, to make you think you made a mistake. The cure for this is to carefully hand them the note and say, *"Billete de cien pesos"* ("Hundred-peso bill").

You must have a valid passport. Visas aren't required in advance. However, if possible, it's a good idea to visit the consulates before you leave and have your passport stamped; you'll save time and extra tip money at the borders. A visa is required by El Salvador and can be obtained free by mail. Without a visa you're required to purchase a tourist card for about $10. Mexican, Guatemalan, Costa Rican, and Honduran Consulates and tourist offices have free road maps for the asking. If you can't get to the consulate or tourist office, request maps by mail.

Don't forget car insurance. Your U.S. or Canadian policy isn't recognized south of the border, but carry it with you anyway, as proof that you have a valid policy, just in case. You need to buy a special insurance policy for Central America. Before you cross into Mexico, contact Chris Yelland of Sanborn's Insurance at (210) 686–0711 (fax: 210–686–0732) or write to P.O. Box 310, McAllen, TX 78505–0310. This company can write Central American policies by telephone and will take credit cards. For a fifteen-day policy (which should be more than ample time to drive all the way to Costa Rica), the cost of full coverage on a vehicle valued at $12,000 would be $201. For fifteen days of liability-only coverage, the cost would be $49. Ask for a *Travelog* with detailed directions, maps, and hotel/restaurant listings for Central America (free with insurance).

Through Mexico

The first country to cross is Mexico. You will be issued a tourist card at the border without hassle, or you can obtain one in advance at your nearest consulate by showing your passport. If your vehicle is financed, you'll need a notarized statement from the bank or finance company with permission to take the vehicle out of the country. Best have it notarized at a Mexican Consulate, if possible. Mexico has been closely checking cars coming into the country to combat a rash of stolen automobiles. Rules are in a state of flux at the moment; you may have to post a small bond to ensure that you don't sell the car in Mexico. (You must use a credit card for this bond; no cash changes hands.) When you exit the country, they'll refund this bond. The Mexican crossing is easy; you don't need a *tramitador*, and you don't have to tip anyone.

If you are carrying household goods or items you will need in Costa Rica, make sure you let customs officials know you are "in transit," and they'll so note on your car papers. Don't let them try to place you in an escorted caravan to the Guatemalan border. You'll have to stay where the police escort says, you'll have to eat where you're told, and the whole thing is rushed and expensive. That's not how you want to travel through Mexico.

Unless you want to visit places like Puerto Vallarta, Acapulco, and other spots on the West Coast, the best route is one of Mexico's new high-speed toll roads. Driving through Mexico on the nontoll highways will add a day or so to your travel time, but you'll see more of Mexico. Figure four or five days to make the trip to the Guatemalan border. You ought to take at least an extra week and enjoy a minivacation, visiting Mexico's recreational and historical sites.

Keep your eye out for speed limit signs and slow down to the posted limit; that way you won't be bothered by cops. They won't stop you unless you're breaking some traffic law. This is pretty much true anywhere in Central America. *Important:* Never drive at night—in Mexico or *anywhere* in Central America. Mexican and Central American highways are generally in fair condition, but they are built as cheaply as possible. The road definitely ends at the edge of the pavement; when there are shoulders, it's purely by chance. In the dark you have no idea what lies alongside the pavement—a stretch of gravel, mud, or a 10-foot dropoff. You might even find a bull sleeping on the pavement. Repeat after me: Don't drive at night! (I have to admit that I violate this rule when using Mexico's toll roads; they are wide and safe, and they have almost no traffic, even in daylight.)

Guatemala

The recommended place to cross into Guatemala is near Tapachula, Mexico—at the Guatemalan town of Tecún Umanán. Good overnight accommodations can be found in Tapachula, so you'll be ready for the Guatemala run in the morning. Start early, since the border closes for siesta from 1:00 to 3:00 P.M.—sometimes earlier if personnel feel in need of a nap.

A typical border crossing was described by Karen Bonis, remembering when she and her husband, Scott, drove their motor home into Guatemala: "From the center of town, we followed a steady stream of taxis filled with customers, heavy trucks, and cars down a potholed highway to the border a few miles south. We crossed a little river and immediately were deluged with young men wanting to change money and lead us through the maze of admittance procedures for Guatemala. We exchanged a few dollars and hired a young man, who led Scott into a small building to pay the bridge tax. They were gone an interminable amount of time, during which I tried unsuccessfully to stop several young men from washing our windows with oily rags, while telling young beggars they weren't going to get any dollars from me. Finally, Scott and the young man returned.

We moved another hundred yards to a modern building where a large sign said: FUMIGACIÓN. They were in this building even longer. Occasionally they would reappear at the rig, clutching even more papers. Eventually someone sprayed the tires and underside of the motor home, and then we were confronted by customs inspectors. They weren't happy about the two TVs, didn't like the cellular phone, and were adamant about not allowing the CB radio into the country. It turns out that CBs were illegal in Guatemala because they don't want rebels in the hills to get them.

It was now well into siesta time, but fortunately, no one seemed to take a break. The inspectors grabbed lunch from various food stands lining the road and continued working. Scott disappeared into the building and was gone for well over an hour, negotiating with customs. He returned smiling; we would be allowed to move in just a few minutes. But the inspector returned to look at the car we were towing. Another problem. Only one vehicle per driver allowed. After showing the inspector my license, offering to drive the car across myself, and solving a few more problems, we finally received permission to enter Guatemala. It was a short haggle over the price with our young man who helped us, settling on $5.00 U.S., which Scott felt was worth the price. The total time spent crossing: four and a half hours.

Alternate Routes to Costa Rica

From Guatemala City to Costa Rica, you have two choices: through Honduras or through El Salvador (which includes a few miles through Honduras). The shortest, quickest route is through El Salvador, yet until the cessation of the civil war here, most drivers preferred the slow, safe route through Honduras. Nowadays travelers describe driving the El Salvador leg as uneventful. By the way, Honduras must have found a lot of extra money somewhere, because the highways are new, wide, and marked with a line in the center, and they actually have shoulders!

The drive from Guatemala City to the city of San Salvador takes about six hours, depending upon the delay at customs at the border. At present the roads through El Salvador are almost as bad as those in Nicaragua, but at last report officials are repairing them rapidly. From El Salvador another early start will get you across a short stretch of Honduras and into Nicaragua. Try to have a full gas tank before entering Nicaragua; gasoline shortages here aren't unknown. It's only a 190-mile trip from the Honduras border to the Costa Rican border. For an overnight stay in Nicaragua, you might consider the beautiful colonial city of Granada.

My favorite way to drive from Guatemala City to Costa Rica is through Honduras, bypassing El Salvador entirely, but it is slower. This route takes you through the town of Copán, where you *must* pause to visit the most fantastic Mayan ruins of all. Although this involves driving several kilometers of dirt road to the Honduras border crossing, there's usually only one customs guy there, so it's a snap to cross. The road was in good shape—for a dirt road—the last time I traveled it, in 1997. It may not be passable in the wet season, however. Make sure the border official knows you're going as far as San Pedro Sula and not just visiting the ruins for the day; otherwise, the official will give you temporary papers and no transit visa. Spend a day or two exploring the ruins, then go on toward San Pedro Sula, turning south to the Honduras capital city of Tegucigalpa. From there you cross into Nicaragua on Highway 3 and head for Chinandega and León.

The other route through Honduras is through Agua Caliente and on to Nueva Ocotepeque, where you'll find satisfactory accommodations if you need them. Understand that all of these border conditions change from day to day; on some days you'll slip through like water through a sieve, whereas on other days it'll be more like molasses. Controlling your temper and putting on a pleasant face will help. But also remember the saying "You can get a lot more with a smile and a $5.00 bill than you can get with just a smile."

By the time you've reached the Nicaraguan border, you'll probably be eager to get to Costa Rica. Driving the length of Nicaragua can be done in a few hours, so there's no real need to stop over there, although you might be tempted to linger in one of the colonial cities or stay at a beach hotel not far from the Costa Rican border. Nicaragua has been plagued with strikes and protests, which can sometimes slow traffic down, so try to make the earliest border crossing possible.

Once in Costa Rica, be sure to make copies of your papers and your passport—and keep them in a separate place, just in case you lose the originals. Be sure to copy the passport page with the entry stamp for the date you entered the country.

Remember that the car permit and your insurance are good for ninety days. Unless you choose to apply for a Tico title and license plates, you'll have to take the vehicle out of the country for seventy-two hours and reapply for admission for another ninety days. There has been talk of clamping down on reentering with a car after the ninety-day period. The plan is to allow a short time to place the car into customs for processing or remove the vehicle from the country permanently. Be sure to check with customs when crossing the border and find out the current policy.

Remember: Don't drive at night!

Touring Costa Rica

Every nook and cranny of Costa Rica has something special to offer, something to dazzle the eyes or gratify the other senses. Newcomers are never satisfied until they have seen it all; longtime residents tend to repeat their travels, to see everything again and again. Fortunately, getting around the country is easy. Within a few hours you can visit just about any section of Costa Rica you choose, and you usually have several modes of transportation available to you.

Air Transportation

The quickest way to travel about the country is by SANSA or Travelair, the airlines serving San José, Quepos, Golfito, Palmar Sur, Barra del Colorado, Nosara, Tamarindo, and Sámara. Ticket prices used to be inexpensive but in the past few years have become costly, and the service often leaves much to be desired. There's a 50 percent discount for residents with *cédulas,* but it's still five to ten times as expensive as bus travel. Travelair tickets cost much more than SANSA tickets, but the bottom line is that Travelair will usually take you to your destination even if you are the only passenger, whereas SANSA has been known to cancel flights if there aren't enough passengers. The air equipment in Costa Rica used to be old reliable, bulky DC-3s, but most planes today are those small foreign jobs that force you to hunch over as you make your way to your seat. Flights to anywhere in the country take far less than an hour, including stopovers.

Because flights are popular, and the planes tiny, they are frequently booked solid. Make reservations in advance, and be sure to reconfirm your reservations even though you have tickets. Someone else could have your boarding pass if you show up at the airport without reconfirming twenty-four hours in advance and arriving early.

Another air option is an "air taxi," which will take you just about anywhere a bush pilot can set down a small plane. The cost is about $300 an hour for a twin-engine plane and five passengers. For a single-engine job, the price drops to $220 an hour for the same five passengers. A $440-an-hour, seven-passenger plane can also be rented. When you consider that the country is small and flying times short, an air taxi isn't as expensive as it might appear. You'll find several companies in the phone book classified pages under the listing "Taxis Aereos."

What if you are a pilot and would like to rent a plane and fly yourself? Not so easy. Even if you are a certified pilot with a license from another country, you can't rent a Costa Rican plane until you've earned a Costa Rican license. You need to show proof of your total air hours logged in your country as well as log a certain amount of time in Costa Rica. If you own a plane, it can be kept in the country for up to six months without having to pay taxes, after which time it must be removed. However, there seems to be a question as to how many six-month permits an individual can obtain. You'll need to check this out with customs.

Trains and Buses

Guidebooks often rave about the scenic wonders of the country's train system. Especially tempting are descriptions of a spectacular railroad trip from San José to the Caribbean city of Limón. However, when you read about train trips in Costa Rica, you know the book is a bit out of date. Since the earthquake of 1991, passenger trains no longer journey to Limón or anywhere else, for that matter. Sad, but true. Some roadbeds and a few ancient bridges slipped downhill—common occurrences in Costa Rica earthquakes—but this time the government decided not to rebuild. The lines were losing money anyway.

It's possible that at some time in the future, service to the Pacific port of Puntarenas could be resumed, and a short commuter run to Cartago started in late 1993. There's also a short excursion to Turrialba. However, there could be a bright side to this story: The government is considering turning over the rail system to the ex-employees of the railroad. Experts are giving them training in management and business practices, in the hope that an employee cooperative might revitalize the train system.

Buses are another story. In addition to excellent city bus service, eight intercity bus companies provide frequent service to just about any place you'd care to go. Unlike the situation in the United States, where monopolistic intercity bus fares border on extortion, tickets between Costa Rican cities are downright cheap. A four-hour ride from San José to Limón, for example, costs little more than $4.00.

San José has no central bus station; bus lines depart from separate terminals, ranging from a new, full-service terminal to a curbside parking place in front of a small ticket office. For example, to go to Quepos and Manuel Antonio, you take the buses that leave from the "Coca Cola" terminal. (The Coca Cola terminal gains its name in a typical Tico fashion: There *used* to be a Coca-Cola bottling plant in the neighborhood.) Buses for Limón, Cahuita, Puerto Viejo, and other Caribbean destinations have their own, modern terminal on Calle Central, 6 blocks north of the Metropolitan Cathedral. Often reservations need to be made a day or two in advance. The better tourist guidebooks list the bus terminals, destinations, and travel times.

A number of smaller bus companies (often with only one or two buses in the fleet) carry passengers to all imaginable sectors of the country. Few towns or villages in the republic lack bus transportation of some sort. Often while I was negotiating impossible backcountry roads, bouncing through deep potholes, skirting boulders in the trail, and wondering whether my rental car could ever make it back in one piece, a passenger-laden bus would appear from out of nowhere, sound its horn impatiently to move me aside, and then rumble past as it hurried on its way.

These country buses tend to be of an older, rattletrap variety, usually secondhand school buses bought at surplus in the United States. Sometimes the owner-drivers don't bother to change the paint, and the bus finishes its transportation career bouncing along dusty trails in Costa Rica with the legend *Maplewood Unified School District* still painted on its side. Sometimes you'll be pleasantly surprised by a small air-conditioned vehicle of late manufacture, which makes the backcountry surprisingly luxurious. (Of course, there's nothing to guarantee the driver will actually turn on the air conditioning, which draws power from the engine.)

Since the distance between San José and any destination in the country is not very far, bus trips don't take too long. From San José to Quepos, a popular tourist destination, bus travel time is less than four hours. By air it is only twenty minutes or so, but by the time you get out to the airport an hour early, wait for the plane to leave (always a half-hour to an hour late), and then wait for a bus to take you from the airstrip to town, you haven't saved all that much time. Plus you've missed a lot of interesting scenery. However, be aware that different bus lines have varying schedules. For example, travel from San José to Puntarenas takes two hours on one bus line but four hours on another line.

I knew Costa Rica had a lot of competing bus companies, but for a while I was astounded at how many different bus lines there appeared to be in and around San José. It seemed that the bus lines' names were very creative. Then I discovered that the name painted on a bus's side or on the back wasn't the name of a bus company at all but, rather, an imaginative name given to the bus by its driver as an expression of his individuality.

The *Tico Times* ran a feature article on these names, at which point I realized that the Papa Lolo bus that passed by my house every morning as I waited for my ride was not owned by the "Papa Lolo Bus Lines" but driven by a driver with the nickname "Papa Lolo." Some buses are named after family members; other names are exercises in imagination. Additional names the article noted were Desert Storm, Krakatoa, El Principe Azul (the Blue Prince), Mil Amores (Thousand Loves), the Dancing Queen, and El Guerrero del Camino (the Road Warrior).

Taxicabs Galore

Costa Rica enjoys an excellent system of taxis, with about 7,000 drivers zipping along the streets of San José and suburbs—double what there were in 1990. Almost all cabs are late-model Japanese imports, usually Toyota or Nissan. Occasionally you'll see a Volkswagen or a Volvo. By law taxicabs are painted bright red. You can't miss them.

Not only is taxi equipment usually in good shape, but fares are inexpensive. At present it costs 165 colones (a little more than 50 cents) to go the first kilometer and 55 colones for every kilometer after that—an absolute bargain! In San José, you can go practically anywhere in the city from downtown for about $3.00. Between 10:00 P.M. and 5:00 A.M., drivers are permitted to charge an additional 20 percent. Drivers don't expect tips, but I always round the bill up to the next 50 colones, and they drive away happy.

All San José taxis are supposed to have meters, and most do. Ticos refer to a taxi meter as a *maría*. Why *maría*? Some years ago Costa Rica's president decided that taxis should have meters, rather than have drivers and clients haggle over the price of each ride. So he ordered a batch of taximeters from a company in Argentina for a trial run. The company's name contained the word *María*-something-or-other. But with typical Costa Rican bureaucracy, customs officials in Limón refused to allow the contraptions into the country until all the proper papers and forms were filled in. By the time all the tax stamps had been fastened, quadruplicate copies made, and signatures affixed, the meters—which were mechanical (as opposed to the electronic ones they use today) had rusted in Limón's damp climate and had to be trashed. Hence the word *maría* for taximeter.

Avoid cabs parked in front of hotels or discos. The drivers will tell you that they don't have to use meters, because they pay more insurance, or some other baloney. The truth is, they charge from two to four times the normal rate. When in doubt, ask, *"Hay una maría?"* If the driver claims the meter isn't working, don't enter the cab until you've established a price (provided, of course, that you know about what the price should be). If the driver quotes a ridiculous price or if you haven't any idea of the correct fare, take another cab with a meter. At certain times of the day, drivers are reluctant to turn on the meters, because they know they can get all the customers they want and don't want the cab's owner to know exactly how much was taken in.

Occasionally you'll find cabs without meters, known as *piratas,* or "pirates," private autos illegally operating as taxis. Usually the fares quoted by these nonmetered cabs are about what you'd pay in a legally operated vehicle. The problem with *piratas* is that some of them aren't in safe operating condition. And unless you know what the fare should be and you know enough Spanish to negotiate, I'd recommend waiting for a cab with a meter. All in all, I think Costa Rican taxi drivers are fairly honest. Rarely have I been overcharged, and that was during times of heavy rains or rush hours—when the extra cost was worth it to me.

Although the law says taxicabs must use meters, bear in mind that any trip over 12 kilometers is exempt. A trip from the airport to San José, for example, should cost between $10 and $15, depending on what part of the city you are going to.

Why are most cabs new? Because one side benefit of owning a taxi is that it can be purchased free of import duties, as long as it is used for three years before selling it as a used car. This means that after three years of generating income, the vehicle can be sold for as much as or more than it cost in the first place.

Up to this point we've been discussing taxicabs around the Meseta Central. Taxis aren't only for city folk; you'll find them all over the country, sometimes in places so isolated that they would seem implausible. Not all villages will have a taxi, but most have access to one from a neighboring village. Away from the city's paved roads, four-wheel-drive taxis are the norm, and in the rainy season, a must. Four-wheel-drive trucks commonly serve as taxis, with the truck bed used to transport furniture, appliances, or more passengers. In rural areas, where buses and taxis are rare or nonexistent, private autos and trucks often provide free rides to local people walking from one village to another. I do the same and find that locals appreciate rides—the hospitality enhances their opinion of foreigners.

Taxi Chauffeurs

Driving a car around San José or through the narrow roads in the immediate countryside isn't exactly a relaxing pastime. I sometimes find myself so involved with traffic and confusion that I see very little. My passengers see even less, since they spend a great deal of their time praying, cursing, or shouting at me: "Watch where you're going, you dummy!" For that reason I rarely drive in downtown San José, even though I own my own car. It takes me ten minutes of sweating and cursing to get from our condo to the center of town, whereas it takes only five minutes of sweating and cursing in the average taxi.

There is a better way to explore the Meseta Central: Rent a cab! Taxi drivers much prefer the idea of one fare for the entire day, instead of wandering all over town waiting for someone to flag them down. One fare isn't nearly as hard on the cab, since passengers always want to stop, get out, and spend time looking around, giving the taxi and driver a deserved rest.

Not only is it convenient to let someone else drive (someone who knows what he's doing), but renting a cab costs about the same as renting a car for the day. A competent, English-speaking cabdriver will chauffeur you around the Meseta Central for five or six hours for about $50. A rental car for one day—with insurance and gasoline—would cost almost $60 and $1 million worth of tension. In other words, after you buy the driver's lunch and give a small tip, you're about even. Most any cabdriver will rent hourly for about $10 per hour, but you're better off making prior arrangements with an English-speaking driver.

Taxicab rental will also save you hours of time and frustration when checking out neighborhoods for real estate. The driver can whisk you to a half-dozen suburbs in less time than you can stumble onto one. This is also a great idea for sightseeing trips around the Meseta Central. Instead of four people paying $25 to $45 per person for a five-hour commercial tour, a cabdriver can show you the same sights, with individual attention, for much less. Some drivers will even take you on longer trips, any place in the country you care to go—Monte Verde or Manuel Antonio, for example—as long as you also take care of their hotel and meal expenses.

Not all drivers are willing to rent by the hour, and not all can speak English well enough to explain what you are seeing. To find one who does, check with your hotel clerk or a travel agency. Many English-speaking drivers are available and eager to show you around the Meseta Central.

Rental Cars in Costa Rica

Renting a car is by far the most convenient way of touring the country. When you get serious about looking for a place to live for a few months or for the rest of your life, renting a car for a week or two allows you to travel about freely in search of your dream location. You don't have to bother with bus schedules; you can check out side streets or country lanes, and you can stop whenever you find a particularly interesting view. With a car you needn't worry about hotel reservations; chances are, if one hotel is full, another will have room. You can drive around, checking out FOR SALE or FOR RENT signs. You can investigate for yourself instead of being under the control of a salesperson, a rental agent, or others with a vested interest in showing you only their own properties.

At present automobile insurance is a government monopoly, and it's mandatory that your rental car insurance be purchased through the government agency. This could change soon, bringing much-needed competition to the field. The way it is now, there's a hefty $750 deductible in case of an accident. Should the car be totaled or stolen, the deductible is $1,500. Since auto theft is at epidemic levels at the time of this writing, this calls for keeping your rental car in a safe place at night.

Check with the rental company as to its policy—don't accept a car with more than $750 deductible (one company tries to impose a $1,000 floor on its liability). If you have a "Gold Card" (such as Visa or American Express), it should cover the deductible in case of an accident. Check with your credit card provider to be certain. Be sure to report a mishap to the credit card company within twenty days, even if the rental agent assures you that the other driver's insurance covers the repairs.

Accessories such as antennas, radios, tires, and mirrors aren't covered by rental insurance; if they are stolen, you are liable. The answer to the insurance problem is to keep your car in a guarded parking lot overnight when in the vicinity of San José. Auto accessory theft is not common in smaller towns, but in San José and other large cities, be aware.

Important: Before you accept a rental car, check the car for dents, scratches, and blemishes, in minute detail! Make sure the rental car employee notes each of them on your contract—no matter how tiny the scar. Unscrupulous employees in some agencies work a scam by charging for the same trivial scratch over and over. If the damage is there but not duly noted, you'll have no recourse but to pay. I've had better luck in this respect with the larger rental companies. Discuss the issue before you sign a contract.

Finally, insist on good tires. A sharp rock can penetrate a tire if the tread is thin and the sidewalls weak. If the tire is destroyed, you're liable for that too. So insist on another car if the tires are not in good shape. If the car rental agency gives you trouble about this, consider finding another such agency.

On the Road

Your regular driver's license is perfectly legal in Costa Rica for ninety days from the time you enter the country. After that you need a Costa Rican license. For residents or for those awaiting *residente* status, a license is relatively easy to get: Simply apply at the local office of the Ministry of Public Works ("MOPT," for us Gringos; ask a friend to help you find one locally) and present several passport-size photos. The license is issued while you wait.

However, as a tourist, you are not permitted to drive after ninety days on your home country's license. You'll have to leave the country long enough to get a fresh stamp on your passport. Take this warning seriously. The rules for foreigners applying for driver's licenses by presenting their passports change from time to time. For a while, it was difficult if not impossible, because of a ruling that only legal residents could get Costa Rican driver's licenses. How strict this ruling was observed is another question. Some MOPT offices issued driver's licenses to nonresidents; some would not do so. However, the advantages of having a driver's license are nebulous unless you are a resident or have made application for residency, since it's illegal to drive if your ninety-day visa or extension has expired.

Always carry your passport when driving; there's a fine for not having it. A photocopy of the passport is sometimes accepted, provided that you have a copy of the page showing the date you entered. The original passport is much preferred. Photocopies of your driver's license are not acceptable.

The first rule of driving in Costa Rica is one that should be followed in any country: Do not leave anything stealable in the car, even out of sight. A favorite trick of thieves is to monitor the car rental desks at the airport and watch who rents a car and fills the trunk with interesting luggage. They then follow the car to the hotel, and while the passengers are inside at the registration desk, the thieves open the trunk and help themselves to the luggage, extra money, cameras, and so on. This trick does not happen often, but why take chances? If possible, leave someone in the car during that crucial first stop. This method of stealing isn't unique to Costa Rica; it was imported from Europe, probably originating in Italy or Spain. Once you are outside of San José, the chance of something like this happening is almost nil.

Driving through the Costa Rican countryside isn't difficult; it's just slower. With all that gorgeous scenery, who wants to travel fast? Be especially careful when passing. Make sure you have time to get around safely, and be cautious near hills and curves. Always drive as though you expect trouble. That's just common sense in any country, but particularly in Costa Rica; too many drivers have a daring, gambling attitude that urges them to pass on hills and curves. For this reason accident rates in Costa Rica are unusually high. Drive defensively and keep an eye on the speedometer. Americans, used to high-speed, paved highways, sometimes have difficulty keeping their speed under 65 miles-per-hour; it doesn't seem normal to drive slower. But you must realize that 65 miles-per-hour is about 110 kilometers-per-hour, an illegal speed anywhere in the country. Most highways have a 75-kilometer-per-hour limit, unless posted with an 80-, 90-, or an occasional 100-kilometer-per-hour limit.

Watch for oncoming drivers who flash their headlights off and on.

That means trouble ahead, usually a radar speed trap or perhaps an accident. Another sign of danger is a tree branch or piece of shrubbery lying across one lane of the pavement. That signifies an accident, a washout, or some other nasty surprise that could await you ahead. Driving in city traffic anywhere around San José can be frustrating. As you get the knack of it and learn the system, it gets easier. Theoretically, finding your way around San José should be easy, because downtown city streets are logically organized on a north-south, east-west grid. *Calles*, or streets, run north to south, and *avenidas*, or avenues, run east to west.

However, nothing in Costa Rica is as simple as it sounds. For one thing, street signs are often missing. Sometimes they'll be posted on the corner of a building or perhaps on a signpost, but just when you need to know exactly where you are, you won't be able to find a clue. Furthermore, most downtown streets are one-way traffic, often without arrows to indicate which way! Perhaps you know that Avenida 9 is a one-way street going west, but how do you know the street you are looking at is Avenida 9 when there are neither street signs nor one-way signs? All you can do is wait to see which way traffic is flowing. If no cars are coming either way, you don't dare take a chance.

In the surrounding towns of the Meseta Central, traffic is lighter than in San José, but the problem of missing street signs becomes even worse. Some streets are one-way and others two-way, but too often there aren't any signs to clue you in as to which is which. An arrow painted on the pavement should indicate which direction is permissible, but sometimes the arrow isn't there. It's especially disconcerting to be driving along what you believe to be a two-way street and suddenly notice that all cars parked on both sides of the street are pointing in your direction. Since parking on either side of the street is OK in Costa Rica, you have no way of knowing if they just happen to be facing your direction or if you are traveling the wrong way again. When in doubt, park and wait for a car to drive past, then follow suit.

Away from the cities and major highways, you find bumpy roads that demand slow driving. Going too fast over rocks can cut tires, marooning you several kilometers from a repair shop. You may have to change a tire yourself! When this last happened to me, I stood around looking perplexed until two young men stopped to change the spare for me. They refused to accept money. Next I drove to a sort of auto repair place where two kids fixed my tire in a jiffy using strips of an old inner tube, some kind of glue, and what appeared to be a steel crochet needle. They didn't even have to take the tire off the rim, as I expected. They charged the equivalent of $1.50; that included putting the repaired wheel on the car and stashing the spare in the trunk.

Automobile Ferry Schedules

Several Costa Rican communities are accessible by car only after a ferry crossing. The longest ferry voyage is across the Gulf of Nicoya from Puntarenas to the southern part of the Nicoya Peninsula. This trip offers a choice of three ferries. Each passage takes about an hour, and you have to allow an hour for waiting in line. If you aren't there at least an hour early, you could find yourself waiting for the next ferry. It always surprises me how many vehicles can fit on one of those small boats. Cargo and cattle trucks, buses, and passenger cars string out in a long line from the ferry terminal in a seemingly impossible mission, yet most seem to fit aboard. Buses have priority, so the last to arrive in line could be a bus, but it will load first. A tip: Truckers can gauge the line pretty accurately and can tell you whether you'll make it aboard, should you arrive late. Just ask, "*Habrá espacio para mí carro?*" ("Will there be room for my car?")

Once aboard you can mingle with the other passengers and practice Spanish with the Ticos or compare travel agendas with the other tourists. I've met some very interesting people this way; something about a slow crossing brings out gregariousness in folks.

You have your choice of three boats to reach the southern portion of the Nicoya Peninsula, to places like Tambor, Tango Mar, Montezuma, and Malpaís. All three leave from Puntarenas; follow the signs.

Puntarenas–Playa Naranjo. This boat leaves Puntarenas at 4:00, 7:00, and 10:30 A.M. and at 1:30 and 4:30 P.M. It leaves Playa Naranjo at 5:15 and 8:30 A.M., noon, 3:00 and 6:00 P.M. The ferry has room for about thirty vehicles, depending on size. Beer, soft drinks, and snacks are sold.

Puntarenas–Paquera. This boat lands farther down the peninsula from Playa Naranjo—near the large village of Paquera—and thus cuts driving time off the trip to Tambor or to the tip of the peninsula. The disadvantage is that it doesn't sell cold beer or soft drinks. It's operated by the Hotel Playa Tambor but is open to the public. It leaves Puntarenas daily at 4:15 and 8:45 A.M. and 12:30 and 5:30 P.M., landing at Paquera, from which it departs at 6:00 and 10:30 A.M. and 2:30 and 7:15 P.M.

Puntarenas–Paquera. A passengers-only ferry departs daily from behind the Puntarenas market at 6:00 A.M. and 3:00 P.M. to Paquera and returns to Puntarenas at 8:00 A.M. and 5:00 P.M.

Río Tempisque Ferry. This ferry crosses to the upper (midpeninsula) region of the Nicoya Peninsula, to the city of Nicoya and the beaches of Nosara and Sámara. It runs from 5:00 A.M. to 6:00 or 7:00 P.M. If you're headed for Playa Flamingo or points to the north, don't bother with the ferry; the quickest way is to continue north on the Pan-American Highway. The Tempisque Ferry takes fifteen minutes to load and about twenty-five minutes to cross. It holds an astonishing number of vehicles, but during busy times you may have to wait for a trip or two. Weekend and holiday traffic is the worst. Again, ask a truck driver what your waiting time will be. If it's horrendous, you might save time by returning to the highway and looping around through Liberia. On each side of the river, several Tico restaurants make the wait somewhat pleasant. A bridge across the river farther upstream has been designed and the access roads built. The only thing holding it up is money. When this bridge finally crosses the river, the peninsula will be much more accessible and property more valuable.

Río Coto Ferry. This is my favorite ferry of anywhere I've driven. You use it when you're headed for Zancudo or Pavones via the shorter route (not always the quickest). The turnoff to the ferry is about halfway between Río Claro and Golfito. The Río Coto crossing isn't very wide at this point, and a steel cable strings across the water to keep the ferry on track. When you arrive at the crossing, if nobody's tending to the ferry, you honk your horn. Soon a teenager or two will come running and start up the old Datsun engine that propels the boat across the water. The capacity is about three cars. The last time we crossed the Río Coto, the engine was broken. How to get across? The solution was simple: Another teenager jumped into a canoe that sat alongside the ferry. He started up an outboard motor, hooked his arm through a projection of angle iron, and revved up the motor. It took some time for the boat to start moving, but the trip went surprisingly fast, once under way.

Golfito–Zancudo. If you don't need to take a car with you, a quicker way to get to Playa Zancudo is via one of the many small "water taxis" that take tourists to and from a wide variety of places around the Dulce

Golfo area. There's also a passenger ferry that sails between Golfito and Puerto Jimenez, on the Oso Peninsula.

Traffic Cops and Speed Traps

I often hear reports of tourists being harassed by Costa Rican traffic cops. No doubt these things happen; as is the case anywhere else in the world, a few bad guys can get on the force. Yet after driving many thousands of miles and receiving numerous traffic tickets (all deserved), I have found the overwhelming majority of Costa Rican traffic police to be courteous and rarely to stop someone without due cause. With all the crazy drivers in this country, cops have little reason to stop somebody for "nothing at all." Let's face it: Issuing a ticket for speeding, illegal passing, no safety belt, or the like, is not "police harassment." In the United States it's known as "law enforcement." Tourists aren't exempt from traffic laws, even if they don't thoroughly understand them. Why should they be?

Yet you'll continually hear Gringos complain that "the cops only stop rental cars. Why not Tico cars?" This is partly true, because Ticos know a little secret: When they see a speed limit sign of 60 kilometers-per-hour (38 miles-per-hour), they slow down, because they know there's a good chance that there's a radar gun ahead. Tourists, used to 65-miles-per-hour highways, blissfully pass the slowpoke Ticos in front of them. And guess what? Most Costa Rican highways have maximum limits of 75 kilometers-per-hour (about 48 miles-per-hour). This may seem ridiculously slow, but Ticos know that those occasional long, straight stretches of good pavement are also favorite places for radar guns. Maybe it seems sneaky, but when 75 kilometers-per-hour is the maximum, you're asking for trouble by going any faster. I've come to love those speed traps; if it weren't for them, all Ticos would be traveling 90 miles an hour! The fine for speeding is about $40 for ordinary violations, or $100 for *velocidad temerario* (120 kilometers-per-hour and above).

Allow me to offer some advice for when you're stopped by traffic police (I've had lots of experience in this department):

1. Be calm, cool, and courteous. After all, a ticket is no big deal. Until you're officially a resident, a traffic ticket doesn't affect your driving record or insurance. I've escaped several well-earned tickets simply by joking with the officers.

2. Do *not* get belligerent or raise your voice. Shouting won't help; it only makes things worse. When a cop feels he's being harassed for doing his job, don't be surprised if he retaliates in kind. I suspect this is where many cases of true police harassment originate: A tourist isn't aware that he's done anything wrong and becomes angry and abusive. The cop loses his temper too.

3. Don't offer a bribe. Even the best cops will accept money if you force it on them. This encourages a bad practice. The department has been undergoing a rigorous campaign of professionalism. Wages have been doubled, crooked cops are being dismissed, and intensive training programs are under way.

4. If the cop suggests that it would be easier to pay him than have to go to some distant place to pay your ticket, just politely decline and calmly wait for the ticket. Don't even discuss it with him. Again, tickets are no big deal, and you can pay at any national bank or simply save them up and turn them in to the rental company with your car. The agency will pay them for you and add the fine to your credit card. Ticos routinely save their tickets and pay them once a year, just before it's time to renew their auto license plates. If a cop tries to insist on a bribe, make a good mental image of him and report the incident to the Ministry of Public Works (MOPT) at (506) 227–2188 or at the MOPT office on Calle 9 between Avenidas 22 and 23.

I might add that since I've grown accustomed to watching the speedometer, I haven't received a ticket in more than three years, even though I make frequent 400-mile-round-trips to the Nicoya Peninsula—past a dozen speed traps—sometimes with California plates, sometimes in a rental car, sometimes with Tico plates. Having no traffic stops in three years is a Central America record for me.

Traffic tickets used to be so ridiculously cheap that drivers routinely ignored traffic laws, preferring to pay the occasional ticket rather than drive safely. This contributed to an appalling accident rate. Speeding tickets were less than $6.00, so why worry? Even with today's $40 fines, people still keep traffic cops busy.

Finding Hotels and Lodging

The tourist bonanza over the past few years made the hotel situation somewhat tight at times. To compensate, new hotels were constructed and private families converted homes into bed-and-breakfasts as quickly as they could. Many North Americans joined this bed-and-breakfast boom, partly financing their retirement by renting out spare bedrooms. In smaller communities hotels and ecotourism facilities raced to accommodate demand. Today you can often find a room in isolated places where camping was the only choice before. This trend seems to have caught up with demand, at least temporarily, because now there's an oversupply of rooms.

The tightest hotel room market in Costa Rica is during the Christmas–New Year's weeks. Not impossible, just tight. During the rush season making reservations before you leave for Costa Rica, even if only for the first couple of nights, is a good insurance policy. After you arrive, you can check around and locate something suitable to your taste and/or the size of your pocketbook.

Around San José, hotels come in all sizes and flavors, with expensive rooms costing $100 a night and up and cheap rooms under $15. For medium-priced hotel rooms, expect to pay from $45 to $65 a night during the tourist season. I looked at one room for under $10 recently, but shivers ran down my spine when I peered into the gloomy-looking room, with dirty linen on the bed, and in a ramshackle wooden building that looked like a firetrap. For my personal tastes a $20.00 room would be my bottom choice, yet many of the younger set and the backpacker brigades believe that anything over $8.00 is far too expensive. My wife's preferences fall into the $40 range or above.

Away from the Meseta Central, fewer hotels are available and rooms can be somewhat expensive for what you get. This is changing as competition grows. Nevertheless, I've found satisfactory accommodations for as little as $30 even in such out-of-the-way places. Understand, what may be satisfactory for me could be unthinkable for someone else!

If you're on a budget—as we long-term travelers usually are—don't expect too much in the way of luxury. You may find an affordable rate for a room with a private bath, only to discover that the shower is plumbed for cold water only. When a hotel advertises hot water, you'll often find one of those rinky-dink electric heaters attached to the showerhead. This contraption has a lever that can be set to one of three positions. The position that says "off" is the only one that works all the time. This encourages short but exhilarating showers, ideal for anyone considering celibacy. The secret is to let the water flow at its lowest possible volume, in the hope of coaxing warmth from the heating element.

Inexpensive hotels habitually use low-wattage light bulbs, so weak that you have trouble reading in bed. The solution is to carry a seventy-five-watt bulb in your luggage and substitute it whenever you feel like reading. (Make sure you aren't into a twelve-volt system!) Other items you might keep in your bag are a drinking cup, a roll of toilet paper, and some nylon string and clothespins so you can wash out undies. *Very important*: Pack a set of earplugs; I've suffered several nights made impossible by inconsiderate people partying all night or standing outside my door making plans for the next day's trip—at 2:00 A.M.! One additional item is insect repellent; whereas a buzzing mosquito can make sleep difficult, a dozen of them can make sleep impossible.

Should you be stranded out in the country, unable to find a place to stay, your ace in the hole is the local *pulpería*. This is the Costa Rican equivalent of a country "general store"; it also serves as the social center of the community. Drinks and snacks are sold, as neighbors congregate to exchange news and tidbits of gossip as well as purchase necessary items ranging from matches to machetes. The proprietor of the *pulpería* can often find you a room with a local family. This is a unique opportunity to see how country folk live in Costa Rica, but don't expect luxury. A *pulpería* is also an excellent place to inquire about real estate. If anything is for sale or rent in the neighborhood, the proprietor will know, and she probably knows the bottom-line price as well as the asking price.

LEGAL MATTERS

In Chapter 9 we discussed the pros and cons of buying real estate in Costa Rica. The nice part is that property ownership is open to anyone, no matter what citizenship; it's fairly easy to gain a clear title; and you can feel absolutely confident about your ownership. The nasty part is that a lot of charlatans and swindlers are out there ready to take advantage of your trusting nature. Don't worry—they haven't a chance if you do things correctly and don't skip any steps in the process.

The following information comes to us courtesy of my friend Carlos Umaña, of Tascan & Umaña law offices in San José. For those of you with connections to the World Wide Web, another source of Costa Rica legal information can be found at http://www.discoverypress. com/crinet/html

Your first step is to cultivate a lawyer who knows what the score is. In Costa Rica it's much easier to become an attorney than it is in the United States or Canada, so just because someone can legally assume the title *licenciado* doesn't guarantee he knows what he's doing, or even that he's ever practiced law. You'll find many people who are entitled to call themselves attorneys but actually practice law as an occasional sideline. A poor attorney isn't necessarily crooked; he could be inefficient or incompetent, which is just as bad.

A second important point: Make certain the lawyer is working for you, exclusively for you. If you use the other person's attorney to represent both interests, you're facing the probability that the lawyer is primarily working for his first client and isn't on your side at all. Unlike the situation in the United States, this is how it can work in Costa Rica. So insist on having *your* attorney handle your part of the sale.

Purchasing Costa Rican Property

To make it easy to check on land ownership, all property, with a few exceptions, must be registered at the Property Department of the Public Record Office. This office is located in Zapote and is open to the public. However, it's best to have your attorney do the checking, because he knows what to look for and where.

The first step, before you hand over any money, is to run a thorough title search of the public records to see whether the property really belongs to the seller, whether the seller is who he claims to be, and whether any mortgages, liens, encumbrances, or easements come attached to the property. Mortgages and liens must be properly registered to have any effect on third parties. So if the title is clear, you needn't worry about outstanding debts. If a lender didn't register a second deed of trust, he's out of luck. A title search should cost about $50, and it is well worth it, because if the seller was untruthful, you won't waste any more time.

You'll remember that all property is registered, with exceptions. These exceptions are important. Let's review the three basic categories of Costa Rican properties.

1. Recorded land. This includes all properties you'll find registered at the Public Record Office. The vast majority of properties for sale today fall into this category.

2. Nonrecorded land. This is property that could be registered at the Public Record Office but has not yet been recorded. This applies to farmland, *fincas* (ranches), or homesteads, places that haven't legally changed hands for many decades, or perhaps changed through a private contract. Nonrecorded land requires an attorney familiar with the procedure. It takes a judicial procedure to register land for the first time into public records. This kind of sale lacks the security granted by the Public Record Office.

3. Nonregisterable land. This is property that cannot be legally recorded at the Public Registry. This is the case with most beachfront property. In some instances, beach properties can be possessed legally by individuals or corporations through a concession granted by the government. The lease is always through the government, but you must acquire possession from the previous possessor, if there is one.

Transferring Recorded Land

Any individual or company, national or foreign, may legally own land sheltered by the Public Record Office system. But for legal and economic reasons, you should consider placing your property in the name of a Costa Rican corporation, or *sociadad anónima* (more about this later in this chapter).

Recorded land transfers must be granted through a public deed. That is, buyer and seller must appear before a Costa Rican notary public (to be chosen by the purchaser), who will insert the title transfer in his protocol. (A notary public is a licensed attorney who is endowed with "public trust" and the right to validate and legalize all contracts and deeds. Again, to protect your investment, you should appoint your own attorney to perform as the notary public in the transaction.)

The purchase deed, as well as any liens or mortgages agreed to by the buyer, is then presented to the Public Record Office to be registered. It's also the notary's duty to complete all recording procedures necessary to provide the title transfer with full efficacy. (This is another reason to have a good attorney working for you, someone who knows what the word *efficacy* means.)

Expenses and legal fees involved can range from 6 to 7 percent of the total amount of the transaction and on the assessed price of the property. These costs are customarily shared by buyer and seller on a fifty-fifty basis—unless agreed otherwise.

Beachfront Property

Because of special regulations some areas are not subject to private ownership. This is the case with most beachfront property, which is leased through concessions granted by the government. This is where things become complicated. Public Law No. 6043 of March 1977 established a restricted coastal zone called the *Zona Marítimo/Terrestre.* This law covers a strip of land, 200 meters deep, along both the Pacific Coast and the Atlantic Coast. The restricted zone is divided into two sections:

1. The Public Zone (Zona Publica) is that first 50-meter strip of land starting at the mean high-tide line. This is public property; the public has full access to the Public Zone.
2. The next 150-meter strip of land is called the Restricted Zone (Zona Restringida).

The law states that no private individual or corporation is allowed to build on or use for private purposes "any portion whatsoever" of the Public Zone. However, it's possible to obtain a lease/concession on Restricted Zone properties for private or business use. Understand, when this happens, it isn't a deed; it's a "lease concession." At first the lease is with the local municipality, and later on, after a procedure, the lease is with the Costa Rica Tourism Institute. Beneficiaries of lease concessions are granted the use, occupation, and possession of the land, including the right to build.

Now comes a sticky point. The law says, "No lease concessions are granted to non–Costa Ricans who have resided in the country less than five years, nor to foreign companies, nor to national companies of which fifty percent or more of its stock is owned by non–Costa Ricans."

While that may be the law, the fact is that many if not most of the desirable Zona Restringida properties are held by Costa Rican corporations that are owned entirely by foreigners. This is, of course, difficult to verify, because ownership of a Costa Rican corporation is impossible to substantiate. (Tips on how to start a corporation are found later in this chapter.)

These lease concessions can be transferred to one person or company to another, subject to the approval of the municipality and the Costa Rican Tourism Institute. Leases are generally granted for periods that range from five to twenty years. The municipality is entitled to charge a small leasing fee. At the end of the leasing period, the lessee can apply for an extension of the lease concession, and extensions are normally granted with the previous approval of the Tourism Institute.

Beachfront land not regulated by this law can be found, but it's extremely unusual to find titled property in areas within the restricted 200-meter zone. True, some beachfront land isn't regulated, because it was in use before the beach laws were passed. These exempt parcels are so-called grandfathered properties. However, be cautious; many people think that their property is grandfathered when it really is not. Some claim it's grandfathered when they know it is not.

Offshore Corporations

For a variety of reasons, banking secrecy laws such as those in Switzerland attract a great deal of interest among certain folks who have motives for hiding assets. As far as I know, there is no law against this as long as these accounts aren't used to defraud creditors or to evade paying taxes. Like Switzerland, Costa Rica has strict rules on nondisclosure of bank accounts.

An interesting angle of financial secrecy is the use of Costa Rican "offshore" corporations. Like bank accounts, these corporations can be started by anyone—citizen, resident, or tourist—and are supposed to be totally secret. Since there's no way of knowing just whose names are on the corporation books, it's almost impossible to discover who actually controls any of these corporations. In fact, the legal term is *sociedad anónima* or "anonymous society." That's why corporation names are appended with "S.A." instead of "Inc." or "Ltd." One common example of a legitimate use of a corporation is when buying or selling real estate. If the property belongs to a corporation, transfer of ownership is simple. You merely transfer the corporation's stock; the property belongs to whoever holds this stock.

Before we go any further, you need to understand a few crucial points. First, I am not an attorney, and even if I were, you would be foolish to accept legal advice from a book—particularly when it comes to activities as complicated as offshore corporations or foreign banking practices. Second, while most corporations and bank accounts in Costa Rica are legal, used for perfectly legitimate purposes, the ones used for illegal schemes are frequently toppled, sending overly creative schemers to jail. I suspect that what happens is that the corporation originally starts off with legal goals in mind and then branches out into a small tax fraud, which grows until it gets out of hand. Some schemes are so obvious that the IRS has little trouble spotting the smoke and flames. My final point is a reiteration of the first: I am not a lawyer, nor am I in any way urging readers to get involved in offshore corporations or secret bank accounts. I am merely reporting what Costa Rican residents and attorneys have passed along to me.

Starting a Costa Rican Corporation

Costa Rica's corporate structure allows any person (Costa Rican or not) to control a company without his or her name appearing in the public records. A Costa Rican lawyer (who must be a specialist in this) sets up a corporation without the real owner's name ever appearing in the record. It is termed a *sociedad anónima con acciones al portador*, or "anonymous society with all stock owned by the bearer." This means that although there is a legal president, secretary, and treasurer (often simply employees of the attorney), the actual ownership of the corporation is invested in whoever physically has the stock certificates in his or her pocket or safe-deposit box. Even the attorney has no way of knowing whether the original client still owns the stock. This arrangement is prohibited in the United States but is perfectly legal in Costa Rica.

This corporation is free to engage in many types of business activities, both in Costa Rica and in other countries. Theoretically, because it is considered a "foreign corporation" as far as the IRS is concerned, it pays no taxes in the United States. (There's talk about changing this.) Because it's a Costa Rican corporation, it pays little or nothing on what it earns outside of Costa Rica. This doesn't relieve the individual of the responsibility of reporting income and paying income taxes in his or her home country. New laws require that a yearly report of a corporation must be filed; should there be no income to report, there are no tax consequences—but not filing the report makes the corporation liable for a large fine. So if you already have a corporation in Costa Rica and haven't been filing reports, see your lawyer.

Advantages of a Corporation

It's always advisable for both foreigners and Costa Ricans to own land through a corporation. Among the advantages is a reduction of personal liabilities and taxes. The ownership of assets, such as real estate, boats, and automobiles, is the main purpose of most registered corporations in Costa Rica. Foreigners aren't supposed to have checking accounts with a national bank, but their corporations can have an account, and checks can be written by the treasurer (you). A foreigner can't engage in commerce, but the corporation can.

A corporation can be owned by a group of shareholders or fully owned by one shareholder. This way a single individual or a small group of people can operate the company in a relatively simple and inexpensive manner. The asset (your house or your car) can be sold or transferred simply by handing over the shares of the corporation, because it is owned by the corporation, not the individual, even though he or she may own all the shares. Your attorney will show you the best ways to ensure control of the company and the overall handling of corporate power.

An important point about corporations is to make sure you are getting a full-fledged corporation; there are shortened versions that have some serious drawbacks. Don't go for a cut-rate, partial incorporation, because you'll not get all the required services, and it could expire at the end of a brief period. Later you'll find you have to go back and spend more money to put the company on a par with other corporations. Most attorneys will charge about $650 to form a complete corporation.

As mentioned above, another advantage of incorporating is that since government banks won't open a colón account unless you are a legal resident, nonresidents work around this by opening a checking account in the name of their Costa Rican corporation. Such accounts are simply for the convenience of bill paying; they pay no interest. Three national banks offer these corporate checking accounts: Banco Nacional de Costa Rica, Banco de Costa Rica, and Banco Credito Agrícola de Cartago. To open an account in a national bank, you'll be asking your attorney for help. Among other things, you'll need the original letters of incorporation of your company, certification of the company's legal representatives, and two recommendation letters from individuals with checking accounts in that bank. At one bank they wanted letters from Costa Rican citizens who regularly lent me money. When I pointed out that if Ticos were gullible enough to lend me money, I wouldn't need a checking account, the bank official agreed to accept a letter from my lawyer instead. The legal charges for something like this should be minimal.

Legal Details

There are four main stages in the process of forming a Costa Rican corporation.

1. A document called the Articles of Incorporation or Constitutive Charter of the company will need to be preapred. This document will be drawn up by your attorney. The Constitutive Charter determines the organization, administration, and bylaws of the company. This is signed by all the shareholders, the appointed members of the board of directors, the controller, and the *agente residente*.
2. Before registration in the Public Record Office, your attorney will announce the company's constitution in Costa Rica's official newspaper, *La Gaceta*. This takes about two weeks. Also, you must make a deposit of the amount of the capital stock indicated in the Constitutive Charter—usually 1,000 colones—in a national bank. The amount of shares in the corporation and their denomination

are determined by the founders. All shares must have equal value and must be worth at least 1 colón, but there's no top limit to a share's value. The money deposited can be withdrawn once the company has been duly recorded.

3. The company must be registered in the Public Record Office. This registration is essential to legally constitute a corporation in Costa Rica. The registration process is performed by the notary public (your lawyer). The whole process takes from one to three months, depending on the time it takes for the Public Registry to approve the company's bylaws, including the books.

4. You'll receive a set of three accounting books (*Diario, Mayor,* and *Inventario y Balances*) and three "legal" books (*Shareholders' Record, Shareholders' Assemblies,* and *Board of Directors' Meetings*). Your attorney will present the books to the Ministerio de Hacienda for their initial authorization. Once duly legalized, these books should register all internal affairs of the company (as well as stock transfers) and are kept privately by the shareholders. You can leave them with your attorney or place them in a secure place, such as a safe deposit box. Remember, whoever has the books in hand also has control of the assets.

To form a Costa Rican corporation, you need a minimum of two initial shareholders. Once the company is formed and properly inscribed in the Public Record Office, the shares can be transferred to a single person, who becomes the sole shareholder of the company.

The name of the company must be in Spanish, Latin, or any native dialect. Of course, a name can't be identical or equivalent to that of an existing corporation. And names with a meaning in a foreign language (such as English or German) are not allowed without special exceptions. Your attorney in charge of preparing the Articles of Incorporation will ask you for a list of names (in Spanish), and he'll research them and determine whether they will be accepted by the Public Record Office.

There must be a board of directors with at least the following offices: president, secretary, and treasurer. The president must be the principal representative of the company. Other members of the board can also be made representatives of the corporation, depending on how the founders of the company decide to do the Articles of Incorporation. The members of the board may or may not be shareholders. The directors must be present when the company is legally formed, to personally accept their designation and sign the Corporation Charter along with the shareholders or power of attorney.

The controller cannot be a shareholder or a member of the board of directors. The person appointed as controller has to sign the Articles of Incorporation. Usually this will be someone on your lawyer's office staff.

Every Costa Rican company must designate an *agente residente*. The *agente residente* will probably be your Costa Rican attorney, who will be a formal representative for official matters. He has no powers to act on the company's behalf. The fee for this service is usually $100 a year.

Taxes on Corporations

Education and culture tax. This tax is payable once a year and is based on the value of the assets owned by the corporation. It isn't expensive, usually somewhere around $100.

Income tax. As with individuals, the corporation must pay income tax depending on the earnings the corporation had during the past fiscal year (from October 1 to September 30). Companies just holding assets do not have to pay anything if there hasn't been any activity. As mentioned earlier, under a recent (1995) tax law all companies must submit a tax declaration on taxes to be paid, if any. So, make sure that the declaration is presented every year before November 1. The fine for not doing so can be heavy. Again, this is why you are paying your lawyer the $100-a-year fee.

Property taxes. If the corporation owns land, it must pay the following taxes:

Territorial tax. A national tax based on the government records of land value, to be paid every four months.

Municipal taxes. Local taxes for public lighting, garbage collection, and so forth, paid locally in the municipality every four months.

Land tax. An annual tax, imposed every January, that is administered on a progressive scale, from 0.30 percent annually for land of 250,000 colones ($1,250) in value, up to 1.05 percent annually for values over 3,000,000 colones ($15,000). This doesn't tell you a whole lot, unless you know the assessed value of your property, which is usually far below market value.

Banking Secrecy

Traditional tax havens—such as the Cayman Islands, Switzerland, Luxembourg, the Channel Islands, and the Netherlands Antilles—have always tempted those looking for ways to hide assets. Secret bank accounts are often used for this purpose. I've been told that medical doctors routinely hide as much of their holdings as possible in these places, to avoid disaster should a multimillion-dollar malpractice suit top their insurance limits. Like the aforementioned countries, Costa Rica maintains a strict policy of banking and commercial secrecy. The amount of money you have in a bank account is supposedly sacrosanct and unavailable to curious outsiders.

One banker said, "If I disclosed information about someone's account—even to a policeman or a government official—I could go to prison." The *Tico Times* illustrated this point with a story about a suspect accused of stealing and forging checks. The crime could easily be solved if authorities could access bank records and see if the stolen checks had been deposited to the suspect's account. But bank officials refused to help the police solve the crime, because in the process they would become criminals themselves!

Do not think that this secrecy deters the IRS from snooping about, and I suspect not without some success. (Realize that failing to report a foreign bank account on your income tax return is a law violation.) Sometimes fraud is so transparent that all the secret bank accounts or anonymous corporations in the world wouldn't help. I suspect that the IRS has its own methods of tracking down fraud without going through the Costa Rican banking system. But there is nothing illegal about U.S. or Canadian citizens owning a bank account or majority stock in an offshore corporation, so long as profits are reported and taxes properly paid.

FREQUENTLY ASKED QUESTIONS

To help readers who desire more information on living, retiring, or investing in Costa Rica, I maintain several Web pages on the Internet. The most interesting for me is my bulletin board, which generates my FAQ Page (FAQ = frequently asked questions). I receive feedback from readers and others about what people want to know about Costa Rica. This chapter covers a range of questions and topics posted on my FAQ Page. To find the page on your computer, enter the Internet address: http://discoverypress.com/faq.html; to reach the bulletin board, type: http://discoverypress.com/talk.html

Below are some of the more frequently asked questions.

How much does it cost to live in Costa Rica?

That depends on your lifestyle and where you want to live. Except for imported items, most goods and services cost from two-thirds to three-fourths of what you would pay in most parts of the United States. Some things cost more, some less. I have friends who pay $250 a month to rent a comfortable apartment; I know others who pay $1,300 for an elegant home. I've looked at some houses for $35,000 and others for $600,000. It's the same back home: If you want to live on the golf course, you pay the price. If you expect Costa Rica to be a supercheap place to live, you're going to be disappointed. Automobiles are very expensive—you'll pay about 100 percent duty on the *Blue-book* value. In short, to live on a tight budget, plan on taking buses and taxis and on walking a lot (it's good for you). I know people here who get by quite well on $800 a month. I know others who barely make it on $2,000 a month. Again, it depends on your lifestyle. If your liquor bill is $800 a month, better plan on the $2,000 budget. There are many reasons for living in Costa Rica, but if living on $300 a month is one of your goals, you can do it, but you won't be happy.

Can I work as a doctor, lawyer, dentist, and so forth in Costa Rica?

Most if not all professionals in Costa Rica protect themselves by belonging to strong associations that discourage "outsiders" from entering the field. It's the same in the United States or Canada. You can't enter practice unless you pass the proper exams and join the association. But the catch here is that you usually can't take the exam unless you are a graduate of a Costa Rican university. Until recently even newspaper writers risked jail by working as journalists unless they belonged to the journalists' association. And, of course, you can't join the association unless you've graduated from a Costa Rican university.

Don't take my word as final on this. For all I know, there may be exceptions in certain fields, particularly for needed skills and specialties. You need to speak with someone in your field who is working in Costa Rica.

Where do most expatriates live?

Unlike in some countries, foreigners in Cost Rica don't feel the need of bunching together in walled compounds or in certain neighborhoods. Most feel comfortable living just about anywhere (common sense will guide you here). But they do tend to congregate in the more expensive neighborhoods, simply because they can usually afford the extra amenities. Around San José these would be places like Rohrmoser, Escazú, Santa Ana, Cariarri, and Curridabat. They seem to like the Arenal and Tilarán areas. Just about anywhere on the Pacific Coast, you'll run into Gringos and Europeans, even down around Golfito, near the Panama border. Not as many live on the Caribbean Coast, but the coast is lightly populated anyway. Don't ask me which is best, because there is no "best place;" that's an individual decision. I'm not going to be responsible for sending you to a place where you will be unhappy. The only way to find your dream home is to investigate thoroughly in person.

Can you supply an Internet listing of names, addresses, phone numbers, and e-mail addresses of North Americans living in Costa Rica?

It would be nice to have an e-mail list of expatriates living in Costa Rica, but think about it: Would you want your name and address spread over the World Wide Web? It's only courteous to respect others' privacy. You'll have no problem meeting people when you go to Costa Rica in person. I can't give out addresses of my friends, not if I want to keep them as friends!

I've been looking at real estate prices on the Internet and in the Tico Times. Prices of $250,000, $400,000, and even higher seem commonplace. Aren't there any affordable properties in Costa Rica?

Sure, there are plenty of places to be found at bargain prices. The problem is, when you look for affordable homes on the Internet, you're looking in the wrong place. When property is a real bargain, it won't be on the Internet and it probably won't be in the Tico Times. Usually it's advertised because the seller is either asking too much money or else having a difficult time selling a luxury property. When the price is much over $60,000, most Ticos and those Gringos with ordinary budgets can't buy. So the advertisement goes into places where well-to-do buyers will see it: on the Internet. The same goes for rents. A house or apartment that rents for $200 a month doesn't need to be advertised in the *Tico Times* or posted on the Internet. But a luxury place that rents for $2,000 needs to be exposed to a different market.

We're thinking about moving to Costa Rica, but we don't want to leave my wife's mother behind. She lives in a nursing home near us; can we take her to Costa Rica and place her in similar accommodations?

Probably not. Before anyone can enter the country on other than a tourist visa, the Costa Rica government requires certification of good health. If your mother-in-law has Alzheimer's or some other debilitating disease, she is unlikely to pass a health examination. Of course, if someone who is already here as a legal resident becomes infirm, that's a different story.

What about investment in reforestation? Teak? Pochote? Exotic wood?

It sounds good on paper. It's possible that, in twenty or thirty years, teak trees planted last year will bring in a profit. Nobody knows for sure, since teak is not native to this hemisphere, and only readers of crystal balls can know whether the price and quality will be high enough to make a profit. It hasn't been done yet. You're going to have to wait a long time to find out whether teak farms will return a profit, or whether they can stand the test of court cases and fraud claims to still be in business when the trees mature. How old will you be in thirty years? Or even twenty years? Will you care? On the other hand, I have friends who are planting teak trees with full confidence in the future. They are honest and well intentioned, as most reforestation promoters probably are. I sincerely hope they make money. But to the best of my knowledge, the only people involved who have ever made a profit are those who planted trees and sold shares to investors. Pochote is a similar story. Yes, it is very profitable to harvest mature pochote trees. I've heard they fetch as much as $5,000. But it takes thirty to fifty years for a tree to grow to that size. I'm sorry, but I can't afford to wait that long to get a return on my investment. Don't take my word for any of this. Check with sources such as back issues of the *Tico Times* or with a knowledgeable Costa Rican attorney.

I've been told that I can bring any personal items with me—such as a computer, small household items, linens, a television, and utensils— when I arrive without paying import tax on them. Is this true? Also, I will be sending these items air freight and they will arrive one day before me. I will be arriving in the evening and the air freight office will be closed. Can I return the next day and pick up my possessions without paying the import tax?

Your information is only partly correct. The generous household customs exemptions of years past are history. Only those who qualified previously are "grandfathered" into the system and can still take advantage of the low tax rates. Customs regulations were completely revised recently, and Costa Rica still has no brochures or documents that detail exactly what you can and cannot bring into the country. Unfortunately, this leaves many decisions subject to interpretation.

Basically, tourists and residents have the right to bring in every six months, tax-free, $500 in merchandise *in addition* to items considered part of the traveler's baggage. The law specifies that personal items that are exempt include clothing; jewelry; handbags; umbrellas; medicines; perfume; toiletry articles; baby carriages and toys; sports equipment, such as a surfboard or fishing equipment; photographic equipment; a tent; a personal computer, calculator, and typewriter; records, a radio, and tapes; portable musical instruments; and books. The handicapped may enter the country with a wheelchair (thank you for being generous). Personal items aren't limited to this list; any article that can be used by the traveler while in the country, whether to work or play, could be considered a personal article. Be prepared to argue about some things, because the customs agent may disagree.

Understand that the $500 exemption is *in addition* to your personal articles. For instance, a used desktop computer should be considered personal equipment if it is packed in an old box and looks used. I say "should" because I've had customs people try to count a used computer against my $500 exemption; it took some arguing to convince them they were wrong. A new computer will be counted against your exemption. If you bring in several identical items—such as two CD players or three radios—they assume you are bringing them into the country to be sold, and therefore you'll pay tax on them.

Goods over the $500 limit and not considered personal articles will be retained in customs until import duties are paid. The amount of duty depends on the type of merchandise; the categories are too numerous to describe. If the value is more than $100, you need a customs broker to handle it. The procedure can be quite complicated.

To qualify for the $500 exemption, merchandise packed in suitcases or boxes does not necessarily have to enter the country at the same time as you do; you have a grace period of three months before or after you arrive. But it's highly recommended that you arrange to bring your things with you on the same flight. If your goodies end up in a customs warehouse, you may not have to pay duty but it could be time-consuming and expensive to employ a customs agent.

Having things shipped to you by someone else can end up in a nightmare scenario. I know folks who received Christmas presents of chocolates from a well-meaning friend—each box of candy was valued at about $10—and they paid about $30 in customs duty for each present.

What about bringing handguns into the country? I have a registered handgun and would like to bring it with me. What are the laws about having guns in a car or on your person?

Firearms, plants, chemicals, and medicines imported for resale all require special permits, issued by specific agencies of the government. And in most cases, these items will be held in customs until the proper permits are obtained. Application for firearms is made through the Control of Arms and Explosives Office (Oficina de Control de Armas y Explosivas) at the Ministry of Public Security. Unless you speak fluent Spanish, you'd best use a customs agent. Under no circumstances should you consider carrying a handgun, either on your body or in your car, without a specific permit. Pistols aren't part of the Costa Rican culture (thank God), and police can become very upset with someone flouting the law in this respect. It's easy to obtain a gun permit, provided that you can show a need for one.

How can I find a job in Costa Rica?

We all know some Gringos who work here, legally and illegally, but I suspect that most of them don't do very well. When you have to compete with local wages of $1.00 or so an hour, you need some special skill that is in high demand. If you can do something nobody else can do, by all means visit Costa Rica and check it out. Then interview, investigate, and make up your own mind. It's as difficult to find a Costa Rican job by mail as it is in the United States or Canada. Employers are hesitant to hire, sight unseen, someone who lives 5,000 miles away and might or might not actually be serious about relocating.

Can you recommend a good realtor in Costa Rica to whom I can write for information?

I have a problem recommending realtors or talking about prices of real estate in Costa Rica. I'm simply not competent to do so, and I don't want to steer anybody wrong. Furthermore, I feel strongly that you are wasting your time pricing property by mail. The *only* way is to go there in person, see what properties are for sale, and not take anybody's word for anything. Go to *all* the realtors and ask to see what they have; often they won't tell you about somebody else's listings. Many real estate people in Costa Rica are rank amateurs and know nothing of real estate professional ethics; therefore they have no established rules to follow. Unless I personally know the realtor, I would much prefer dealing with a private party and a good lawyer.

What about starting a business in Costa Rica?

If you ask any Gringo who has gone into business in Costa Rica, "What's the best part of being in business here, and what's the worst part?" almost all of them will say, "The best part is I can live in Costa Rica. The worst part is I don't make enough money to live well." The big problem is that profit margins are low, because the purchasing power of the Ticos is low. The trick is to find some niche that deals with affluent foreigners. Once you find this niche, you'll probably discover that others got there first. Don't bother paying for "expert advice" from sages who live in the United States, or subscribing to Internet newsletters about how to enter a profitable business in Costa Rica. (If they knew, they would be in Costa Rica, making money.) The long and short answer to finding business opportunity in Costa Rica is this: Go there in person, do a lot of investigating, and believe one-third to one-tenth of what people tell you about why they're trying to get rid of the business.

I'm a schoolteacher and would like to teach in Costa Rica, maybe English. Are there any paying jobs in this field?

There are some jobs for teachers but mostly in highly specialized fields or in teaching English as a Second Language. Remember, teachers are not highly paid in Costa Rica, and there are hundreds of Gringos willing to teach English for a chance to live in Costa Rica for whatever wages. You face a lot of competition for low-paying jobs. If you have some specialty that's needed in one of the universities, that may be another story. But the pay will still be far less than you earned as a beginning teacher years ago.

Why did the Costa Rican government renege on is Pensionado Program? The government took away tax-free benefits from elderly retirees. Is this ethical?

It used to be that folks who qualified for residency received a ton of tax breaks when they entered the program. They could bring in $7,000 in household goods tax-free, and every few years they could import an automobile tax-free. Refrigerators and other appliances, same deal. This caused a lot of resentment among Costa Rican citizens—can you blame 'em? They had to pay twice as much for an automobile as the Gringo who lived next door and who paid no taxes other than a small property assessment. Furthermore, the International Monetary Fund threatened to cut off loans if Costa Rica didn't put its financial house in order; the Pensionado Program was one of the mandates. However, the government didn't renege; the way I understand it, those who qualified under the existing program were "grandfathered" in. Those coming after that cutoff date knew full well that they were not included. They weren't tricked; they knew exactly what they were entitled to before they made application for residency. From a personal standpoint, I'd love to buy an automobile tax-free. Since I can't, I don't think it's unfair that I have to pay as much as a Costa Rican. Costa Ricans don't think so either.

We want to visit Costa Rica next year. Where would you recommend we visit, and which hotels should we stay in?

I receive e-mails every day requesting travel information. I don't mind answering e-mail, but I don't feel competent to plan travel schedules. There's no substitute for a good travel book to answer these questions. I refuse to take responsibility for recommending a hotel or sending you to some tourist trap just because I once had a good time there. The fact is, I do little traveling in Costa Rica; I'm too busy writing, working on volunteer projects in my home village, and trying to break Zonker's world record in the Tanning Olympics. What do I know about travel? Ask me about suntans and Imperial beer.

I've read that you have to keep an armed guard at your home when you're gone or squatters will take over your house. Is this true?

No, it's absurd. There are laws in Costa Rica that confirm the principle that if land is abandoned, it's open to be used and eventually claimed by whoever uses and improves the land. These laws apply only to agricultural land. If someone tries to take over your house, you can have him or her arrested, just as you would back home. Further, the law applies only to land that's been abandoned. If someone tries to squat on your property, you simply call the police.

If Costa Rica doesn't have an extradition treaty with the United States, isn't the country a haven for criminals?

Many countries don't have extradition treaties with the United States. Why should they? Our Supreme Court has ruled that if we want to arrest a criminal and bring him back to the United States for trial, we have every right to send our police into that country and take the prisoner by force (in the case of the Mexican doctor who was kidnapped by Drug Enforcement Administration agents), and we can even send soldiers into a country to make an arrest (in the case of President Noriega in Panama). With this power who needs a treaty? But in fact what happens in Costa Rica is this: Each request for extradition is judged by certain criteria, such as, "Would the offense be considered a crime in Costa Rica?" and "Is the country requesting the extradition legally entitled to bring the person to trial?" Rarely is a reasonable request turned down. For example, a few years ago Costa Rica returned a California ex-legislator who had been indicted for extortion. But Costa Rica also rejected a request by Israel for a Ukrainian accused of being a death-camp guard. Why? Because the crime occurred in the Ukraine and the government of the Ukraine still refuses to issue an extradition request. Costa Rica regularly sends back people accused of selling drugs, but not someone accused of "conspiracy" to sell drugs, because in Costa Rica a person hasn't broken the law until he or she actually sells or attempts to sell drugs. In the United States conspiracy is a catch-all charge that means anything the prosecutor wants it to mean.

Having said all this, I have to report that in April 1997, Costa Rica came to an agreement with the U.S. government to the effect that "You promise not to break our laws by kidnapping suspects in our country and we'll reinstate our extradition agreement."

What does an average house in Costa Rica sell for? Near the beach?

This is like asking what an average house costs in the United States. I've seen homes in the United States selling for under $15,000 (I wouldn't want to live there, but someone might). I've also seen them selling for

$150,000 (I wouldn't mind living there, but many people would consider such property too cheap). I've also seen houses selling for $1.5 million (I can't afford that, but it's well worth it to some people). So, what's an average house sell for in the United States? You tell me. It's the same in Costa Rica: location, location, location. I've seen places for sale for $5,000 (I'm not sure I'd want to live there, but then I can afford better). I've also seen many places for sale for more than $500,000. So knowing the "average" cost is meaningless. My personal observation—and remember, I'm an amateur when it comes to real estate—is that homes suitable for North Americans generally cost less in Costa Rica than they would in similar locations back home. But they are not give aways. My impression is that properties I like cost about a third of what they would cost in my California neighborhood. On the other hand, homes in many California neighborhoods cost three times what they would cost in a similar neighborhood in the Midwest or the South. So maybe it's a wash. I've met people who come to Costa Rica and are shocked to find that homes cost almost as much as they do back home. But when I find out where such persons come from, I realize that the only way I'd live there would be at gunpoint. The bottom line is that in Costa Rica you will pay for location and quality, just as you would back home.

Do you know of any preretirement tours to Costa Rica? My wife and I would like to check out the highlights but don't want to waste time doing a strictly tourist thing.

As a matter of fact, a tour company in Costa Rica—called *Explore Costa Rica Tours*—has put together a five-day package that takes you to several of the more popular retirement locations. They've asked me to accompany the group for the first three days of each tour. Included will be visits to homes of retired North American couples, where we will have luncheons and cocktails with local retirees; a seminar on retirement, with lectures by a Costa Rican attorney and other experts; visits to various communities preferred by retirees; and visits to some of the more popular tourist sites. See the Web site at http://discoverypress.com /explore.html for more information.

APPENDIX

Business Contacts

American Chamber of Commerce of Costa Rica: P.O. Box 4946, San José 33102–1033. U.S. mailing address: SJO 1576, P.O. Box 025216, Miami, FL 33102.

Associación Nacional de Fomento Economico: Apdo. 3577, San José.

Camara de Industrias de Costa Rica: Calle 13 y 15, Avenida 6, San José; (506) 223–2411.

Costa Rica Export Investment Promotion Center: International Trade Mart, New Orleans, LA 70130; (504) 529–2282.

Dirección General de Aduanas (General Customs Bureau): Ministerio de Hacienda, Avendia 1–3, Calle 14, San José.

Economic Development Offices: c/o Embassy of Costa Rica, 2112 S Street, NW, Washington, DC 20008; (202) 328–6628.

Ministerlo de Industrias: Calle 10, Avenida 2, San José; (506) 257–8511.

Costa Rican Consulates

Albuquerque, New Mexico: 7033 Luella Anne Drive, NE, 87109; (505) 822–1420

Atlanta, Georgia: 1870 The Exchange, Suite 100, 30339; (404) 951–7025

Austin, Texas: 1730 E. O. Horf, Unit 320, 78741; (512) 445–0023

Chicago, Illinois: 8 South Michigan Avenue, Suite 1312, 60603; (312) 263–2772

Denver, Colorado: 1633 Fillmore Street, Suite 100, 80206; (303) 377–0050

Durham, North Carolina: 3516 University Drive, Suite A, 27707; (919) 490–1817

Honolulu, Hawaii: 819 Koko Isle Circle, Suite 1130, 96825; (808) 395–7772

Houston, Texas: 2901 Wilcrest Drive, Suite 347, 77042; (713) 266–1527

Las Vegas, Nevada: 5436 Mountain View Drive, 89102; (702) 363–2925

Los Angeles, California: 3540 Wilshire Boulevard, Suite 404, 90010; (213) 380–7925

Miami, Florida: 1600 North West Le Jeune Road, Suite 300, 33126; (305) 871–7485

Minneapolis, Minnesota: 2400 Energy Park Drive, St. Paul, 55108; (612) 645–3401

New Orleans, Louisianna: 4532 West Napoleon Avenue, Suite 112, Metaire, LA 70001; (504) 887–8131

New York, New York: 80 Wall Street, Suite 718–19, 10005; (212) 425–2620

Philadelphia, Pennsylvania: 1411 Walnut Street, Suite 200, 19102; (215) 564–4415

San Antonio, Texas: 6836 San Pedro, Suite 206B, 78216; (210) 308–8623

San Diego, California: 4007 South Camino del Rio, Suite 107, 92108; (619) 563–6441

San Francisco, California: 870 Market Street, Room 546–548, 94102; (415) 392–3745

San Juan, Puerto Rico: Urb. Rio Piedras Heights, 1732 Yenisey Street, Rio Piedras, 00926; (809) 282–6747

Washington, D.C.: 2114 South Street, NW, 20008; (202) 234–2945

Books and Periodicals

Costa Rica: A Natural Destination (1994), by Ree Strange Sheck. A guidebook for those travelers especially interested in ecology. (John Muir Publications, Santa Fe, NM.)

Costa Rica Adventures (1996). This video features fifteen thrilling adventures, from hikes and horseback rides to bungee jumping and sportfishing. (Away from It All Press, P.O. Box 5573, Chula Vista, CA 91912–5573; 800–365–2342.)

Costa Rica Guide, 6th Ed; (1996), by Paul Glassman. Information on travel in Costa Rica, with regional maps. (Open Road Publishing, New York, NY.)

Costa Rica Today. Excellent full-color newspaper geared to the foreign traveler. Widely available in hotels and the like. (P.O. Box 025216, Miami, FL 35102; $59.95 annual subscription.)

The Costa Rica Traveler (1988), by Ellen Searby. Covers travel in Costa Rica and descriptions of the country's attractions. (Windham Bay Press, Occidental, CA.)

Costa Rican Outlook. An upbeat newsletter with insightful background stories and handy tidbits for travelers. Subscribers receive an ID card for discounts for restaurants and other places in Costa Rica. (Away from It All Press, P.O. Box 5573, Chula Vista, CA 91912; phone/fax: 619–421–6002 or 800–365–2342.)

Exploring Costa Rica (1997). This *Tico Times* publication is available in Costa Rican bookstores and has extensive coverage of tourist activities.

Investor's Guide to Costa Rica (1996). General information on investment, banking, finance, and business opportunities. (Costa Rican–American Chamber of Commerce.)

Legal Guide to Costa Rica (1997), by Roger A. Petersen. Answers many questions about laws, from buying property to writing a will. (Centro Legal R&M, S.A. Interlink 553, P.O. Box 02–5635, Miami, FL 33102.)

Living in Costa Rica (1996), written and produced by employees of the U.S. Embassy. This book gives excellent information on rules, regulations, customs, and shopping in Costa Rica. (Mission Association.)

Retire in Costa Rica (1996). An excellent video of what it's like to retire in Costa Rica, with scenes in various parts of the country popular with retirees. (Great Plains Library Distribution Co., P.O. Box 685, Liberty, MO 64089.)

The New Key to Costa Rica (1996), by Beatrice Blake and Anne Becher. A popular travel guide for residents and tourists and a must for anyone considering visiting Costa Rica for more than a short vacation; (Ulysses Press, Berkeley, CA.)

Tico Times. This weekly English-language newspaper is published in San José, Costa Rica; a three-month trial subscription is $21, and a six-month one is $33. In the United States or Canada, write Department 717, P.O. Box 025216, Miami, FL 33102. In Costa Rica write Apdo. 4632, San José, or call (506) 222–8952.

INDEX

About the Author

During the past decade John Howells has written eleven books on places, at home and abroad, that make for comfortable, stimulating retirement. He has become increasingly well known as an authority on this subject and is much in demand as a lecturer and seminar leader on retirement strategies and retirement places. He is a member of the board of directors of the American Association of Retirement Communities and is a featured speaker at that organization's quarterly conferences.

Howells was born in New Orleans and raised in suburban St. Louis. He now divides his time between homes in California and Costa Rica. At any time, however, he is just as likely to be on the road in the United States, Europe, or Latin America, gathering material for a new book or for an update of an older one.

He has worked on newspapers from coast to coast—more than forty newspapers in all–and at various times has been a Linotype operator, an English teacher, a silver miner, and a travel and feature writer—not to mention the author of books on subjects ranging from tramp printers to prospecting for gold, in addition to those on retirement.